The
Communicator's
Commentary

Leviticus

THE COMMUNICATOR'S COMMENTARY SERIES
OLD TESTAMENT

Lloyd J. Ogilvie

General Editor

The Communicator's Commentary

Leviticus

Gary W. Demarest

WORD BOOKS, PUBLISHER • DALLAS, TEXAS

Library of Congress Cataloging in Publication Data
Main entry under title:

The Communicator's commentary.

      Bibliography: p.
      Contents: OT3. Leviticus / by Gary Demarest
      1. Bible. O.T.— Commentaries. I. Ogilvie, Lloyd John. II. Demarest, Gary
BS1151.2.C66 1986 221.7'7 86–11138
ISBN 0–8499–0408–0 (v. OT3)

Printed in the United States of America

  3 4 9 AGF 9 8 7 6 5 4 3 2

To

Howard Congdon, D.D.

whose friendship and partnership
in life and ministry
have enriched my living and my worship

Contents

Editor's Preface

God has called all of His people to be communicators. Everyone who is in Christ is called into ministry. As ministers of "the manifold grace of God," all of us — clergy and laity — are commissioned with challenge to communicate our faith to individuals and groups, classes and congregations.

The Bible, God's Word, is the objective basis of the truth of His love and power that we seek to communicate. In response to the urgent, expressed needs of pastors, teachers, Bible study leaders, church school teachers, small group enablers, and individual Christians, the Communicator's Commentary is offered as a penetrating search of the Scriptures of the Old and New Testament to enable vital personal and practical communication of the abundant life.

Many current commentaries and Bible study guides provide only some aspects of a communicator's needs. Some offer in-depth scholarship but no application to daily life. Others are so popular in approach that biblical roots are left unexplained. Few offer impelling illustrations that open windows for the reader to see the exciting application for today's struggles. And most of all, seldom have the expositors given the valuable outlines of passages so needed to help the preacher or teacher in his or her busy life to prepare for communicating the Word to congregations or classes.

This Communicator's Commentary series brings all of these elements together. The authors are scholar-preachers and teachers outstanding in their ability to make the Scriptures come alive for individuals and groups. They are noted for bringing together excellence in biblical scholarship, knowledge of the original Hebrew and Greek, sensitivity to people's needs, vivid illustrative material from biblical, classical, and contemporary sources, and lucid communication by the use of clear outlines of thought. Each has been selected to contribute to this series because of his Spirit-empowered ability to help people live in the skins of biblical characters and provide a "you-are-there" intensity to the drama of events of the Bible which have so much to say about our relationships and responsibilities today.

The design for the Communicator's Commentary gives the reader an overall outline of each book of the Bible. Following the introduction, which reveals the author's approach and salient background on the book, each chapter of the commentary provides the Scripture to be exposited. The New King James Bible has been chosen for the Communicator's Commentary because it combines with integrity the beauty of language, underlying Hebrew and Greek textual basis, and thought-flow of the 1611 King James Version, while replacing obsolete verb forms and other archaisms with their everyday contemporary counterparts for greater readability. Reverence for God is preserved in the capitalization of all pronouns referring to the Father, Son, or Holy Spirit. Readers who are more comfortable with another translation can readily find the parallel passage by means of the chapter and verse reference at the end of each passage being exposited. The paragraphs of exposition combine fresh insights to the Scripture, application, rich illustrative material, and innovative ways of utilizing the vibrant truth for his or her own life and for the challenge of communicating it with vigor and vitality.

It has been gratifying to me as editor of this series to receive enthusiastic progress reports from each contributor. As they worked, all were gripped with new truths from Scripture — God-given insights into passages, previously not written in the literature of biblical explanation. A prime objective of this series is for each user to find the same awareness: that God speaks with newness through the Scriptures when we approach them with a ready mind and a willingness to communicate what He has given; that God delights to give communicators of His Word "I-never-saw-that-in-that-verse-before" intellectual insights so that our listeners and readers can have "I-never-realized-all-that-was-in-that-verse" spiritual experiences.

The thrust of the commentary series unequivocally affirms that God speaks through the Scriptures today to engender faith, enable adventuresome living of the abundant life, and establish the basis of obedient discipleship. The Bible, the unique Word of God, is unlimited as a resource for Christians in communicating our hope to others. It is our weapon in the battle for truth, the guide for ministry, and the irresistible force for introducing others to God.

A biblically rooted communication of the Gospel holds in unity and oneness what divergent movements have wrought asunder. This commentary series courageously presents personal faith, caring for individuals, and social responsibility as essential, inseparable dimensions of biblical Christianity. It seeks to present the quadrilateral Gospel in its fullness which calls us to unreserved commitment to Christ, unrestricted self-esteem in His grace, unqualified love for others in personal evangelism, and undying efforts to work for justice and righteousness in a sick and suffering world.

A growing renaissance in the church today is being led by clergy and laity who are biblically rooted, Christ-centered, and Holy Spirit-empowered. They have dared to listen to people's most urgent questions and deepest needs and then to God as He speaks throughout the Bible. Biblical preaching is the secret of growing churches. Bible study classes and small groups are equipping the laity for ministry in the world. Dynamic Christians are finding that daily study of God's Word allows the Spirit to do in them what He wishes to communicate through them to others. These days are the most exciting time since Pentecost. The Communicator's Commentary is offered to be a primary resource of new life for this renaissance.

It has been very encouraging to receive the enthusiastic responses of pastors and teachers to the twelve New Testament volumes of the Communicator's Commentary series. The letters from communicators on the firing line in pulpits, classes, study groups, and Bible fellowship clusters across the nation, as well as the reviews of scholars and publication analysts, have indicated that we have been on target in meeting a need for a distinctly different kind of commentary on the Scriptures, a commentary that is primarily aimed at helping interpreters of the Bible to equip the laity for ministry.

This positive response has led the publisher to press on with an additional twenty-one volumes covering the books of the Old Testament. These new volumes rest upon the same goals and guidelines that undergird the New Testament volumes. Scholar-preachers with facility in Hebrews as well as vivid contemporary exposition have been selected as authors. The purpose throughout is to aid the preacher and teacher in the challenge and adventure of Old Testament exposition in communication. In each volume you will meet Yahweh, the "I AM" Lord who is Creator, Sustainer, and Redeemer in the unfolding drama of His call and care of Israel. He is the Lord who acts, intervenes, judges, and presses His people into the immense challenges and privileges of being a chosen people, a holy nation. And in the descriptive exposition of each passage, the implications of the ultimate revelation of Yahweh in Jesus Christ, His Son, our Lord, are carefully spelled out to maintain unity and oneness in the preaching and teaching of the Gospel.

I am pleased to introduce the author of this commentary on Leviticus, Dr. Gary Demarest. Throughout his lifetime he has ministered in a variety of positions, including pastor, seminary teacher, missionary advocate, author, and denominational leader. After more than twenty years as pastor of the La Canada Presbyterian Church, Dr. Demarest now serves as associate director of the Evangelism and Church Development Division for the Presbyterian Church (USA). Although I miss his pastoral partnership in Southern California, I am delighted by the strong, Christ-centered leadership which he brings to our denomination.

Many readers will already be familiar with Gary Demarest from his noteworthy contribution to the New Testament portion of The Communicator's Commentary. His exposition of several Pauline epistles has been acclaimed by pastors and teachers for its close study of the text and vivid application for the contemporary Christian. Dr. Demarest's excellent work on this earlier volume encouraged me to ask him for an encore in the Old Testament series.

Leviticus, with its chronicle of sacrifices and rituals, is not an easy book for today's communicator. Yet it deserves careful, expert scrutiny. Upon the foundation of solid linguistic and historical analysis, Dr. Demarest builds a challenging theological and practical synthesis. He has produced a commentary that bridges the gap between worship in ancient Israel and discipleship in our day.

Gary Demarest writes "to enable the contemporary pastor and lay teacher to help people come to a practical and enriching experience of the word of God given to us in Leviticus." Several salient issues emerge, including: the holiness of God, the presence of God in all facets of life, and the challenge for God's people to live holy lives. Dr. Demarest allows the Word of God embodied in Leviticus to speak incisively to our yearning for genuine, impelling worship. Since renewal in worship is a major emphasis throughout the church today, this commentary speaks the right word at just the right time.

LLOYD OGILVIE

Author's Preface

What you are about to read represents a much more difficult and arduous task than I realized when I responded affirmatively to Lloyd Ogilvie's invitation to write this volume for the Communicator's Commentary series. In writing Volume 8 for the New Testament Commentary, I experienced nurturing joy in working with texts from which I had taught and preached for years. In agreeing to do this volume, I assumed the continuation of the same joy. Such has not been the case!

If you allow me to be your guide through Leviticus, you need to know at the outset that I am a pastor by profession, not an Old Testament scholar. And I must confess that I have largely ignored and avoided preaching and teaching from Leviticus until I tackled this project. I wish I could tell you that it has been a sheer delight to have written this volume. It hasn't! I wish I could tell you that I have come to love Leviticus as my favorite book in the entire Bible or at least in the Old Testament. I haven't! At times, I have resented Dr. Ogilvie for asking me to do this, and, more often, I have pitied myself for having accepted. And since I'm in a confessing mood, I should add that I've missed several promised publishing deadlines and have no doubt added to the aging process of the editors and publishers. For this I ask forgiveness and would even be willing to attempt some kind of sin offering.

However, I can tell you that I'm truly grateful for having been asked and for having done the study. I'm grateful for challenges and insights that have come to me in so many ways from this ancient and often difficult-to-interpret-and-apply section of Scripture.

I know now that in the past I have ignored Leviticus to my own loss. Working through it in its entirety has, indeed, been richly rewarding, and I write these words with the prayer that you will experience the same enrichment in tackling this strange and difficult book.

The first difficult choice was in the development of my hermeneutical approach to Leviticus. After considerable reading and reflection upon the text itself, I probed some of the major commentaries, Jewish and Christian, along with many analytical and overview studies. It seemed to me that the scholarship on and preaching from Leviticus in recent years fall into two major categories, which I choose to call the typological and the historical.

The typological was the primary approach used by the fundamentalist and evangelical preachers and teachers, particularly in the nineteenth and early twentieth centuries. This approach places little emphasis upon the meaning of Leviticus to the faith and life experience of the ancient Hebrews, whether in the time of Moses or in the postexilic period and beyond. Such interpretations are based upon the view that, to varying degrees, most everything in Leviticus was given as a "type" of Christ. The sacrifices, the shedding of blood for the forgiveness of sins, the priests, and the high priest all have meaning primarily as signs pointing to Christ. As we shall see, the New Testament writers, particularly the writer of the Book of Hebrews, portray crucial aspects of Christ's death on the cross in rich images drawn from Leviticus. But to see Leviticus only, or even primarily, from our side of the Cross, seems to me to miss much of the rich meaning of Leviticus itself. I urge you to attempt to get into the experience and thinking of the Hebrews on their side of the Cross. For me, the typological approach has been of limited help in doing that.

But I have also found the historical approach to be less than fulfilling. Since the advent of the various documentary theories (which hold that the writings of the Pentateuch are a product of various writers and editors over a long period of time), the emphasis has been upon the proper dating of the rituals and codes, and upon the development of Israel's faith and worship. With due respect for the importance of this aspect of scholarship, I have found it, likewise, to fall short of bringing into play for us the full meaning of Leviticus.

For most of its history, whenever you date its origin(s), Leviticus was the primary reader and textbook for Jewish children. Only in recent history has it receded into virtual neglect. And, certainly, in most Christian circles that I know, it has been totally ignored (or abused), with the exception of two isolated texts. It is now my firm conviction, after months of trying to live into and teach out of this beleaguered Book, that we do well, as learners and teachers, to try to discover and experience its rich and deep meanings.

I make no claim that this study constitutes a comprehensive and complete work on Leviticus. I do not believe that to be possible by any individual. Though I grappled with many of the critical and technical issues involved in the scholarship of Leviticus and many of my applications and conclusions have been shaped by a particular view of such scholarship, I chose not to deal with these issues in this study. I have tried to deal with the text in ways which enable the contemporary pastor and lay teacher to help people come to a practical and enriching experience of the word of God given to us in Leviticus.

Before us are profound insights into the reality and seriousness of sin, many of which desperately need to be recovered in our time. Here is the foundation of our experience of the grace of God in the divine provision for atonement and forgiveness. There's much, much more than a mere "God loves you, no matter what" here! Here are the clues to a much deeper understanding of the meaning of Christ's death on the cross at the sacred time of the Passover. Here is the expanded definition of the statement, to all too many a thoughtless cliché, "Christ died for our sins." Here, above all, is a ringing call to personal and collective holiness to individuals and to the people of Christ's church. And here is a call to reflect upon our understanding and practice of the worship of God, a rethinking desperately needed in contemporary American churches.

A nineteenth-century preacher portrayed Leviticus as "the gospel of the Pentateuch, glistening with purity, turning law into music, and spreading a banquet in the wilderness." I now share his appreciation for this unique part of Scripture. And my prayer is that this modest effort, with whatever faults you will find it to have, will be useful to you in the renewal and growth of your experience of God's unlimited love and grace, both in your life and worship as a responsible member of the Body of Christ, and in your witness and service in the world.

GARY W. DEMAREST
March, 1990

Introduction

In his excellent, though very brief, volume on Leviticus in the *Knox Preaching Guides*, Professor Lloyd Bailey begins by saying that it may surprise readers of a series of books on preaching to discover a volume on Leviticus. He points out that most preachers have probably never heard a sermon based upon it, much less having felt the necessity of preparing one! He points to a current lectionary that draws upon Genesis fifteen times and upon Isaiah forty-five times, but uses Leviticus only twice (13:1-2, 44-46 and 19:1-2, 15-18).

During the past two years, I have asked numerous pastors, both individually and in groups, "How many of you have either preached or worked in Leviticus in the past two years?" The most frequent response is laughter, and rarely has a hand been raised! Some of my closest friends have said, "Why bother to write a commentary on Leviticus? Who's going to read it?"

The present neglect (and even disregard) of Leviticus by the Christian community stands in stark contrast to its place in the life of Israel across the centuries. For centuries, Jewish children began their memorization of Scripture with Leviticus at age three! Some 40 percent of the Talmud discusses guidelines for life and worship from Leviticus. It has been pointed out that of the 613 commandments numbered in the Scriptures by rabbinic Judaism, 247 appear in Leviticus.

Why is it that we who affirm the Bible as the word of God written virtually ignore this Book? Will we Christians ever take Leviticus seriously as Scripture? Probably not, unless we give serious thought to some basic assumptions that have shaped our uses of Scripture, especially in the Protestant evangelical community.

Let's face it. All too many of us have majored upon being "New Testament" Christians. Without declaring ourselves Marcionites, we have at least in practice endorsed the heresy. Marcion, you recall, insisted in the third century that the Old Testament was no longer needed by the church. With the advent of Christ, the Old Testament was declared incomplete and nonessential. The early church fathers overwhelmingly rejected Marcion's views as heretical, and the church universally has affirmed the essential unity of the Scriptures of the Old and the New Testaments.

And yet, in practice, we are closer to Marcionism than most of us would ever want to admit. Frequently, in conferences or retreats, when I ask people to open their Bibles for a lesson, I become aware, if working with an Old Testament passage, that many of them only have a New Testament with them. At times, I wish that we could ban the publication of the New Testament as a solo volume. At the same time, I must confess that probably more than 80 percent of my preaching in more than twenty-three years in one congregation was essentially New Testament preaching. *Mea culpa.*

I think it can be said also that many of us, when we have worked from the Old Testament, have tended to turn more to the Psalms and the prophets than we have to the Pentateuch. And even our use of the Pentateuch has often been restricted to the opening chapters of Genesis and to the Ten Commandments. Have we not created the impression that the Old Testament is law and the New Testament is grace with this kind of selectivity? If we do believe that God speaks through *all* of Scripture, then it's long past time to demonstrate such a faith through our preaching and teaching.

Recall that Jesus responded to the question of a scribe, "Which is the first commandment of all?" with the words: "The first of all the commandments is: 'Hear, O Israel, the LORD our God, the LORD is one. And you shall love the LORD your God with all your heart, with all your soul, with all your mind, and with all your strength' [Deut. 6:4]. This is the first commandment. And the second, like it, is this: 'You shall love your neighbor as yourself' [Lev. 19:18]. There is no other commandment greater than these" (Mark 12:29–31).

And remember that the writings of the New Testament have an abundance of the ideas and vocabulary of Leviticus. These facts call us to a recovery of our sense of the wholeness of Scripture and to a recovery of Leviticus in our preaching and teaching.

The Title

The title "Leviticus" was never used on an ancient scroll and would never have been recognized by anyone in ancient Israel. The title of the Book in the Hebrew Bible was the first word of the first verse, *Wayyiqra*, translated "Now the Lᴏʀᴅ called." The English title "Leviticus" was first adapted from the Latin Vulgate translation which had taken it from the Septuagint, the early Greek translation of the Hebrew Pentateuch.

The English title Leviticus may well be at the root of some of our negative attitudes toward the Book itself. For the title suggests that its contents have to do primarily with the Levites, implying that this is a manual for the Levitical priesthood. And since none of us aspire to be Levitical priests, the fate of the Book is sealed.

The title Leviticus is misleading. Far from being a manual for the exclusive use of the priests, the Book was much more a guide for the laity — for all of the people — regarding their role in worship. Here were the principles for when and where they were to worship, what they were to bring, and what they were to expect of the priests when they arrived. Leviticus thus had powerful implications for the life of every member of the community, making it a book known as well or better than any other part of their Scriptures. This Book had vital implications for their life and worship, as it might well have for ours.

Authorship and Date

The oldest traditions in synagogues and churches hold the Mosaic authorship of the first five books of the Bible. Thus, in our translation, the title is *The Third Book of Moses Called Leviticus*. If Moses was the author of the Book, the date must be fixed in the thirteenth century before Christ, and this we call the traditional view. The scholarship that has focused upon the Pentateuch in general and upon Leviticus in particular has called the traditional view into serious question on many counts, and no serious inquiry into the authorship and dating of Leviticus can ignore the scholarship of the past few decades.

We must begin any such inquiry with a recognition of the deep complexity of the entire issue of the dating and authorship of the Pentateuch. Few areas of biblical scholarship have been so passionately debated for so long. For our purposes, we can only point to some of the arguments for and against some of the major views that have been proposed relating to the dating and authorship of Leviticus.

We must begin by recognizing that the Book throughout claims to record what God disclosed to Moses. Again and again, we will read,

"Now the LORD called to Moses," or "Now the LORD spoke to Moses." This is obviously the most common phrase throughout the Book and might well be called its unifying theme. Yet, nowhere in the Book does it ever make any statement that Moses wrote down what was said, nor is there any claim to Mosaic authorship.

The traditional view holds either that Moses wrote or compiled the Book of Leviticus, or that the Book, in its final form, dates back to Moses. The main argument supporting this view is the consistent use of the unifying theme just stated. Here it is pointed out that the laws and sacrifices throughout the Book are clearly set within the framework of the wilderness experience under Moses. In the first seventeen chapters, the sacrifices are offered in the tabernacle, not in the temple. The general context is clearly that of people who are on the move, as were the Israelites for forty years in the wilderness prior to their entry into Canaan under Joshua. Another defense of the traditional view holds that the sacrificial systems and rituals in Leviticus have parallels in the ancient Near East prior to Moses' time and need not be regarded as later developments of Israelite worship and life.

Proponents of the traditional view argue further that much of what is in Leviticus is actually less at home in the postexilic period than in the Mosaic period. Here comparisons are offered between Leviticus and Ezra/Nehemiah. For example, Leviticus 18 and 20 deal comprehensively with questions relating to marriage, and yet nothing is said about intermarriage with the people of Canaan, a severely critical issue in the period of Ezra and Nehemiah, following the exile. Also, the Book of Ezekiel has numerous quotes from or allusions to Leviticus. While this does not require Mosaic dating, it would seem to establish that the practices in Leviticus were in place well before the exile.

The view that stands at the extreme opposite of the traditional view is generally called the "critical" view, growing out of what has come to be called higher criticism, derived from J. Wellhausen's *Prolegomena to the History of Israel* (1878). This was the classic exposition of the documentary hypothesis in which those portions of the Pentateuch relating to priestly matters (Leviticus and sections of Genesis, Exodus, and Numbers) were assigned to the period following the exile, in other words during the late sixth and early fifth centuries before Christ.

More recent commentaries tend to take this position for granted and seldom give arguments supporting it. Many of us recall the phrase from seminary days: "The settled results of higher criticism." While those results have not remained as settled as once assumed, they certainly require thoughtful interaction by any serious student of Leviticus.

According to this view there was a clearly discernible development in the worship life of Israel from quite simple and unstructured to rigid and ritualistic. One gets a picture, for example, of sacrifice as an unstructured, joyous kind of celebration with the parents of Samson (Judges 13). In Leviticus, however, sacrifice is clearly and thoroughly prescribed with priestly functions and a central place of worship.

In the early times, it is argued, there was simple freedom to sacrifice pretty much wherever one wished, as when Samuel was told to take his sacrifice to Bethlehem and offer it in the presence of Jesse in what became the anointing of David (1 Sam. 16:1–13). Leviticus, on the other hand, assumes and requires that all sacrifices are to be offered in the tabernacle according to the carefully prescribed rituals. (In the most extreme critical views, the tabernacle and the worship described in Leviticus are but projections of the temple in Jerusalem back into the time of Moses.)

It is also argued that differentiation among Levites, priests, and the high priest, and the elevation of the high priest did not take place until after the return from the exile. It is further argued that the requirement of bringing gifts to the priests, such as tithes, sacrifices, and firstfruits, was also a late development in the worship of Israel. Further argument for the late date of Leviticus and the priestly documents in the Pentateuch results from the differences between Chronicles and Kings. Kings, probably written during the period of the exile, has little to say about the worship in Jerusalem, while Chronicles, probably written much later, describes worship much more akin to that in Leviticus.

In sum, the critical view stands or falls on the development of the worship of Israel over a long period of time from simple, free, and unfettered expressions to worship that was highly structured and ritualized. Thus, in this view, the worship set forth in Leviticus has to be dated in the later period, following the return from the exile in the last quarter of the sixth century. More recently, some proponents of the critical view admit to the possibility that even though Leviticus in its final form was not completed until late in the fifth century, its practices may well reflect those in the temple in Jerusalem prior to the exile (587 B.C.).

Recent scholarship, as might be expected, seems to be moving to positions between the traditional and the critical. The work of Y. Kaufmann in *The Religion of Israel* (1961), is often cited as the primary source of this moderating view. The fundamental assumption of the critical view that worship always moves from the simple to the structured is both challenged and rejected. Structured forms of worship are not seen necessarily as indicating later development.

In this school, Leviticus and the priestly writings are dated much earlier, as early as the seventh century, but not as early as Moses. Contrary to the Wellhausen school, it is argued strongly that the forms and styles of worship in Leviticus simply do not fit into the period following the exile. The priestly writings are seen as coming from an earlier period. This view points out that Deuteronomy and Joshua frequently quote Leviticus and other priestly writings, while Leviticus never quotes Deuteronomy or Joshua.

Further arguments for an earlier dating of Leviticus than allowed in the critical school link some of the concepts of Leviticus quite directly to Judges and Samuel. The requirement in Leviticus 17, for example, that all animals must be killed in the tabernacle could only occur during the wilderness period. The ban on eating blood (Lev. 17:10-14) is also articulated in 1 Sam. 14:31-35 at the time when Saul built his first altar to the Lord.

It seems to me that those of us who preach and/or teach Leviticus to contemporary Christians owe it to them to bring them an awareness of the complex issues surrounding the questions of the dating and authorship of Leviticus. At the same time, we should have no hesitation in stating our own views, along with our reasons for holding them, or in articulating our ambiguity if we do not feel that we can hang our hat completely on any one view.

I find myself most comfortable with those who recognize the difficulties with the traditional view, as well as with the critical view, but who also recognize that many, if not all, of the practices and traditions in the worship of Israel in Leviticus, could certainly have their roots in the wilderness period under Moses. I personally feel confident in the validity of preaching and teaching from Leviticus with this perspective. I'm most convinced that dogmatism in these matters is unhelpful and uncalled for.

The Structure of Leviticus

I learned long ago, when beginning to move around in a city that is new to me, to get a map and familiarize myself with the general plan and layout of the city. I have found that cities like New York and Philadelphia, laid out on north-south and east-west grids are much simpler to learn than cities like Washington or London whose plans seem much more diverse — and at times downright devious!

The plan of Leviticus is well-organized, simple, and straightforward. It is divided into two basic sections, chapters 1–16 and 17–27, and each theme logically follows the one before. Thus, one can learn to move around in Leviticus with relative ease. It's not a bad idea to plant in your mind at the outset that there are only two brief narrative sections in the entire text (chaps. 8–10 and 16). (Critical scholarship generally holds that only these narrative sections were in the original priestly documents and that the rest of the material was later added from other sources. For our purposes, I think it safe and fair to say that all efforts to nail down the sources of Leviticus with precision are, at best, quite tentative.)

I have found it most helpful, in teaching Leviticus, to spend at least one session reviewing the closing chapters of Exodus before moving into the structure of Leviticus. Without the picture of the tabernacle clearly in mind, it's much more difficult to enter into the flow of Leviticus.

Exodus 25 is the appropriate place to begin our introduction to Leviticus. Moses has received the Law at Mount Sinai (Exod. 19–23), the people have affirmed the Covenant at the altar that Moses had made at the foot of the Mount (Exod. 24:1–8), and Moses has spent forty days and forty nights on the mountain with God in his final preparation by God for the leadership of Israel under the Covenant (Exod. 24:9–18). While on the mountain, Moses was given detailed instructions for the building of the tabernacle, beginning with the words:

> Then the LORD spoke to Moses, saying: "Speak to the children of Israel, that they bring Me an offering. From everyone who gives it

willingly with his heart you shall take My offering. And this is the offering which you shall take from them: gold, silver, and bronze; blue and purple and scarlet yarn, fine linen thread, and goats' hair; rams' skins dyed red, badger skins, and acacia wood; oil for the light, and spices for the anointing oil and for the sweet incense; onyx stones, and stones to be set in the ephod and in the breastplate. And let them make Me a sanctuary, that I may dwell among them. According to all that I show you, that is, the pattern of the tabernacle and the pattern of all its furnishings, just so you shall make it."

Exod. 25:1–9

From this point in Exodus 25 through Exod. 31:18, God is recorded as having given Moses the instructions for building the tabernacle, for consecrating Aaron and his sons as priests, for the daily offerings, and for the selection of the artisans for the building of the tabernacle. The final articulation to Moses on the mountain was the Sabbath law, after which was given to him "two tablets of the Testimony, tablets of stone, written with the finger of God" (Exod. 31:18).

As Moses returned to the people from the mountain, he was met with the all too boisterous and idolatrous scene of the people dancing around the golden calf, to which Moses responded by shattering the tablets of God and grinding the golden idol into powder (Exod. 32:1–24). Then followed the tragic scene in which the sons of Levi gathered with Moses and carried out his instructions to slay the unfaithful men. On that dark and fateful day, about three thousand of their men were slaughtered (Exod. 32:25–29). Moses then returned to the Lord on the mountain with his confession on behalf of the people. He received new instructions, new tablets to replace the former, and the covenant was renewed by God with a repentant people.

In the midst of this renewal, there is a delightful passage which gives us an anticipatory sense of the tabernacle that is to come:

Moses took his tent and pitched it outside the camp, far from the camp, and called it the tabernacle of meeting. And it came to pass that everyone who sought the LORD went out to the tabernacle of meeting which was outside the camp. So it was, whenever Moses went out to the tabernacle, that all the people rose, and each man stood at his tent door and watched Moses until he had gone into the tabernacle. And it came to pass, when Moses entered the tabernacle, that the pillar of cloud descended and stood at the

24

> door of the tabernacle, and the LORD talked with Moses. All the
> people saw the pillar of cloud standing at the tabernacle door, and
> all the people rose and worshiped, each man in his tent door. So
> the LORD spoke to Moses face to face, as a man speaks to his friend.
> And he would return to the camp, but his servant Joshua the son
> of Nun, a young man, did not depart from the tabernacle.
>
> *Exod. 33:7–11*

The offerings for the tabernacle are received and presented (Exod. 35:4–29), the artisans are called (35:30–36:1), and the construction of the tabernacle and its furnishings is completed (36:2–40:33), with the closing words, "So Moses finished the work." The narrative of the building of the tabernacle is complete, and Exodus concludes with these dramatic words:

> Then the cloud covered the tabernacle of meeting, and the glory
> of the LORD filled the tabernacle. And Moses was not able to enter
> the tabernacle of meeting, because the cloud rested above it, and
> the glory of the LORD filled the tabernacle. When the cloud was
> taken up from above the tabernacle, the children of Israel went
> onward in all their journeys. But if the cloud was not taken up,
> then they did not journey till the day it was taken up. For the
> cloud of the LORD was above the tabernacle by day, and fire was
> over it by night, in the sight of all the house of Israel, throughout
> all their journeys."
>
> *Exod. 40:34–38*

I consider it imperative, therefore, to regard Exodus 25–40 as a part of the structure of Leviticus. Only with this narrative of the construction of the tabernacle and its central role in the life of the Hebrews well established in their minds can people hope to understand and appreciate the Book of Leviticus. The very opening words of Leviticus demand this background: "Now the LORD called to Moses, and spoke to him *from the tabernacle of meeting.* . . ." One can then see that the narrative of Exodus is followed by the teaching of chapters 1–7, giving the instructions for the five types of offerings that will be given regularly in the tabernacle. The narrative then resumes in chapters 8–10 with the story of the consecration of Aaron and his sons to the priesthood, into which is included the strange and frightening story of Nadab and Abihu. The complex matters of ceremonial cleanness and uncleanness are dealt with in chapters 11–15, at which point the narrative form is resumed in chapter 16 with the instructions for Aaron on the great Day of Atonement.

The second main section of Leviticus takes us through the rest of the text with what is generally called the Holiness Code (chaps. 17–27). As we shall see, these are numerous laws and regulations, along with a section directed specifically to the priests (chaps. 21–22), all pertaining to the life and worship of the community during its time in the wilderness under Moses.

Leviticus and Us

Before anyone begins a journey involving time and work, one has a perfect right to ask, "What's in it for me?" Before beginning, one must have some hope that the study will be worthwhile. Having lived with Leviticus, off and on, for many months in the preparation of this volume, I give you my word that this book is worth studying. It will be different, say, from the immediate enrichment that one receives from studying John or Luke. You will have to take the long view — believing that as you study this portion of Scripture, you will learn, perhaps more by absorption than by analysis, more about the living God and what it means to be a part of God's family.

It's a good idea to begin your journey in Leviticus by remembering the words of Paul that "*all* Scripture is given by inspiration of God, and is profitable for doctrine, for reproof, for correction, for instruction in righteousness, that the man of God may be complete, thoroughly equipped for every good work" (2 Tim. 3:16–17). The implication is that continued neglect of *any* portion of Scripture leaves a deficiency in one's development. And Paul would further add: "For whatever things were written before were written for our learning, that we through the patience and comfort of the Scriptures might have hope" (Rom. 15:4).

To me, the greatest value of the journey will be a heightened sense of the holiness of God and of the need for our own personal and collective holiness. Certainly, the theme of holiness is central to the entire Book. The Hebrew word *qadosh*, translated "holy," "holiness," "sanctify," occurs 152 times. The word for "unclean" is found 132 times in Leviticus, more than half of all its occurrences in the Old Testament. The word translated "clean" occurs 74 times. "You shall be holy, for I am holy" is certainly the password of Leviticus. In a day when the criterion for behavior seems all too often to be "does it feel good?" the call of Leviticus to holiness based upon the nature of God's holiness needs to be heard as never before.

In Hebrew thought, everything was either holy or profane, clean or unclean. The passion of Leviticus was to enable people to discern the difference. Perhaps the key verse of the entire book is found in the words "that you may distinguish between holy and unholy, and between unclean and clean, and that you may teach the children of Israel all the statutes which the LORD has spoken to them by the hand of Moses" (10:10–11). This business of discernment is critical, especially among those who all too casually sum up the gospel with the words, "God loves you, no matter what." A study of Leviticus may be the best hope for enabling us to make distinctions between the holy and the profane, the clean and the unclean in our day.

Yet another great value of this journey through Leviticus can be a heightened awareness of the presence of God in every dimension of life and existence. Whatever else informed their consciousness, the reality of God's presence in every aspect of life is pervasive in Leviticus. They knew no distinction between God's presence in worship or in sex, in prayer or in personal hygiene, in spirituality or in relationships with neighbors. God's visible presence in glory on special occasions in no way diminished the fact that to them God was always and ever present in reality. The unapproachableness of God in the Holy of Holies, except by the high priest once a year, in no way diminished their sense of God's presence with them at all times and in every place. To those of us who have made such sharp distinctions between the sacred and the secular, the religious and the political, the spiritual and the physical, the insights of Leviticus are a much needed corrective for our thinking, being, and doing.

And does not our generation need to explore in new ways the meaning of sacrifice as assumed and understood in the Old Testament? The entire concept of atonement, in which the death of an animal in some way substituted for the death of a guilty person, is so foreign to contemporary, Western thought that proclaiming that Jesus Christ died for our sins may have very little meaning to the vast number of people around us. It seems as though our inability to probe the meaning of sacrifice for the atonement of the guilt of sin has resulted in our presenting the gospel primarily as a means by which people may find meaning or self-fulfillment. The meaning of sacrifice in the Old Testament is our only way to understand the meaning of Christ's death on the cross for us. And yet, one listens in vain for meaningful and intelligible articulation of this great theme from our preachers and teachers. Serious grappling with Leviticus may be our best way to recover this essential and fundamental truth at the core of the gospel.

Our journey in Leviticus should lead to a recovery of the essence of public worship and an understanding of its crucial nature for the believer. If worship to the average Christian simply means a not-always-meaningful option for a Sunday morning, the church is doomed to cultural captivity. If the planners and leaders of worship simply plug in different hymns and lessons into predictable, dull routines, the people of God are doomed to boredom. Worship in Leviticus is essential and vital, lively and dynamic. It is the means by which the love and the mercy of God are reenacted and offered anew each day. It is the point at which response to God is demanded and given. It is the wellspring from which the presence of God in every other aspect of life flows into thoughts and actions in every relationship between and among people. However, the integrity of worship is not guaranteed by the exaction of the ritual but by the sense of need and inadequacy brought by the worshiper and by the subsequent response of gift and obedience through the life of the worshiper. Leviticus may well be the ground of our hope for a recovery of the meaning of the worship of God.

With joy, hope, and prayerful anticipation, let's begin the journey! It just might change our lives.

An Outline of Leviticus

I. Introduction (Exod. 25-40)
II. The Offerings (1:1-7:38)
    A. Instructions for the People (1:1-6:7)
        1. The burnt offering (1:1-17)
        2. The grain offering (2:1-16)
        3. The peace offering (3:1-17)
        4. The sin offering (4:1-5:13)
        5. The guilt offering (5:14-6:7)
    B. Instructions for the Priests (6:8-7:38)
        1. The law of the burnt offering (6:8-13)
        2. The law of grain offerings (6:14-23)
        3. The law of the sin offering (6:24-30)
        4. The law of the trespass offering (7:1-10)
        5. The law of peace offerings (7:11-27)
        6. The portion for the priests (7:28-36)
        7. The summary (7:37-38)
III. The Priesthood (8:1-10:20)
    A. Aaron and His Sons Consecrated (8:1-36)
    B. The Priestly Ministry Begins (9:1-24)
    C. The Profane Fire of Nadab and Abihu (10:1-7)
    D. Conduct Required of Priests (10:8-20)
IV. Definitions and Treatments of Uncleanness (11:1-15:33)
    A. Definitions of Clean and Unclean Foods(11:1- 47)
    B. Purification After Childbirth (12:1-8)
    C. Diagnosis and Treatment of Leprosy (13:1-14:57)
        1. Diagnosis by the Priest (13:1-46)
        2. Concerning Leprous Garments (13:47-59)
        3. Cleansing of Healed Lepers (14:1-32)
        4. Concerning Leprous Houses (14:33-57)
    D. Laws Concerning Bodily Discharges (15:1-33)

V. The Great Day of Atonement (16:1-34)
VI. The Holiness Code (17:1-27:34)
   A. The Sanctity of Blood (17:1-16)
   B. Laws of Sexual Morality (18:1-30)
   C. Laws of Relationships (19:1-37)
   D. Punishment for Serious Violations (20:1-27)
   E. Rules for the Priests (21:1-22:33)
      1. Rules on mourning and marriage (21:1-9)
      2. Rules for the high priest (21:10-15)
      3. Physical standards for priests (21:16-24)
      4. Rules about priests' food (22:1-9)
      5. Kin's rights to priests' food (22:10-16)
      6. Blemishes in sacrifices (22:17-30)
      7. Concluding exhortation (22:31-33)
   F. Feasts of the Lord (23:1-44)
      1. The proclamation (23:1-2)
      2. The Sabbath (23:3)
      3. The Passover and Unleavened Bread (23:4-8)
      4. The Feast of Firstfruits (23:9-14)
      5. The Feast of Weeks (23:15-22)
      6. The Feast of Trumpets (23:23-25)
      7. The Day of Atonement (23:26-32)
      8. The Feast of Tabernacles (23:33-44)
   G. The Care of the Tabernacle (24:1-9)
   H. The Penalty for Blasphemy (24:10-23)
   I. The Sabbath and Jubilee Years (25:1-55)
   J. Promises of Blessing and Retribution (26:1-46)
   K. Redeeming Vowed Gifts (27:1-34)

CHAPTER ONE

ISRAEL'S WORSHIP AND OURS

LEVITICUS 1:1–7:38

The writer of Leviticus either ignored or didn't have a good editor. For every editor will insist that the opening paragraph be designed to capture the attention and interest of the reader. In reality, not only the opening paragraph, but the first seven chapters of Leviticus, are almost certain to discourage the modern reader from getting into this book.

Of what possible interest could the details of how various ritual sacrifices were made long ago be to me? What does the killing of animals in religious rites have to do with me and my world? What do I care about the world of priests and altars? These are the obvious questions that confront the contemporary Christian reader of Leviticus in deciding whether to invest time and energy in this particular book of the Bible.

Though sacrifice is a term used often in everyday vocabulary, its meaning in Leviticus is essentially different from its meaning to us. When we use the word, we usually refer to something that we do for someone else at some cost to ourselves. As a pastor, I sometimes ask our people to sacrifice some comfort or luxury in order to give money to feed hungry people nearby or abroad. This may mean doing without some legitimate pleasure or activity for the sake of helping someone in need. It is sacrificial because it is costly.

As a parent, I have become very aware of the sacrifices required to provide higher education for our children. We have chosen to forego or postpone certain things in order to provide for their needs.

When we go to Dodger Stadium to root for our favorite baseball team, we will likely hear the language of sacrifice. With a runner on first base, with no outs, it's probable that the hitter will attempt a sacrifice bunt to advance the runner to second. Though the batter be thrown out at first, he will not be charged with an at-bat, in recognition of his intentional sacrifice.

In everyday language, sacrifice is commonly used in reference to some costly action taken in order to benefit someone else.

But the language of sacrifice meant something much more specific to the people of the Bible. The word *sacrifice* would have brought to mind, specifically and exclusively, that which was central to their lives — the offering of sacrifices in their central place of worship. Until the time of Solomon, the sacrifices were offered in the tabernacle, a rustic and portable structure described in the Book of Exodus. With the building of the first temple by Solomon, the sacrifices were offered in that center of worship.

From the time of Moses, the life of Israel centered in the offering up of sacrifices to God. Daily, the people brought their animals and food for the sacrifices as set forth primarily here in Leviticus. Daily, the priests performed the sacrifices as prescribed in these writings.

Without some effort on our part to understand the central role of the sacrifices, our understanding of the faith and life of our Hebrew ancestors will be deficient. And this deficiency will be reflected in our understanding of the life, death, and resurrection of Jesus, as well as the faith of the New Testament writers.

The Offerings: Instructions for the People

In studying the first seven chapters of Leviticus, we must emphasize the linkage between Leviticus and the books of Exodus and Numbers. Exodus brings to us the giving and shaping of the covenant at Sinai followed by the erection of the tabernacle. Both the covenant and the tabernacle are fundamental to our understanding of the theology of Leviticus as well as to our understanding of Jesus and the gospel. And the practical applications of the worship of Leviticus are expanded in the Book of Numbers, a reminder that the life of the people of God is always seen as an extension of their worship.

Life that is not shaped by the worship of God becomes futile, and worship that does not shape the quality of life is irrelevant ritual. The very structure of the middle three books of the Pentateuch is a powerful statement of this reality.

The worship of Israel revolved around five basic sacrificial offerings: the burnt offering, the grain offering, the peace offering, the sin offering, and the trespass offering. All but the grain offering involved the killing of animals, followed by carefully prescribed actions with the blood of those animals and then the burning of all or part of them.

We cannot approach the sacrificial system without recognizing that these people regarded sin as a serious matter. Sin was not something that could be ignored or casually dismissed. God could not be approached apart from bringing some animal or food as an offering to be sacrificed in a prescribed ritual. Such an act of worship, performed with the proper spirit of contrition, must have been a powerful experience in the life of the worshiper. By the same token, one could go through the ritual as nothing more than an outward performance and quite miss the deeper, inner meaning intended by the sacrifice.

The sacrificial offerings were hypocritical and meaningless unless accompanied by subsequent obedience to the living God in lives of righteousness and justice. Thus, the prophet Amos portrayed God saying in anger:

> "I hate, I despise your feast days,
> and I do not savor your sacred assemblies.
>
> Though you offer Me burnt offerings
>   and your grain offerings,
> I will not accept them,
> nor will I regard your fattened peace offerings.
>
> Take away from Me the noise of your songs,
> for I will not hear the melody
> of your stringed instruments.
>
> But let justice run down like water,
> and righteousness like a mighty stream."
>   *Amos 5:21–24*

We will do well as we study the five types of basic offerings in Leviticus 1–7 to keep these two focal points in mind: (1) the need to take sin seriously, and (2) the importance of our acts of worship being expressed through lives committed to righteousness and justice.

I have found it helpful to keep before me a chart of the distinctives of the four animal sacrifices we now study:

33

The Four Animal Sacrifices of Leviticus

Name	Text	Elements	Purpose
Burnt Offering	Lev. 1:1–7 6:8–13	Young bull without defect Sheep or goat ram without defect Dove or young pigeon Burned throughout the night, ashes removed by priest wearing special garments	Basic expression of continual worship of God Basic atonement for human sin by placating God's wrath
Peace Offering	Lev. 3:1–17 7:11–36	Male or female animal without defect Additional breads of various types Fat to be burned upon the altar. Meat to be eaten on same day or next day	An expression of thanksgiving or as an expression of a vow; resulted in a type of communal meal
Sin Offering	Lev. 4:1–5:13 7:11–36	1. A young bull without defect for the priest 2. A young bull for the community 3. A male goat for a leader 4. A female goat for a member of the community, or a female lamb 5. Two doves or young pigeons for a poor person 6. Some flour for a very poor person	To be eaten by the priest or a male in the priest's household The basic offering of atonement for a wide variety of sins by priest and people
Guilt Offering	Lev. 5:14–6:7 7:1–10	A ram without defect Silver in value to 20% of the restitution to be made	To be eaten by priest or a male in the priest's household A sacrifice to atone for sins against holy things in the worship

THE BURNT OFFERING

1:1 Now the LORD called to Moses, and spoke to him from the tabernacle of meeting, saying,

2 "Speak to the children of Israel, and say to them: 'When any one of you brings an offering to the LORD, you shall bring your offering of the livestock — of the herd and of the flock.

3 'If his offering *is* a burnt sacrifice of the herd, let him offer a male without blemish; he shall offer it of his own free will at the door of the tabernacle of meeting before the LORD.

4 'Then he shall put his hand on the head of the burnt offering, and it will be accepted on his behalf to make atonement for him.

5 'He shall kill the bull before the LORD; and the priests, Aaron's sons, shall bring the blood and sprinkle the blood all around on the altar that *is by* the door of the tabernacle of meeting.

6 'And he shall skin the burnt offering and cut it into its pieces.

7 'The sons of Aaron the priest shall put fire on the altar, and lay the wood in order on the fire.

8 'Then the priests, Aaron's sons, shall lay the parts, the head, and the fat in order on the wood that *is* on the fire upon the altar;

9 ' but he shall wash its entrails and its legs with water. And the priest shall burn all on the altar as a burnt sacrifice, an offering made by fire, a sweet aroma to the LORD.

10 'And if his offering *is* of the flocks — of the sheep or of the goats — as a burnt sacrifice, he shall bring a male without blemish.

11 'He shall kill it on the north side of the altar before the LORD; and the priests, Aaron's sons, shall sprinkle its blood all around on the altar.

12 'And he shall cut it into its pieces, with its head and its fat; and the priest shall lay them in order on the wood that *is* on the fire upon the altar;

13 ' but he shall wash the entrails and the legs with water. And the priest shall bring *it* all and burn *it* on

the altar; it *is* a burnt sacrifice, an offering made by
fire, a sweet aroma to the LORD.

14 'And if the burnt sacrifice of his offering to the
LORD *is* of birds, then he shall bring his offering of
turtledoves or young pigeons.

15 'The priest shall bring it to the altar, wring off its
head, and burn *it* on the altar; its blood shall be
drained out at the side of the altar.

16 'And he shall remove its crop with its feathers
and cast it beside the altar on the east side, into the
place for ashes.

17 'Then he shall split it at its wings, *but* shall not
divide *it* completely; and the priest shall burn it on
the altar, on the wood that *is* on the fire. It *is* a burnt
sacrifice, an offering made by fire, a sweet aroma to
the LORD.

Lev. 1:1–17

The structure of chapter 1 is simple: introduction(vv. 1–2), burnt
offerings of bulls (vv. 3–9), burnt offerings of sheep and goats (vv.
10–13), and burnt offerings of birds (vv. 14–17).

Since we have discussed the matters growing out of 1:1–2 in the
Introduction, we will move directly to the first of the five types of
sacrificial offerings: the burnt offering. This offering could be made
with a bull, a sheep, a goat, a turtledove, or a young pigeon. Animal
sacrifice was common to most of the religions in the Near East, and
ancient religions articulated their reasons for sacrificing animals to
their gods. But in Leviticus, we have an entirely different approach.
The rationale for the sacrifices is never articulated. It is simply a given
that these sacrifices are to be offered. Thus, in the burnt offerings, as
with those to follow, we are not given explanations of the *why* of the
sacrifices. We are simply given the *how*.

Though the burnt offering is described first, we will see that it was
often given in conjunction with other offerings, in which case it followed the other offering. It has been suggested that the sacrifices are
ordered according to their theological concepts, so that it is easier to
recall their particular features.

It may be that the burnt offering is listed first because it is the
sacrifice that signifies total commitment. It is the only offering in

36

which the entire animal is burned upon the altar, and the emphasis is repeated three times that it creates "*a sweet aroma to the* LORD" (vv. 9, 13, 17). The priests were charged with the responsibility to keep the fire burning at all times (6:9, 12, 13), for it was to be a perpetual offering to God with its aroma ever ascending heavenward.

Central to this offering is the concept of costliness. While only a few could afford a bull, more could afford a sheep or a goat, and most everyone could afford a dove or a young pigeon. But everyone accepted the fact that this basic offering to God was to represent a sacrifice of one's substance. It was inconceivable to them that one could enter into God's presence without making a costly sacrifice.

In making the offering, the worshiper brought the animal into the outer court of the tabernacle (or later, the temple), at "*the door of the tabernacle of meeting before the* LORD" (1:3). This was the tent which housed the ark and other sacred furniture (Exodus 37). Outside the tabernacle of meeting was the large altar for the burnt offerings where the various offerings were presented.

If the offering was a bull, sheep, or goat, it was to be "*a male without blemish.*" We need not read this as a statement of male superiority, for it is likely that the reason for this was quite pragmatic. Male animals were more expendable than females, since fewer males were needed to maintain the herds and flocks. While males were used occasionally for breeding, the females were the continuous providers of milk as well as the nurturers of the newborn.

The first act of the worshiper in arriving at the entrance of the tabernacle of meeting was to lay his hand on the head of the animal (v. 4). It is possible that the worshiper may have participated in some kind of liturgy at this point, such as the singing of a psalm.

Next, the worshiper was required personally to kill the animal on the north side of the altar (vv. 5, 11). This most likely involved a specially prescribed technique in which all of the blood was carefully drained from the animal and collected in a container by the priest. The priest would then sprinkle the blood against the four sides of the altar (vv. 5, 11).

The worshiper would then cut the animal into pieces while the priest burned them, piece by piece, upon the top of the altar, beginning with the head and the fat. The viscera and the hind legs were washed by the worshiper in the laver (vv. 8, 13), presumably to insure the removal of impurities from the offering.

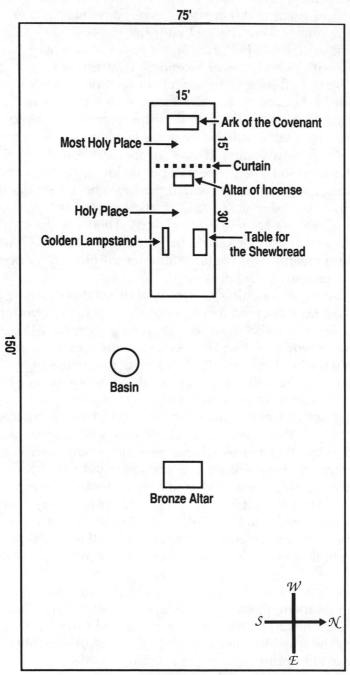

The Tabernacle

38

In the case of animals, the actions of the worshiper and the priest were carefully delineated, whereas with birds, the priest did virtually everything (vv. 14 –17), since with such a small animal the operation was much more delicate. With a bird, the worshiper was to remove the crop and the feathers and throw them into the ash pit (v. 16). This was similar to the act of washing the hind legs and viscera of the animal sacrifice. In each case the worshiper did the messier tasks so that the priest could be kept from physical uncleanness during the sacrifices.

Though we are only given a sketchy outline of the act of worship involved in the burnt offerings, we can't miss the fact that our contemporary services of worship are pale and anemic compared to the worship of Israel. If you add some music, prayers, and liturgy to the outline we have, you have a worship experience which truly involved the worshiper, mentally, physically, and emotionally!

Such worship was costly. It involved a sacrificial gift of significant economic value to the worshiper. Recall the time that David went to Araunah the Jebusite to purchase his threshing floor in order to build an altar to make sacrifices to God. When David met Araunah and offered to buy the threshing floor, Araunah offered the property and everything needed for burnt offerings as a gift to David. But David replied, "No, but I will surely buy it from you for a price; nor will I offer burnt offerings to the LORD my God with that which costs me nothing" (2 Sam. 24:24). The cost never deterred these worshipers because they believed that their offerings brought genuine pleasure to God. Note again the repitition of the phrase "*a sweet aroma to the LORD*" (vv. 9, 13, 17). The fire was never to go out because it was their conviction that God was pleased with the unceasing aroma of the burnt offerings.

While the purpose of the burnt offering is not spelled out in detail here, there is little question in my mind that we are given the clue in verse 4: "*Then he shall put his hand on the head of the burnt offering, and it will be accepted on his behalf to make atonement for him.*" While the burnt offering was costly to the worshiper, the central meaning of the sacrifice was in the atonement for the sins of the worshiper. The burnt offerings throughout the Old Testament are always linked with the atonement for sin.

In the incident with David and Araunah mentioned above, a plague had come upon Israel because of David's disobedience to God in taking a census. It stopped after David had made burnt offerings and peace offerings (2 Sam. 24:25). Here, as in other places, the idea is expressed that God's anger is appeased by the burnt offering. Though the burnt offering does not remove sin or alter human proclivity to sin, it does open the way for fellowship between sinful people and a holy God.

The burnt offering was the most common of all of the Old Testament sacrifices. Its primary function was to atone for human sin by placating God's wrath. In the death of an animal, most frequently a lamb, the seriousness of sin was continually portrayed, as was the fact that the life of the animal was a substitute for the life of the sinner. Atonement (at-one-ment) with God was the gracious result of the burnt offering.

The idea of atoning for sin is central to the message of the Bible. The history of theology and biblical interpretation abounds with efforts to develop a theory of atonement, especially with regard to the meaning of Christ's sacrificial death on the cross. One of the most debated questions in theories of the atonement revolves around the concept of Christ's death as a ransom for sin. The most simplistic theories begin with the idea that some price must be paid in order to satisfy the wrath of God. Thus, atonement becomes appeasement: finding some way to appease the wrath of an angry God. While it was Jesus Himself who said, "For even the Son of Man did not come to be served, but to serve, and to give His life as a ransom for many" (Mark 10:45), we must be careful not to erect a theological theory on what was essentially a statement of love. To say that the death of Jesus was the price that had to be paid for our sins is to say that His love for us was so great that nothing would hold Him back from living out that love for our benefit.

Trying to determine the recipient of the ransom only distracts from the power of Christ's cross. Let us affirm the mystery of Christ's atoning death. Let us celebrate the costly sacrifice made for us. Let us proclaim the mystery that it took the life of Jesus to bring us back from our sin and rebellion into fellowship with God. Beyond this we need not go.

The Burnt Offering and Us

Does this ancient practice have meaning for us today? Obviously, no, in the sense that we should be making such animal sacrifices in our contemporary worship. But, yes, in the sense of enriching our understanding of Christ's death on the cross and enhancing our corporate worship.

Though there is scant reference in the New Testament to the burnt offering, the basic concept of the burnt offering is crucial to our understanding of the meaning of Jesus' death. Only in Mark 12:33 and Heb. 10:6–8 do we have specific references to the burnt offering, and each is a quote from the Old Testament pointing out that burnt offerings in themselves are secondary in importance to living out the will of God. But the concept of Jesus as the sacrificial lamb is central to New Testament thought.

The sacrifice of bulls, goats, sheep, or birds is no longer necessary because of the sacrifice of Christ, once and for all. We shall come later to the Day of Atonement (Leviticus 16) and the subsequent interpretation by the writer of the Book of Hebrews. The burnt offering stands as a reminder of what Christ has done for us. Whatever else our study of Leviticus will accomplish, it will give us a profound theology of the Cross! Without such a theology, it is all too easy to avoid the central issue of the necessity of the forgiveness of sin, instead making the gospel an approach to peace of mind, mental health, good adjustment, or even a sure road to success. A genuine theology of the Cross is sadly lacking in much that comes out of our pulpits and churches these days. Social activists without a theology of the Cross find their energies and efforts sadly lacking in the transforming power of God's love. And those at the other extreme, offering what Bonhoeffer called "cheap grace," salvation without costly demands of love and obedience to Christ in the real world, find few parallels between the lives of the early disciples and comfortable "Christians" using the gospel as a means of self-fulfillment. Perhaps the most needed thing for our lives today is a genuine theology of the Cross.

And there are elements of the worship through the burnt offerings that need to be recovered in our worship experiences. It would never have occurred to the ancient worshiper that one could enter into the presence of God without a costly offering. Yet we come and go to our worship services pretty much as we please with little or no sense that we should approach God with sacrificial gifts and service. Folks whose worship participation is a matter of convenience, embellished with an occasional small donation, are not likely to discover the life-transforming power of authentic worship of the living God!

And what a difference it might make if we ever captured the sense of the ancient worshiper in the awareness that the smoke of the burnt offerings rose constantly as *"a sweet aroma to the LORD "* (vv. 9, 13, 17). The fire was to be kept burning at all times because it was their conviction that God was pleased with their devotion. I find increasing joy in the awareness that as I join with the congregation for worship on Sunday morning, we are doing that which brings pleasure to God. We pastors and leaders of worship do well to remind our people continually that our corporate worship is not only for our well-being, but for the pleasure of God as well. It is at this point that worship can become a joyous dialogue with God. And what greater satisfaction could there be than bringing a smile to the face of God?

THE GRAIN OFFERING

2:1 'When anyone offers a grain offering to the LORD, his offering shall be *of* fine flour. And he shall pour oil on it, and put frankincense on it.

2 'He shall bring it to Aaron's sons, the priests, one of whom shall take from it his handful of fine flour and oil with all the frankincense. And the priest shall burn *it as* a memorial on the altar, an offering made by fire, a sweet aroma to the LORD.

3 'The rest of the grain offering *shall be* Aaron's and his sons'. *It is* a most holy *offering* of the offerings to the LORD made by fire.

4 'And if you bring as an offering a grain offering baked in the oven, *it shall be* unleavened cakes of fine flour mixed with oil, or unleavened wafers anointed with oil.

5 'But if your offering *is* a grain offering *baked* in a pan, *it shall be of* fine flour, unleavened, mixed with oil.

6 'You shall break it in pieces and pour oil on it; it *is* a grain offering.

7 'And if your offering *is* a grain offering *baked* in a covered pan, it shall be made *of* fine flour with oil.

8 'You shall bring the grain offering that is made of these things to the LORD. And when it is presented to the priest, he shall bring it to the altar.

9 'Then the priest shall take from the grain offering a memorial portion, and burn *it* on the altar. *It is* an offering made by fire, a sweet aroma to the Lord.

10 'And what is left of the grain offering *shall be* Aaron's and his sons'. *It is* a most holy *offering* of the offerings to the Lord made by fire.

11 'No grain offering which you bring to the Lord shall be made with leaven, for you shall burn no leaven nor any honey in any offering to the Lord made by fire.

12 'As for the offering of the firstfruits, you shall offer them to the Lord, but they shall not be burned on the altar for a sweet aroma.

13 'And every offering of your grain offering you shall season with salt; you shall not allow the salt of the covenant of your God to be lacking from your grain offering. With all your offerings you shall offer salt.

14 'If you offer a grain offering of your firstfruits to the Lord, you shall offer for the grain offering of your firstfruits green heads of grain roasted on the fire, grain beaten from full heads.

15 'And you shall put oil on it, and lay frankincense on it. It *is* a grain offering.

16 'Then the priest shall burn the memorial portion: *part* of its beaten grain and *part* of its oil, with all the frankincense, as an offering made by fire to the Lord.

Lev. 2: 1–16

This chapter divides into three sections: grain offerings of uncooked grain (vv. 1–3), cooked grain offerings (vv. 4–10), and rules about grain offerings (vv. 11–16).

This offering has been given various names in English translations of the Bible. It is called the "meat" offering in the King James Version, for at the time of that translation *meat* was a term used for any and all kinds of food. Later translations called this a "meal" offering, and more recent translations use "cereal" or "grain." I prefer "grain" since "cereal" in our house brings to mind a prepared breakfast food. *Grain* is the term used in our translation.

The official daily burnt offering was followed by the grain offering (Numbers 28). With the burnt offering and the peace offering (Leviticus 3), it is one of the three offerings that produce "*a sweet aroma to the LORD*" (vv. 2, 9, 12). The grain offering was different from the burnt offering in two essentials: it was not an animal sacrifice, and only part of it was burned by the priest. It could be offered on its own or in conjunction with other sacrifices.

Verses 1–3. The basic ingredient in every grain offering was fine flour (from wheat or barley) to which olive oil and incense were added. It could be brought in this simple form (vv. 1–2), or it could be baked as bread or as a wafer (v. 4), or prepared on a griddle (v. 5), or cooked in a pan (v. 7). Even the very poorest of the poor could participate in this offering.

In its simplest form, the worshiper brought the offering to the priest, who took a handful of the grain, with special care to include all of the incense (actually, frankincense). This handful was called the "*memorial portion*" and was burned in the fire on the altar. The rest of the grain was a provision for Aaron and his sons, the priests, though they were to eat it without yeast only in the courtyard of the taber-nacle of meeting (6:16), because it was "*a most holy offering of the offer-ings to the LORD made by fire*" (vv. 3, 10).

Verses 4–10. If the worshiper preferred, the grain offering could be cooked. Provision is made for bringing it in the form of dough flat-tened out by hand and then baked in an oven, or made into a wafer, probably much thinner and smaller than the traditional bread. Bread is still made this way in Arab villages today.

It could be cooked on a griddle, much like our way of making pancakes. The standard griddle would be made of ceramic ware, though in the Middle Bronze Age (1950–1550 B.C.), copper griddles were not uncommon. By the time of David (1000 B.C.), iron griddles were used by people of relative affluence.

It could also be cooked in a pan, a reference to a ceramic or metal cooking pot used as a deep fat cooker. This would be similar to our making of doughnuts.

As with the grain offering in its uncooked form, the worshiper took the offering to the priest, who burned "*the memorial portion*" (v. 9) on the altar and kept the rest for his own sustenance with the same restrictions as noted above.

Verses 11–16. Three substances, leaven, honey, and salt, now receive special attention. Leaven was a substance like yeast used to produce fermentation in dough and make it rise. Under no circumstances was leaven to be used in any burnt offering. The use of leaven was forbidden at the Passover and with sacrifices. However, as we shall see later, leaven was used in the loaves of firstfruits (Lev. 23:17). Leaven is not to be regarded as symbolic of evil. Jesus used leaven as symbolic of both good and evil. On one occasion He used leaven as a symbol of the Kingdom of God (Matt. 13:33), and on another as a symbol of the insidious teaching of the Scribes and Pharisees (Matt. 16:6, 11–12). As a matter of fact, leaven used in baking enhances the quality of the product. Thus, to regard leaven, in this context, as a symbol of corruption seems unwarranted. Perhaps the prohibition against leaven was primarily in the interest of the purity of the offering itself from the fermentation process initiated by leaven.

The same could be the case with regard to honey. Honey was the basic sweetening agent for ancient Jews as sugar is for us. There is good reason to believe that honey was regarded in the pagan world as a favorite food of the gods and was often incorporated in the sacrifices to pagan deities. This in itself would be adequate reason to avoid the use of honey in Israel's worship of the true and living God. Honey was also an agent of fermentation, and the purity of the offering may have been the issue here as with leaven.

All grain offerings were to be seasoned with salt. The delightful statement: *"you shall not allow the salt of the covenant of your God to be lacking from your grain offering"* (v. 13) gives us a clue as to the symbolism of salt in the offering. In the ancient world, salt was used as a preservative, as a cleansing agent, and as a seasoning. It was a symbol of permanence, purity, and flavor. The idea of God's covenant as salt is a rich and beautiful metaphor. The covenant of God is, indeed, eternal and abiding. God is always faithful to the covenant made with God's people. Through the pain of an unfaithful wife, Hosea understood the anguish of God with the infidelity of Israel. And yet, it was Hosea's message that God would never abandon the unfaithful, whoring spouse. Instead, God will pursue the unfaithful one in covenant love that avows:

> "I will betroth you to Me forever;
> Yes, I will betroth you to Me

> In righteousness and justice,
> In lovingkindness and mercy;
> I will betroth you to Me in faithfulness,
> and you shall know the LORD"
> *Hos. 2:19–20*

A final provision for a grain offering *"of your firstfruits to the LORD"* is made in verses 14–16. Such an offering consisted of crushed heads of new grain roasted in the fire. This was the common staple of food among the poor. The idea of the firstfruits was dear to the hearts of the people of Israel. Living in an agrarian economy, every harvest was the difference between life and death. Thus, the initial fruit of a harvest was an occasion for joy and celebration. But they never forgot that the God of creation was also the God of the harvest. Every harvest was a reminder of God's providential care for them. They believed that the initial fruit of the harvest was a promise from God for a full harvest yet to come. The priest was to burn the memorial portion of the grain, mixed with oil and frankincense, retaining the rest.

We are not given any definitive guidance in Leviticus 2 as to the meaning of the grain offerings, either in terms of the purpose in presenting them, or in their results. The Hebrew word for them is *minhah*, which is also the tribute that a vassal king would pay to his overlord. It may mean something as simple as a gift, though on occasion it is used for a gift that is given out of fear, such as when Jacob sent a *minhah* to his brother Esau (Gen. 32:19ff.), hoping to appease him.

It seems reasonable to view the grain offering as a tribute that the servant brings to his or her divine King. Unlike an animal sacrifice, the grain offering represented a product of the worshiper's endeavor. While God was regarded as the source of the grain, it was the worshiper who planted, cultivated, harvested, and ground the grain into flour, and who then brought it to the priest, cooked or uncooked. Thus, the grain offering seems to represent the consecration to God of the fruit of one's labor.

The Grain Offering and Us

Would we not do well to adopt in our living and worship the same attitude with which the ancient worshiper brought the grain offering?

Living in a world that places such emphasis upon private wealth and property, we are prone to forget that the work of our hands really belongs to God. And for those of us who make our living, not so much by what we do with our hands, but by what we do with our minds, we are in even greater danger of distancing ourselves from God. How easily we fall into the traps of self-sufficiency and self-satisfaction. We begin to think that what we have belongs to us. And we find it easy to believe that we have every right to accumulate for ourselves as much as we can.

Living in the midst of people of affluence, I experience the deepening anguish of self-afflicted pain. Our culture promises us in a thousand ways that self-sufficiency is the only route to personal fulfillment. As we are able to make and accumulate wealth, sometimes by hard work and often by the good luck of having been born to the right parents in the right part of the world, it is only natural that we take some of the credit for our good success. And as we do so, we become more and more convinced that we have done it by ourselves. We defend more and more our right to the ownership of our property and wealth, and, bit by bit, we remove ourselves from any direct responsibility to help the poor and the needy. Then fear begins to grow — the fear of losing what we have, the fear that someone or something will take what is ours away from us. Eventually we are gripped by the constant fear of what might go wrong. Our defensiveness becomes abrasive to us, as well as to others, and our loneliness grows beyond our understanding.

Perhaps it's long past time for most of us to seek a grain-offering mentality by bringing to God each day our recognition with tangible offerings that everything that we are and have belongs to God. Even if we do grow in this grace, we must avoid the pitfall of ever believing that God has chosen us as special recipients of our material abundance. Otherwise, we would have to conclude that the poor were neglected or uncared for by God. Let the poor among us and throughout the world be a reminder to us that God expects us to be the distributors, not the sole beneficiaries, of God's wealth and abundance.

And let us sprinkle our offerings generously with the salt of God's covenant love for us all!

The Peace Offering

3:1 'When his offering *is* a sacrifice of peace offering, if he offers *it* of the herd, whether male or female, he shall offer it without blemish before the Lord.

2 'And he shall lay his hand on the head of his offering, and kill it *at* the door of the tabernacle of meeting; and Aaron's sons, the priests, shall sprinkle the blood all around on the altar.

3 'Then he shall offer from the sacrifice of the peace offering an offering made by fire to the Lord. The fat that covers the entrails and all the fat that *is* on the entrails,

4 'the two kidneys and the fat that *is* on them by the flanks, and the fatty lobe *attached to* the liver above the kidneys, he shall remove;

5 'and Aaron's sons shall burn it on the altar upon the burnt sacrifice, which *is* on the wood that *is* on the fire, *as* an offering made by fire, a sweet aroma to the Lord.

6 ' If his offering as a sacrifice of peace offering to the Lord *is* of the flock, *whether* male or female, he shall offer it without blemish.

7 ' If he offers a lamb as his offering, then he shall offer it before the Lord.

8 'And he shall lay his hand on the head of his offering, and kill it before the tabernacle of meeting; and Aaron's sons shall sprinkle its blood all around on the altar.

9 'Then he shall offer from the sacrifice of the peace offering, as an offering made by fire to the Lord, its fat *and* the whole fat tail which he shall remove close to the backbone. And the fat that covers the entrails and all the fat that *is* on the entrails,

10 'the two kidneys and the fat that *is* on them by the flanks, and the fatty lobe attached to the liver above the kidneys, he shall remove;

11 'and the priest shall burn *them* on the altar *as* food, an offering made by fire to the Lord.

12 'And if his offering *is* a goat, then he shall offer it before the Lord.

13 'He shall lay his hand on its head and kill it
before the tabernacle of meeting; and the sons of
Aaron shall sprinkle its blood all around on the altar.
14 'Then he shall offer from it his offering, as an
offering made by fire to the LORD. The fat that covers
the entrails and all the fat that *is* on the entrails,
15 'the two kidneys and the fat that *is* on them by
the flanks, and the fatty lobe *attached to* the liver above
the kidneys, he shall remove;
16 'and the priest shall burn them on the altar *as*
food, an offering made by fire for a sweet aroma; all
the fat *is* the LORD's.
17 '*This shall be* a perpetual statute throughout
your generations in all your dwellings: you shall eat
neither fat nor blood.'"

Lev. 3: 1–17

The chapter has three paragraphs: peace offerings of cattle (vv. 1–
5), peace offerings of sheep (vv. 6–11), and peace offerings of goats
(vv. 12–17). It's obvious that each of the three paragraphs sets forth
the same pattern. The most striking difference lies in that the offering
of cattle or sheep could be male or female, whereas the burnt offering
required a male animal. The reason for this is not stated. The striking
similarity between the peace offerings and the burnt offerings is the
emphasis upon the offering made by fire as "*a sweet aroma to the LORD*"
(vv. 5, 16).

The peace offering, unlike the burnt and grain offerings, was a
voluntary offering, to be brought by the worshiper if and when he or
she chose. Unlike all other sacrifices and offerings, it was followed by
a dinner party, with parts of the sacrificial animal as the entree. Three
reasons are given in Lev. 7:12ff. for bringing this offering. It could be
an occasion of special thanksgiving, a time for making a special vow
to God, or a time for just plain spontaneous celebration of God's
goodness. We will deal with these occasions in more detail in that
section.

Scholars continue to debate whether this offering should be called
the "peace" offering or the "fellowship" offering. Some even refer to it
with other terms, such as "shared" offering or "thank" offering. The
differences revolve around the interpretation of the Hebrew name for

the offering: *shlamim*. In Hebrew *shlamim* is a common root with a wide variety of meanings, thus the difficulty of nailing one down.

The traditional connotation of peace offering relates *shlamim* to *shalom*, the broad word for peace. To many of us, *shalom* is one of the most beautiful words in any language. It means much more than the absence of conflict. It means good health, well-being, wholeness, prosperity, salvation, closeness with God. It means life as God intended it to be. Relating this offering to *shalom* certainly appeals to me the most.

Verses 1–5. There is not enough detail in this paragraph to cover all of the things that would have happened in the sacrifice of the peace offering. And there is no mention of the meal that accompanied this offering nor of the grain offering that was to accompany it. These aspects will appear in chapter 7.

The worshiper is to participate in the same symbolism as in the burnt offering by laying his hand on the head of the cow or bull to be sacrificed. While the meaning of this symbol is never articulated, it seems quite clear that this act was one of identification. Imagine the feelings of the worshiper, conscious of his own need for cleansing in order to enter into the presence of God, as he lays his hand on the head of the animal to be sacrificed, knowing that the death of the animal will be a substitution for the death that is rightfully his. Imagine the feeling of release that must have come to the worshiper as, symbolically, he transferred his own sin and guilt onto the animal. As with the burnt offering, this was done at the entrance to the tabernacle of meeting.

The animal was killed by the worshiper. The priest sprinkled the blood on the sides of the altar. Then, the animal was cut up, presumably after being skinned.

At this point the process departs from that followed in the burnt offering. Instead of the entire animal being burned on the altar, only the kidneys, the fat covering the intestines, and the fatty lobe of the liver were to be burned. We shall learn in chapter 7 that the priest is to be given the breast and the right thigh of the animal.

The service concluded with the worshiper and his family and invited guests joining in a celebrative meal, not mentioned here, in which the rest of the animal was eaten.

Verses 6–11. The procedure for the offering of a sheep is the same, with the exception of the cutting up of the animal. As before, the fat, the kidneys, and the fatty lobe of the liver are to be burned. In addition, *"the whole fat tail"* (v. 9) is to be cut off and burned as a part of the offering. To us city folks not acquainted with different kinds of sheep, the Palestinian breed of Oriental fat-tailed sheep may be regarded as an oddity. These sheep have an extra long tail that serves to store body fat. A tail weighing fifteen or twenty pounds is not uncommon and is regarded as the choice part of the animal for eating, much as we regard a filet mignon or prime rib of beef. Such sheep still exist in the Middle East today, and stories are told of little two-wheeled devices attached to the tail to support it as the sheep moves around.

Verses 12–17. The procedure for offering a goat is the same as for an offering from the herd, with the concluding statement that *"all the fat is the LORD's"* (v. 16). Verse 17 is of special significance: *"This shall be a perpetual statute throughout your generations in all your dwellings: you shall eat neither fat nor blood."*

To me, there are two questions of interest regarding the specifics of the peace offerings. The first is the question of why only parts of the animals were burned in this offering while all of the animal was burned in the burnt offering. What was the special significance of the fat, the kidneys, and the fatty lobe of the liver? The answer is never really given in the Bible. As I have indicated, Leviticus deals almost entirely with the how of the offerings, hardly at all with the why. That creates a real problem because we are now much more interested in the why than in the how.

The second question focuses more specifically upon why the blood and the fat were singled out. Why such a strong and perpetual ban upon the eating of blood or fat? We can only guess.

Perhaps the most logical conjecture can be made regarding the blood. As we shall see in Lev. 17:11, the blood was regarded as the source of life and regarded as the essential element in atonement. As such, it was to be devoted wholly to God in the sacrifice, and thus not to be eaten. As we shall see in later chapters, ancient Hebrews held the blood in awe. It was rightly seen as vital to life, and since God was the author of life, blood was virtually akin to God. Since blood participated in the sacred, its consumption was unthinkable.

With regard to the fat, the logic is not as clear. John Calvin assumed that these people regarded the fat as the very best part of the animal, as, for example, the fat tail of the special sheep. Therefore, to give God the fat was to give Him the very best. Calvin could not have anticipated any more than the ancients that we would eventually discover that the consumption of too much fat is detrimental to good health. I don't think we would be justified to suggest that the Bible was merely a few centuries ahead of its time in this matter. Regarding the fat as the choice part of the animal seems to me to be the best conjecture.

As to the kidneys and liver, we may not be pushing the symbolism too hard to suggest that to these people the kidneys and liver were regarded as the seat of the emotions, just as the heart was regarded as the seat of the mind and will. Since the peace offering was a time of deep emotional expression with one's friends and family, some connection of this sort may have been felt.

Perhaps the wise counsel of John Calvin could be applied to many aspects of our studies in Leviticus. He said, in effect, that to spend too much time inquiring about things that we cannot know which do not lead us into greater piety is neither wise nor helpful.

THE PEACE OFFERING AND US

As the writer of the Book of Hebrews emphasizes, there is no longer any need for sacrifices such as these because Christ, in his sacrificial death on the cross, has completed all of the sacrifices once and for all time and for all people.

But do we not need to recover the spirit and essence of these offerings in our worship? Where better to begin than with the peace offering?

When there is something for which you are especially thankful, when you feel called to enter into a new depth of your relationship with and service to God, or when you just feel like praising God, why not invite some special friends to join you in a special service of making some special offering to God? What if we were to create some new liturgy in our own fellowships that would recover the equivalent of the ancient peace offering?

It's not uncommon for many of us to have some friends over or take them out to dinner on a special occasion. Why not make it into an occasion that would focus on the worship and praise of God and that would make "a sweet aroma to the Lord"?

One of my most memorable pastoral occasions was an invitation to "bless" a new home for one of our families. They came from an

Orthodox background, which has a regular liturgy for such an occasion. Never having been asked to do this before, I was somewhat hesitant, and even a bit fearful of what might be something of a superstitious rite to me. I agreed to the invitation, and had a very special evening. It was a delightful family occasion with relatives, neighbors, and children all included. After dinner, we went through the house, room by room, offering prayers of thanksgiving, petition, and intercession and singing hymns of praise and worship. It was a beautiful evening of "peace offerings."

I keep wanting to find the strength and courage to bring the very best of what I have to God. It would be easier to cut a fat tail off of a sheep than it is to give God the best of my energy, the best of my talents, the best of my time and money. Why is this so difficult?

THE SIN OFFERING

4:1 Now the LORD spoke to Moses, saying,

2 "Speak to the children of Israel, saying: 'If a person sins unintentionally against any of the commandments of the LORD *in anything* which ought not to be done, and does any of them,

3 'if the anointed priest sins, bringing guilt on the people, then let him offer to the LORD for his sin which he has sinned a young bull without blemish as a sin offering.

4 'He shall bring the bull to the door of the tabernacle of meeting before the LORD, lay his hand on the bull's head, and kill the bull before the LORD.

5 'Then the anointed priest shall take some of the bull's blood and bring it to the tabernacle of meeting.

6 'The priest shall dip his finger in the blood and sprinkle some of the blood seven times before the LORD, in front of the veil of the sanctuary.

7 'And the priest shall put some of the blood on the horns of the altar of sweet incense before the LORD, which is in the tabernacle of meeting; and he shall pour the remaining blood of the bull at the base of the altar of the burnt offering, which is at the door of the tabernacle of meeting.

8 'He shall take from it all the fat of the bull as the sin offering. The fat that covers the entrails and all the fat which *is* on the entrails,

9 'the two kidneys and the fat that *is* on them by the flanks, and the fatty lobe *attached to* the liver above the kidneys, he shall remove,

10 'as it was taken from the bull of the sacrifice of the peace offering; and the priest shall burn them on the altar of the burnt offering.

11 'But the bull's hide and all its flesh, with its head and legs, its entrails and offal—

12 'the whole bull he shall carry outside the camp to a clean place, where the ashes are poured out, and burn it on wood with fire; where the ashes are poured out it shall be burned.

13 'Now if the whole congregation of Israel sins unintentionally, and the thing is hidden from the eyes of the assembly, and they have done *something against* any of the commandments of the LORD *in anything* which should not be done, and are guilty;

14 'when the sin which they have sinned becomes known, then the assembly shall offer a young bull for the sin, and bring it before the tabernacle of meeting.

15 'And the elders of the congregation shall lay their hands on the head of the bull before the LORD. Then the bull shall be killed before the LORD.

16 'The anointed priest shall bring some of the bull's blood to the tabernacle of meeting.

17 'Then the priest shall dip his finger in the blood and sprinkle *it* seven times before the LORD, in front of the veil.

18 'And he shall put *some* of the blood on the horns of the altar which *is* before the LORD, which *is* in the tabernacle of meeting; and he shall pour the remaining blood at the base of the altar of burnt offering, which is at the door of the tabernacle of meeting.

19 'He shall take all the fat from it and burn *it* on the altar.

20 'And he shall do with the bull as he did with the bull as a sin offering; thus he shall do with it. So the priest shall make atonement for them, and it shall be forgiven them.

21 'Then he shall carry the bull outside the camp, and burn it as he burned the first bull. It *is* a sin offering for the assembly.

22 'When a ruler has sinned, and done *something* unintentionally *against* any of the commandments of the LORD his God *in anything* which should not be done, and is guilty,

23 'or if his sin which he has sinned comes to his knowledge, he shall bring as his offering a kid of the goats, a male without blemish.

24 'And he shall lay his hand on the head of the goat, and kill it at the place where they kill the burnt offering before the LORD. It *is* a sin offering.

25 'The priest shall take some of the blood of the sin offering with his finger, put *it* on the horns of the altar of burnt offering, and pour its blood at the base of the altar of burnt offering.

26 'And he shall burn all its fat on the altar, like the fat of the sacrifice of peace offering. So the priest shall make atonement for him concerning his sin, and it shall be forgiven him.

27 'If anyone of the common people sins uninten-tionally by doing *something against* any of the com-mandments of the LORD *in anything* which ought not to be done, and is guilty,

28 'or if his sin which he has sinned comes to his knowledge, then he shall bring as his offering a kid of the goats, a female without blemish, for his sin which he has sinned.

29 'And he shall lay his hand on the head of the sin offering, and kill the sin offering in the place of the burnt offering.

30 'Then the priest shall take *some* of its blood with his finger, put *it* on the horns of the altar of burnt offering, and pour its remaining blood at the base of the altar.

31 'He shall remove all its fat, as fat is removed from the sacrifice of peace offering; and the priest shall burn it on the altar for a sweet aroma to the LORD. So the priest shall make atonement for him, and it shall be forgiven him.

32 'If he brings a lamb as his sin offering, he shall bring a female without blemish.

33 'Then he shall lay his hand on the head of the sin offering, and slay it as a sin offering at the place where they kill the burnt offering.

34 'The priest shall take *some* of the blood of the sin offering with his finger, put *it* on the horns of the altar of burnt offering, and pour its remaining blood at the base of the altar.

35 'He shall remove all its fat, as the fat of the lamb is removed from the sacrifice of the peace offering. Then the priest shall burn it on the altar, according to the offerings made by fire to the LORD. So the priest shall make atonement for his sin that he has committed, and it shall be forgiven him.

5:1 'If a person sins in hearing the utterance of an oath, and *is* a witness, whether he has seen or known *of the matter*—if he does not tell *it,* he bears guilt.

2 'Or if a person touches any unclean thing, whether *it is* the carcass of an unclean beast, or the carcass of unclean livestock, or the carcass of unclean creeping things, and it is hidden from him, he also shall be unclean and guilty.

3 'Or if he touches human uncleanness, whatever *sort of* uncleanness *it is* with which a man may be defiled, and it is hidden from him—when he realizes *it,* then he shall be guilty.

4 'Or if a person swears, speaking thoughtlessly with *his* lips to do evil or to do good, whatever *it is* that a man may pronounce by an oath, and it is hidden from him—when he realizes *it,* then he shall be guilty in any of these *matters.*

5 'And it shall be, when he is guilty in any of these *matters,* that he shall confess that he has sinned in that *thing;*

6 'and he shall bring his trespass offering to the LORD for his sin which he has sinned, a female from the flock, a lamb or a kid of the goats as a sin offering. So the priest shall make atonement for him concerning his sin.

7 'If he is not able to bring a lamb, then he shall bring to the LORD, for his trespass which he has

committed, two turtledoves or two young pigeons:
one as a sin offering and the other as a burnt offering.

8 'And he shall bring them to the priest, who shall
offer *that* which *is* for the sin offering first, and wring
off its head from its neck, but shall not divide *it*
completely.

9 'Then he shall sprinkle *some* of the blood of the
sin offering on the side of the altar, and the rest of the
blood shall be drained out at the base of the altar. It *is*
a sin offering.

10 'And he shall offer the second *as* a burnt offering
according to the prescribed manner. So the priest
shall make atonement on his behalf for his sin which
he has sinned, and it shall be forgiven him.

11 'But if he is not able to bring two turtledoves or
two young pigeons, then he who sinned shall bring
for his offering one-tenth of an ephah of fine flour as a
sin offering. He shall put no oil on it, nor shall he put
any frankincense on it, for it *is* a sin offering.

12 'Then he shall bring it to the priest, and the
priest shall take his handful of it as a memorial
portion, and burn *it* on the altar according to the
offerings made by fire to the LORD. It *is* a sin offering.

13 'The priest shall make atonement for him, for
his sin that he has sinned in any of these matters; and
it shall be forgiven him. *The rest* shall be the priest's as
a grain offering.'"

Lev. 4:1-5:13

In this section, we come to the fourth of the five sacrificial offerings
in the worship of Israel. The structure of this section can be outlined
as follows: introduction (4:1–2), the sin offering for the high priest
(vv. 3–12), the sin offering for the congregation (vv. 13–21), the sin
offering for a tribal leader (vv. 22–26), the sin offering for an individual member (vv. 27–35), and the sin offering for specific sins (vv.
5:1–13).

Verses 4:1–2. As with the previous offerings, there are different
views regarding their appropriate titles. The most common and
widely used title is that of "the sin offering." This is certainly correct

because the Hebrew words *hattath* and *hatta* are regularly translated "sin." The root of this word means "to miss the mark." The primary Greek word used in the New Testament for sin has the same meaning. Or, in the words of the Westminster divines, "Sin is any lack of conformity to the will of God."

But the title "sin offering" is somewhat misleading, for, as we shall see, this offering is fundamentally concerned with the purification of the place of worship so that God can be present there among his people. In the deepest sense, the burnt, cereal, and peace offerings all deal with the problem of sin as it disrupts the relationships between persons and God and between persons themselves. This offering is concerned with the question of the pollution of the place of worship caused by sinful people who frequent it. Sin makes God's sanctuary unclean, and a holy God cannot dwell in an unclean place. Thus, Wenham prefers the title "purification offering."

In verse 2, the phrase translated "through ignorance," "inadvertently," or "unintentionally" can be misunderstood, because in the sins that bring impurity into the sanctuary, some degree of conscious disobedience was inevitable. The entire question of intentional and unintentional sins is at best ambiguous. As an example, Numbers 35 has regulations about murder which distinguish between premeditated killing and death that results from unintentional actions, making much the same distinction that we make between murder and manslaughter. In the latter cases, cities of refuge were provided to shelter those who were guilty, and, interestingly, they had to live in the city of refuge until the death of the high priest. If they were to leave the city of refuge prior to that event, they were subject to the death penalty the same as intentional murderers.

Thus, the question of intentional and unintentional sinning is not a simple one on which to rule, and it is certainly not intended as the primary emphasis of this section. The reality is that as the priests, the entire community, tribal leaders, and individuals come and go in and out of the sanctuary, they will bring pollution into the sanctuary, not by intent or design, but simply because they are sinful people. Something must be done to cleanse the sanctuary from this uncleanness — thus the sin offerings.

Verses 3–12. The phrase "the anointed priest" is generally interpreted to mean the high priest, who in the time of Moses was Aaron.

This is not the regular way of referring to the high priest, however, and some commentators believe this phrase to apply to the sons of Aaron. who were also anointed as priests. You will recall that only the direct descendants of Aaron were anointed as priests. The other members of the tribe of Levi were commissioned to assist the priests, thus the common distinction between the priests and the Levites.

Whether the reference is to the high priest, or to any of the anointed priests, there was a fundamental belief that the priest represented the whole nation. This meant that one priest's sin had consequences for the entire nation. We cannot conclude from this section whether the reference was only to the actions of the priest or high priest in his official capacity in the offerings and worship, or whether it included his private life as well. In either case, the importance of exemplary life on the part of the priests was always stressed, and the gravity of their sins is here stated.

The priest, or high priest, was to bring a bull for this offering, the largest and costliest of animals prescribed. As with other offerings, he was to lay his hand on the head of the animal prior to killing it at the entrance to the tabernacle of meeting. What follows was different from the burnt and peace offerings. Emphasis was upon the sprinkling of the blood of the bull, first upon the front of the sanctuary curtain, then upon the horns of the altar of fragrant incense, followed by the pouring out of the remaining blood at the base of the altar of the burnt offering. Then the fat and kidneys were to be burned on the altar of the burnt offering, as with the peace offering. The skin, the head and legs, the flesh and intestines, and the rest of the bull were to be taken outside the camp to a ceremonially clean place where it was burned on the ash pile.

Clearly, the symbolic emphasis was upon the cleansing of the key places and objects in the sanctuary outside of the holy of holies, into which the high priest alone entered only once each year on the Day of Atonement (Leviticus 16).

The fact that the blood was sprinkled on the curtain and on the incense altar, both inside the Holy Place, indicates that the sins of the anointed priest were regarded as more serious than those of the lay people. The curtain separated the Holy Place from the Holy of Holies. Only the high priest ever passed beyond this curtain, and then only on the Day of Atonement. Seven was the number of completeness; thus the sprinkling of the blood seven times would symbolize the

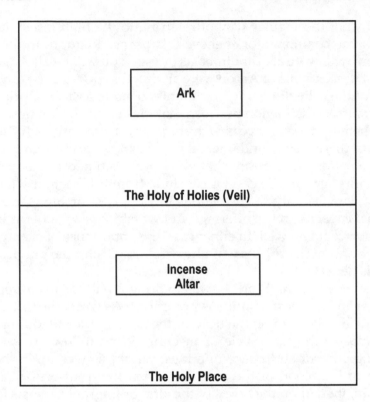

Ark

The Holy of Holies (Veil)

Incense
Altar

The Holy Place

complete cleansing of the curtain. It was this curtain that was torn from top to bottom at the time of Jesus' crucifixion.

The "horns" (v. 7) on the incense altar were projections at each corner of the altar that looked like horns. The purpose of these horns, if for anything more than decoration, has never been clear. Ancient tradition suggests that they were to direct the attention of the worshipers upward toward heaven as the incense was burned. Exodus 30 describes both this altar inside the Holy Place and the twice-daily ritual of burning the incense. This altar was not open to view to the people as was the altar of burnt offering in front of the Holy Place. There has been considerable discussion as to the exact make-up of the incense as described in Exod. 30:34–38. The ingredients consisted of fragrant substances such as frankincense, different kinds of balsam, and various gums and spices, tempered with salt. The burning of the incense became symbolic of prayer rising to God.

Verses 13–21. When the whole congregation had sinned "unintentionally," the same process was required as had been for the anointed priest, and in this paragraph, the details are repeated in abbreviated form.

There are two words in Hebrew in this paragraph referring to the people, *hethah* and *kahal*. They are translated "community," "congregation," and "assembly." Some translations (e.g., NIV) use the word "community" for both words as they occur in vv. 13, 14, 15, and 21. Others, such as AV and RSV translate *hethah* as "congregation," and *kahal* as "assembly." Traditional Jewish interpretation has been that the congregation *hethah* refers to the Sanhedrin, the supreme court of ancient Israel. Most Christian commentators have held the terms to be interchangeable, referring to a large gathering of people.

It seems appropriate to view the terms separately, with the congregation as a representative body with certain legal functions, possibly containing representatives from all of the families, or tribes, of Israel. The assembly is the broader term for the entire gathering of the people. If so, the situation here seems to be that the congregation, representing all Israel, is guilty of some sins that have been unknown by the assembly in the course of its daily worship. The congregation begins to feel guilty; the guilt is known by the assembly, which in turn brings the young bull for a sacrifice.

Again, the symbolic emphasis is upon the cleansing of the curtain, the altar of incense, and the burnt offering altar. Unlike the previous offering for the priest, the language of atonement is used in verse 20, and the community is assured of forgiveness.

Verses 22–26. The "ruler" or "leader" referred to in this paragraph is most likely a leader of a tribe of Israel. His sin is not as serious as that of the priest or of the congregation, for his offering is less costly, a male goat. He is to be told of his sin, perhaps by the high priest.

Though the procedure is similar to the preceding two sin offerings, it differs in that the blood is placed only on the horns of the burnt offering altar and poured at the base of the altar. It is not taken into the Holy Place. Again, the language of atonement is used, and the forgiveness of sin is assured.

Verses 27–35. In descending order of status, we now come to the common, ordinary member of the community, who is neither a priest, a member of the congregation, or a tribal leader. In this case, the offering is less costly, a female goat (v. 28) or a female lamb (v. 32). In the event that he can afford neither, provision is made to bring two doves or two young pigeons (5:7), or if he is poorer yet, a small amount of fine flour (5:11). The flour offering is not to be mixed with oil or incense, keeping it distinct from the grain offering.

The procedure is the same as in the preceding offering for tribal leaders, the blood not being taken into the Holy Place. The phrase "*a sweet aroma to the LORD*" appears in verse 31, for the first time in the description of the sin offerings. Atonement is made and sin is forgiven.

Verses *5:1–13*. In this section, we have a listing of three types of sin that require a sin offering by the guilty individual. The first is that in which the person fails to speak up in public testimony about something of which he has heard or seen. Later (6:5), restitution in such cases will be required.

In the second instance the person comes in contact with something or someone who is unclean. The entire matter of cleanness and uncleanness will be dealt with in much detail in chapters 11–15. Here the sin of contact with uncleanness brings pollution into the sanctuary and must be cleansed and forgiven.

The third specific situation is that of taking an oath thoughtlessly, whether for good or evil. The idea here is that of a rash oath to do anything, often uttered in the ancient world under the influence of alcohol.

The appropriate offering is that of a female lamb, though ample provision is made for those who cannot afford a lamb. They may substitute two doves or young pigeons. If that cannot be afforded, a measure of fine flour will do.

If two birds were brought, the first is to be offered as a sin offering and the second as a burnt offering. In the case of a flour offering, the priest is to offer a handful of it as a memorial offering to be burned on the top of the altar and keep the rest for himself as with the grain offering.

The Sin Offering and Us

As with the preceding three types of offerings, we do well to try to enter into the world of ancient Israel in order to identify with their sense of God, of sin, and of worship. And here the identification may be more difficult, for we have little sense of God as dwelling in our church sanctuaries. As a matter of fact, some prefer to call them auditoriums so as not to imply that God dwells in these houses made with human hands. For us who have come to know that God dwells in our hearts through faith in Jesus Christ, we can only resist the idea of God dwelling in buildings.

But does this not bring us to a very real point of application in our own lives? For, though we may not agree with the Israelites' view of the tabernacle of meeting or, later, the temple as being God's dwelling place, might we not learn something profound from their view that God could not dwell in the midst of uncleanness? Is it not always the case that God must dwell in a sanctuary cleansed from sin? God cannot dwell in the midst of people where there is sin. We could use some recovery of a sense that God does dwell somewhere. We have so spiritualized God that the idea of God dwelling in a building is unacceptable to us. But having lost that sense, have we not also lost our sense of God dwelling within our bodies? Or even within our world?

But we do affirm our belief that God dwells within us, that the Holy Spirit is present and alive within the life of every believer. Thus, we need the equivalent of the sin offerings to cleanse these dwelling places of God. This was precisely what Paul had in mind when he wrote to the Corinthians: "Do you not know that your body is the temple of the Holy Spirit who is in you, whom you have from God, and you are not your own? For you were bought at a price; therefore glorify God in your body and in your spirit, which are God's" (1 Cor. 6:19–20).

Confession of sins to God through another is perhaps as close to the ancient sin offerings as we can come. The Protestant reformers rightly abandoned the sacrament of confession which required a human priest as an intermediary between humans and God. They rightly affirmed that Christ is the sole mediator of God's forgiveness. And yet there is still much to be said for the act of confession to God in the presence of another. "Confess your trespasses [or sins] to one another, and pray for one another, that you may be healed" (James 5:16). In such practice, however, confidentiality is of the highest order. That's why people often come to us pastors with their confessions, discovering that one can be more readily assured of God's forgiveness through the forgiveness of another. Pastors are as much in need of this as all others, and that's why I encourage pastors to enter into covenant relationships with others who can be trusted to serve faithfully as their "confessors."

As it was necessary for priests, governing bodies, tribal leaders, and just plain folks to bring sin offerings for the cleansing of the sanctuary from time to time, so it becomes essential for us regularly to apply the sacrifice of Christ for our own cleansing and forgiveness, knowing that God cannot dwell in unclean temples. We need others near us to incorporate these graces and disciplines into our lives.

And let us not ignore that the sins of the leaders were considered more serious than those of the common folks. This need not set up a double standard of values and behavior. But for those of us who have been called by God to positions of special responsibility "to whom much is given, from him much will be required; and to whom much has been committed, of him they will ask the more" (Luke 12:48). James insisted that teachers "shall receive a stricter judgment" (James 3:1).

The personal and public tragedy of the brokenness and moral failures of numerous Christian pastors and leaders in recent years is a matter of widespread public knowledge. We are right to expect and demand high standards of integrity and morality from all who commit themselves to leadership in Christ's church. But we must be as insistent that we provide for each other the kind of preventive support and care needed so desperately.

Certainly, the crucial moment in the sin offering was the moment at which the worshiper laid his hand on the head of the animal to be sacrificed. For the man and woman in Christ, the way into the offering is the confession of our sin: "if we confess our sins, He is faithful and just to forgive us our sins and to cleanse us from all unrighteousness" (1 John 1:9). Both the public and shared confession of sin in our worship services and the development of trusting relationships for personal and deeper confession are in need of serious attention by us.

THE GUILT OFFERING

14 Then the LORD spoke to Moses, saying:
15 "If a person commits a trespass, and sins unintentionally in regard to the holy things of the LORD,
then he shall bring to the LORD as his trespass offering
a ram without blemish from the flocks, with your
valuation in shekels of silver according to the shekel
of the sanctuary, as a trespass offering.

16 'And he shall make restitution for the harm that he has done in regard to the holy thing, and shall add one-fifth to it and give it to the priest. So the priest shall make atonement for him with the ram of the trespass offering, and it shall be forgiven him.

17 'If a person sins, and commits any of these things which are forbidden to be done by the commandments of the LORD, though he does not know *it*, yet he is guilty and shall bear his iniquity.

18 "And he shall bring to the priest a ram without blemish from the flock, with your valuation, as a trespass offering. So the priest shall make atonement for him regarding his ignorance in which he erred and did not know *it*, and it shall be forgiven him.

19 "It is a trespass offering; he has certainly trespassed against the LORD."

6:1 And the LORD spoke to Moses, saying:

2 "If a person sins and commits a trespass against the LORD by lying to his neighbor about what was delivered to him for safekeeping, or about a pledge, or about a robbery, or if he has extorted from his neighbor,

3 "or if he has found what was lost and lies concerning it, and swears falsely — in any one of these things that a man may do in which he sins:

4 "then it shall be, because he has sinned and is guilty, that he shall restore what he has stolen, or the thing which he has deceitfully obtained, or what was delivered to him for safekeeping, or the lost thing which he found,

5 "or all that about which he has sworn falsely. He shall restore its full value, add one-fifth more to it, *and* give it to whomever it belongs, on the day of his trespass offering.

6 "And he shall bring his trespass offering to the LORD, a ram without blemish from the flock, with your valuation, as a trespass offering, to the priest.

7 "So the priest shall make atonement for him before the LORD, and he shall be forgiven for any one of these things that he may have done in which he trespasses."

Lev. 5:14 – 6:7

This section consists of three paragraphs: sin against holy things (vv. 14–16), sin against God's commands (vv. 17–19), and sin against a neighbor (6:1–7).

This brings us to the last of the five offerings in the Levitical sacrificial system of worship. There has been some confusion regarding the meaning of this offering because of its title and its relationship to the sin offering. Some commentators choose to call this the "reparation" offering, since one of its distinctions is that of restitution requiring an additional 20 percent of the value of the failure or of the offense. Is this guilt offering to be regarded as another type of sin offering? Probably not, inasmuch as the two sacrifices are different, requiring different animals and having a different ritual. The function of the sin offering, as we have seen, was related to the cleansing of the place of worship, the place where God dwelt and met with his people. The function of this offering, the guilt or reparation offering, has to do with sins committed against "*holy things*" (5:15), "*things which are forbidden . . . by the commandments of the LORD*" (17), or sins against a neighbor (6:2).

Sinning against holy things apparently had to do with things involved in the sacrificial worship. The details are not given here, but perhaps eating holy food already dedicated in the worship or failing to fulfill a vow or bring a full tithe might be the kinds of things at issue.

The "forbidden" things, again not specified, may have been related to one of the most feared sins of all: the fear of an unintentional sin against some sacred object. Some suggest that this particular offering really served to pacify oversensitive consciences regarding sacred worship.

The third occasion for this offering was in relation to defrauding one's neighbor, with special emphasis on swearing falsely with regard to the fraudulent action.

This was a costly offering, a ram from the flock. And, in the case of sins against sacred property, a penalty of 20 percent was to be paid as restitution to the priest, who presumably had not received his share of the offering as provided. In the case of defrauding one's neighbor, full restitution was to be made, plus a 20 percent assessment, plus the costly ram sacrifice.

The Guilt Offering and Us

To be sure, we moderns have little sensitivity about holy things and places, and the possibility of feeling guilt in such matters is not likely.

And yet, again in this offering of old, we must not overlook the message of God's gracious willingness to forgive sins taken with utmost seriousness by the ancient worshipers. While we may write off some of their compunctions as superstitions, they were given provision for the removal of sin and guilt by God Himself.

While sins against sacred places may not be our concern, we need to recognize our many ways of sinning against others. In the ancient prayer of confession, sins of omission were included with sins of commission. We do well to heighten our sense of the seriousness of the "things that we have left undone," especially with regard to family, friends, and neighbors.

In the case of fraudulent behavior toward others, the phrase in 6:2 has timeless significance: "*If a person sins and commits a trespass against the LORD by lying to his neighbor . . .*" Here is an awareness too often missing in human relations. Sin against a neighbor is sin against God. We are to regard the rights, property, and interests of others as we regard God. To defraud or deceive one's neighbor is to defraud or deceive God.

But even here, the grace of God shines forth. There is an offering for this sin by which forgiveness may be received. To us who are familiar with the rich meaning of the sacrifice of Jesus on the cross, that grace is all the more a source of overwhelming wonder and gratitude. Without being casual about the seriousness of our sins, we must also live with absolute confidence in God's gracious forgiveness. We can live in confident trust that God has forgiven us for all of the sins we have yet to commit in that unknown future. This is the ultimate paradox of God's grace.

THE OFFERINGS: INSTRUCTIONS FOR THE PRIESTS

8 Then the LORD spoke to Moses, saying,

9 "Command Aaron and his sons, saying, 'This *is* the law of the burnt offering: The burnt offering *shall be* on the hearth upon the altar all night until morning, and the fire of the altar shall be kept burning on it.

10 'And the priest shall put on his linen garment, and his linen trousers he shall put on his body, and take up the ashes of the burnt offering which the fire

has consumed on the altar, and he shall put them beside the altar.

11 'Then he shall take off his garments, put on other garments, and carry the ashes outside the camp to a clean place.

12 'And the fire on the altar shall be kept burning on it; it shall not be put out. And the priest shall burn wood on it every morning, and lay the burnt offering in order on it; and he shall burn on it the fat of the peace offerings.

13 'A perpetual fire shall burn on the altar; it shall never go out.

14 'This *is* the law of the grain offering: The sons of Aaron shall offer it on the altar before the LORD.

15 'He shall take from it his handful of the fine flour of the grain offering, with its oil, and all the frankincense which *is* on the grain offering , and shall burn *it* on the altar *for* a sweet aroma, as a memorial to the LORD.

16 'And the remainder of it Aaron and his sons shall eat; with unleavened bread it shall be eaten in a holy place; in the court of the tabernacle of meeting they shall eat it.

17 'It shall not be baked with leaven. I have given it *to them as* their portion of My offerings made by fire; it *is* most holy, like the sin offering and the trespass offering.

18 'All the males among the children of Aaron may eat it. *It shall be* a statute forever in your generations concerning the offerings made by fire to the LORD. Everyone who touches them must be holy.'"

19 And the LORD spoke to Moses, saying,

20 "This *is* the offering of Aaron and his sons, which they shall offer to the LORD, beginning on the day when he is anointed: one-tenth of an *ephah* of fine flour as a daily grain offering, half of it in the morning and half of it at night.

21 "It shall be made in a pan with oil. *When it is well* mixed, you shall bring it in. *And* the baked pieces of the grain offering you shall offer *for* a sweet aroma to the LORD.

22 "The priest from among his sons, who is anointed in his place, shall offer it. *It is* a statute forever to the LORD. It shall be wholly burned.

23 "For every grain offering for the priest shall be wholly burned. It shall not be eaten."

24 And the LORD spoke to Moses, saying,

25 "Speak to Aaron and to his sons, saying, 'This *is* the law of the sin offering: In the place where the burnt offering is killed, the sin offering shall be killed before the LORD. It *is* most holy.

26 'The priest who offers it for sin shall eat it. In a holy place it shall be eaten, in the court of the tabernacle of meeting.

27 'Everyone who touches its flesh must be holy. And when its blood is sprinkled on any garment, you shall wash that on which it was sprinkled, in a holy place.

28 'But the earthen vessel in which it is boiled shall be broken. And if it is boiled in a bronze pot, it shall be both scoured and rinsed in water.

29 'All the males among the priests may eat it. It *is* most holy.

30 'But no sin offering from which *any* of the blood is brought into the tabernacle of meeting, to make atonement in the holy *place,* shall be eaten. It shall be burned in the fire.

7:1 'Likewise this *is* the law of the trespass offering (it *is* most holy):

2 'In the place where they killed the burnt offering they shall kill the trespass offering. And its blood he shall sprinkle all around on the altar.

3 'And he shall offer from it all its fat. The fat tail and the fat that covers the entrails,

4 'the two kidneys and the fat that *is* on them by the flanks, and the fatty lobe *attached to* the liver above the kidneys, he shall remove;

5 'and the priest shall burn them on the altar *as* an offering made by fire to the LORD. It *is* a trespass offering.

6 'Every male among the priests may eat it. It shall be eaten in a holy place. It *is* most holy.

7 'The trespass offering *is* like the sin offering; *there is* one law for them both: the priest who makes atonement with it shall have *it.*

8 'And the priest who offers anyone's burnt offering, that priest shall have for himself the skin of the burnt offering which he has offered.

9 'Also every grain offering that is baked in the oven and all that is prepared in the covered pan, or in a pan, shall be the priest's who offers it.

10 'Every grain offering mixed with oil, or dry, shall belong to all the sons of Aaron, to one *as much* as the other.

11 'This *is* the law of the sacrifice of peace offerings which he shall offer to the LORD:

12 'If he offers it for a thanksgiving, then he shall offer, with the sacrifice of thanksgiving, unleavened cakes mixed with oil, unleavened wafers anointed with oil, or cakes of *finely* blended flour mixed with oil.

13 'Besides the cakes, *as* his offering he shall offer leavened bread with the sacrifice of thanksgiving of his peace offering.

14 'And from it he shall offer one cake from each offering *as* a heave offering to the LORD. It shall belong to the priest who sprinkles the blood of the peace offering.

15 'The flesh of the sacrifice of his peace offering for thanksgiving shall be eaten the same day it is offered. He shall not leave any of it until morning.

16 'But if the sacrifice of his offering *is* a vow or a voluntary offering, it shall be eaten the same day that he offers his sacrifice; but on the next day the remainder of it also may be eaten;

17 'the remainder of the flesh of the sacrifice on the third day must be burned with fire.

18 'And if *any* of the flesh of the sacrifice of his peace offering is eaten at all on the third day, it shall not be accepted, nor shall it be imputed to him; whoever offers it shall be an abomination, and the person who eats of it shall bear guilt.

19 'The flesh that touches any unclean thing shall not be eaten. It shall be burned with fire. And as for the *clean* flesh, all who are clean may eat of it.

20 'But the person who eats the flesh of the sacrifice of the peace offering that *belongs* to the LORD, while he is unclean, that person shall be cut off from his people.

21 'Moreover the person who touches any unclean thing, *such as* human uncleanness, *any* unclean beast, or any abominable unclean thing, and who eats the flesh of the sacrifice of the peace offering that *belongs* to the LORD, that person shall be cut off from his people.'"

22 And the LORD spoke to Moses, saying,

23 "Speak to the children of Israel, saying: 'You shall not eat any fat, of ox or sheep or goat.

24 'And the fat of a beast that dies *naturally,* and the fat of what is torn by wild animals, may be used in any other way; but you shall by no means eat it.

25 'For whoever eats the fat of the beast of which men offer an offering made by fire to the LORD, the person who eats *it* shall be cut off from his people.

26 'Moreover you shall not eat any blood in any of your dwellings, *whether* of bird or beast.

27 'Whoever eats any blood, that person shall be cut off from his people.'"

28 Then the LORD spoke to Moses, saying,

29 "Speak to the children of Israel, saying: 'He who offers the sacrifice of his peace offering to the LORD shall bring his offering to the LORD from the sacrifice of his peace offering.

30 'His own hands shall bring the offerings made by fire to the LORD. The fat with the breast he shall bring, that the breast may be waved *as* a wave offering before the LORD.

31 'And the priest shall burn the fat on the altar, but the breast shall be Aaron's and his sons'.

32 'Also the right thigh you shall give to the priest *as* a heave offering from the sacrifices of your peace offerings.

33 'He among the sons of Aaron, who offers the blood of the peace offering, and the fat, shall have the right thigh for *his* part.

34 'For the breast of the wave offering and the thigh of the heave offering I have taken from the children of Israel, from the sacrifices of their peace offerings, and I have given them to Aaron the priest and to his sons from the children of Israel by a statute forever.'"

35 This *is* the consecrated portion for Aaron and his sons, from the offerings made by fire to the LORD, on the day when Moses presented them to minister to the LORD as priests.

36 The LORD commanded this to be given to them by the children of Israel, on the day that He anointed them, *by* a statute forever throughout their generations.

37 This *is* the law of the burnt offering, the grain
offering, the sin offering, the trespass offering, the
consecrations, and the sacrifice of the peace offering,
38 which the LORD commanded Moses on Mount
Sinai, on the day when He commanded the children
of Israel to offer their offerings to the LORD in the
Wilderness of Sinai.

Lev. 6:8–7:38

This section is puzzling to the contemporary reader, because it
repeats much of that which has preceded (1:1–6:7). The same five
sacrifices are dealt with somewhat redundantly, though the order
of the offerings is changed, with the peace offering being moved
from third to last. A separate cereal offering by the priests is added in
6:19–23.

At least two questions come to our minds. Why this repetition?
And why this variance? The simplest suggestion is that the repetition
may be due to the possibility that Lev. 6:7–7:38 was written immediately after Exodus 29. If this was the case, the sequence began with
Exodus 29 setting forth the ordination of Aaron and his sons as priests
with the sacrifices required on that occasion. Then followed Lev. 6:8–
7:38, giving the details of the rituals involved in those sacrifices.
Finally came Lev. 1:1–6:7 clarifying how the lay people were to bring
their sacrifices. While this may at first appear to be an unnecessary
manipulation of the texts, it does resolve some of the problems created by the variances. This in no way need question the integrity of
the text itself, granted one's willingness to accept the possibility of
such gathering and editing of the material.

The variances are explained by the instructions given to Moses in
each of the two sections. In the first section, he is told to address the
instructions to "*the Israelites,*" the people in general. In the second
section, he is told to give the instructions to "*Aaron and his sons.*" Thus,
in 1:1–6:7, we have instructions for the lay people in the bringing of
their offerings and sacrifices. In 6:8–7:38, we have instructions for the
priests in their role in the sacrifices. The reason for the variance in the
order of the offerings is not clear.

The section consists of nine paragraphs:
the burnt offering (vv. 8–13),
the grain offering (vv. 14–18),

the priest's grain offering (vv. 19–23),
the sin offering (vv. 24–30),
the guilt offering (vv. 7:1–10),
the peace offering (vv. 11–21),
the prohibition of eating fat or blood (vv. 28–36),
the priest's share (vv. 28–36), and
the summary (vv.37–38).

Verses 6:8–13. The emphasis, repeated three times, is clear: *the fire on the altar must be kept burning.* The symbolism expresses the heart of Israel's worship and life. Their worship to God is to be unceasing. The perpetual smoke rising from the burnt offerings is to be a constant reminder that all of life flows from their worship of God.

There have been three major schools of thought regarding the need for this perpetual fire. John Calvin noted that the first burnt offerings were ignited by fire from heaven (Lev. 9:24). Continual fire was required so that the subsequent offerings would be consumed with the fire from heaven. Others emphasize the symbolism of perpetual and uninterrupted worship of God by His people. Others see this as a symbol of our perpetual need for atonement and forgiveness. I am personally drawn to the second, finding here a beautiful picture of the life in Christ. How often, in special times of renewal and commitment, I find myself needing a reminder to keep the fire burning.

Though we no longer are required to bring burnt offerings, the symbolism of perpetual fire is a powerful expression of our life in Christ. When Paul wrote to his young friend and colleague, Timothy, he urged him "to stir up the gift of God which is in you" (2 Tim. 1:6). Paul used the same word that would be used to describe rearranging the sticks on a fire to rekindle the flames. I love Clarence Jordan's translation of this as "I'm reminding you to shake the ashes off the God-given fire that's in you." There's no reason to believe that Timothy's fire had gone out—for when it has gone out, no amount of stirring does any good. But every fire needs repeated stirring and rearranging to keep it burning brightly.

How do you rekindle the fire? Make some changes. Do some rearranging. If your prayer and devotional life no longer burns brightly, try some different approaches or different times. If your joy in Christ has cooled, try forming a small group for regular sharing and study. If you've gotten turned in on yourself, initiate a mission group to serve the needs of others. Don't be discouraged or surprised when the flames go down—just knock off some ashes and get some new kindling. Don't let the fire go out!

The priests are given specific instructions regarding the clothing they are to wear in performing these rituals. When the priest approached the altar, he was to be clothed with special linen, even while removing the ashes. When he took the ashes out to a special disposal site, he was to wear other clothes. Thus continued the clear distinction between that which was holy and that which was common.

Verses 14–18. The grain offering is called *"most holy"* (v. 17), as are the sin offering (v. 25) and the guilt offering (7:6). These three offerings are to be eaten only by the priests and within the sanctuary, as already indicated in chapter 2.

The statement in the closing sentence, *"Everyone who touches them must be holy"* (6:18), is widely regarded by commentators as a phrase of uncertain meaning. The same phrase occurs in connection with the sin offering (v. 27). As we shall see with Nadab and Abihu in chapter 10, these offerings are not to be approached casually or carelessly. It seems to me that two meanings are possible. On the one hand, no one dare handle the offerings but those who have been set apart for the priestly tasks. At the same time, even the priests must be meticulous in following the prescribed patterns for worship.

Verses 19–23. This offering was not mentioned in chapters 1–5. Here the focus is upon the need for the priests to make offerings for themselves. This grain offering by the priest is not to be eaten but completely burned. The writer of the Book of Hebrews emphasizes that with the human priesthood it was necessary for the priests first to offer sacrifices for their own sins. Christ's priesthood was unique because he was without sin; therefore he was a priest who did not need to offer sacrifices for his own sin. His superiority and uniqueness shine forth by contrast.

Verses 24–30. The same basics are set forth as before in Chapter 4, with special emphasis on what is to be eaten. The importance of not touching any portion of the sacrifice, as described in verse 18, is repeated in verse 27. The same principle prevails of maintaining a sharp distinction between what is holy and what is common.

Verses 7:1–10. The ritual of the sin offering is described more fully here than in chapter 5. Here the hide of the animal is to be given to the priest. The picture begins to emerge of a well-fed and well-provided-for priesthood. Presumably the details of the sin offering are expanded here because this passage was written primarily for the priests.

Verses 11–21. We have already learned that the peace offering was the only one which lay people were allowed to eat. The occasions for the peace offerings were those in which the worshiper wished to make a special offering of thanks to God or to renew a special vow.

This section gives details about the purpose and ritual of the peace offerings not found anywhere else in Leviticus. The meaning and significance of some of these details defy clear or simple explanations, and commentators offer a wide range of options, none of which give assured conclusions.

An interesting feature connected with these offerings is the requirement of eating the flesh of these sacrifices promptly, some on the same day, some on the next day, but none on or after the third day. Various reasons have been suggested for this strict regulation. The most obvious has to do with sanitation. It is likely that after the second day putrefaction might have set in, and the meat would be dangerous for consumption. Others suggest that the rule may have prevented the offering coming in contact with something ceremonially unclean. Still others suggest that the rule requiring immediate consumption would preclude storing up the meat, thus encouraging the worshiper to invite the poor to share the meal. Or there is the possibility that being required to eat the meat immediately would remind the worshiper that God would provide tomorrow's needs just as surely as he had provided today's.

None of these interpretations explains fully why some had to be eaten on the very day, while some could be kept for two days. What must not be overlooked is the seriousness with which these matters were to be taken, as in the threat of being "cut off" from the people for eating the meat of the offering while unclean. These matters will become the focus of chapters 11–15 and 22.

Verses 22–27. The prohibition of eating the fat or blood of the sacrifices has already been established in chapter 3. Under no circumstances was meat to be eaten from which the blood had not been drained. This has become the basis for the tradition of kosher meats in Jewish culture. The fat could be used for other purposes, but not for eating. The punishment for violation was also the "cutting off," which indicates divine judgment, possibly resulting in death.

Verses 28–36. The concept of the "wave" offering also has received many explanations, the most common of which suggests that the waving of the offering toward the altar and back again in a horizontal motion symbolized the giving of the offering by the worshiper and the reception of the offering by God. The giving of the breast and the right thigh of the sacrificial animal to the priests seems to indicate that the prime parts of the sacrifice were involved, suggesting that God made special provision for the priests.

Verses 37–38. This concluding sentence of the entire section of chapters 1–7 is of special interest to scholars because of its literary form. It is written like a colophon of a Mesopotamian tablet. The colophon on such a tablet contained what we are accustomed to place on the title page of a book, only it was appended to the end of the tablet. The parallels of this sentence with a Mesopotamian colophon are well developed by W. K. Harrison in his commentary on Leviticus and are significant from the standpoint of the early dating of Leviticus.

Instructions for the Priests and for Us

Though this section was clearly addressed to the priests, the sons of Aaron, who led the worship of ancient Israel, those who are called to lead the worship of the new Israel, the Church of Jesus Christ, do well to reflect upon some of the principles from long ago.

Though animal and grain sacrifices are no longer needed because of the meaning of Christ's sacrificial death, the seriousness with which we take our worship of God is still a measure of our devotion. Attention must be given to the quality of our worship, though we now recognize a rich diversity of forms and styles of worship. Paul took the Corinthians to task for their sloppiness in worship. The writer of the Book of Hebrews calls us to "serve God acceptably with reverence and godly fear. For our God is a consuming fire" (12:28, 29).

Too often, mere spontaneity that disdains preparation is equated with spirituality in worship. But this section of Leviticus reminds us that attention and care for the proper preparation and conduct of worship is as ancient as our faith and just as essential now as then. Since God is holy, far above all that we can imagine, the planning and leadership of worship demand and deserve our thoughtful best.

But this need not mean that we must get locked into the same repetitions to the point of boredom. Why are we so afraid of introducing new songs and hymns to our congregation? Many are discovering that people enjoy learning new songs when given the opportunity and encouragement. Some churches structure some time prior to the beginning of the worship service, after the people have arrived, for learning new songs and reviewing any other unusual aspects of the upcoming service. Why not vary the way in which the corporate confession of sin is shared? Some are finding that confession can be made through a hymn or psalm. Extending the use of silence in confession is often helpful. Exploring the many different ways of praying as a congregation can be most fruitful. Often, I have been impressed with the response of people to the invitation to pray aloud with "one-word" prayers. To hear people articulating their prayers all at the same time can be a moving experience.

These suggestions are an appeal to the planners and leaders of worship to give much more time to the specific, prayerful planning of each Sunday morning worship service and to allow creative imaginations a chance to be stirred and led by the Holy Spirit. I have been joyously surprised by God when participating with people in the release of creative imagining. And it's not a bad idea to send some folks out to other nearby churches just to experience ways that other congregations are praising and worshiping God.

In all of this, we must not succumb to the temptation to cross the line from planning worship into planning entertainment. Soren Kierkegaard used the analogy of the theater in regard to worship. Too often, he suggested, we regard the preacher and choir as the performers with the congregation as the audience. In reality, the preacher and the choir are to be regarded as the prompters, the congregation as the actors, and God as the audience. I'm convinced that there will come genuine renewal in worship to any congregation that begins to think of worship as our performance before God. To come into the house of the Lord on the Lord's day to bring to God our praise, our worship, and our adoration can and must be the basis for all of our living, being, and doing.

CHAPTER TWO

The Centrality of the Priesthood

Leviticus 8:1–10:20

Had we not already noticed the relationship between Leviticus and Exodus, we would be surprised to move from the regulations concerning the sacrifices directly to a narrative describing the ordination of Aaron and his sons to the priesthood. But we are aware that the stage was set for this part of the narrative beginning in Exodus 25.

Moses, while up on Mount Sinai, was told to instruct the people to bring offerings to God and to make a sanctuary, the tabernacle, as a movable worship center to take with them on their journey through the wilderness (Exodus 25–27). Aaron and his sons were to be ordained as priests (chaps. 28–31). After the episode with the golden calf (chaps. 32–34), work on the tabernacle progressed (chaps. 35–40). At this point (Leviticus 1–7) instructions for the worship were given before resuming the historical narrative in Leviticus 8.

In studying and teaching this section, it is crucial that we avoid either interpreting the text as only a record of a particular stage of development in the religious life of Israel or as a mandate for the form and structure of worship for all God's people, past and present. We need to be reminded that the story of the Bible is that of God's redemptive work in the course of history in forming a people who would know and do His will. Central to the life of this people were the observance and practice of a system of worship in which God would be praised and honored, in which people could experience the forgiveness of sin, and through which they could live in harmonious fellowship with God and with each other.

Thus, as we are learning in Leviticus, the tabernacle and the priesthood became the center of their lives, the constant and unfailing reminder of God's presence. Eventually, the temple would replace the tabernacle, but the priesthood would continue. The purpose of all of this was expressed in Exod. 29:42–46,

"This shall be a continual burnt offering throughout your generations at the door of the tabernacle of meeting before the LORD, where I will meet you to speak with you. And there I will meet with the children of Israel, and the tabernacle shall be sanctified by My glory. So I will sanctify the tabernacle of meeting and the altar. I will also sanctify both Aaron and his sons to minister to Me as priests. I will dwell among the children of Israel and will be their God. And they shall know that I am the LORD their God, who brought them up out of the land of Egypt, that I may dwell among them. I am the LORD their God."

Aaron and His Sons Consecrated

In this section of Leviticus, great emphasis is placed upon the fact that the commands given in Exodus 28 and 29 were carefully and meticulously carried out. More than fifteen times in these three chapters, we read the phrase, "as the Lord commanded Moses." With detail and fidelity, God's plan was carefully implemented.

THE VESTMENTS OF THE PRIESTS

8:1 And the LORD spoke to Moses, saying:
2 "Take Aaron and his sons with him, and the garments, the anointing oil, a bull as the sin offering, two rams, and a basket of unleavened bread;
3 "and gather all the congregation together at the door of the tabernacle of meeting."
4 So Moses did as the LORD commanded him. And the assembly was gathered together at the door of the tabernacle of meeting.
5 And Moses said to the congregation, "This *is* what the LORD commanded to be done."
6 Then Moses brought Aaron and his sons and washed them with water.
7 And he put the tunic on him, girded him with the sash, clothed him with the robe, and put the ephod on him; and he girded him with the intricately woven band of the ephod, and with it tied *the ephod* on him.

8 Then he put the breastplate on him, and he put
the Urim and the Thummim in the breastplate.
9 And he put the turban on his head. Also on the
turban, on its front, he put the golden plate, the holy
crown, as the LORD had commanded Moses.

Lev. 8:1–9

Before engaging the Leviticus text itself, we must go back to Exodus 28–29 for the original instructions to Moses for the ordination of Aaron and his sons as priests. The instructions for ordination began in Exod. 28:1–5 with the identification of Aaron and his sons Nadab, Abihu, Eleazar, and Ithamar as the five persons to be singled out for the priesthood. Special garments were to be made for them "for glory and for beauty" (Exod. 28:2), perhaps better translated "dignity and honor" (NIV). The attire for Aaron, the high priest, will be more elaborate than that for his sons. Special craftsmen, singled out by God, are to be enlisted for this unique task. There are to be six separate garments: (1) A breastplate, (2) An ephod, (3) A robe, (4) A skillfully woven tunic, (5) A turban, and (6) A sash.

The materials to be used for the priestly garments are gold; blue, purple, and scarlet yarn; and fine linen. The instructions for making each of these garments constitute the rest of Exodus 28 (vv. 6–43), and the actual making of the garments is described in Exod. 39:1–31. The ephod and the breastplate are described initially and in much greater detail than the other garments, suggesting their special importance. The ephod (Exod. 28:6–14) was something like a vest that covered the upper half of the body from the shoulders down to the waist. It was the outer garment, worn over the robe, upon which was attached the breastplate. It was a very colorful garment with gold, with blue, purple, and scarlet yarn, and with finely twisted linen. It required the work of a skilled craftsman. It was to have two shoulder pieces attached to its two upper corners for securing to the shoulders and a waistband woven into the ephod with the same materials. It was to be decorated with two elaborate onyx stones set in gold filigree, attached to the shoulder pieces of the ephod by two gold rope chains. Upon each of the stones was to be engraved, carefully and professionally, the names of six of the sons of Israel in the order of their birth. Thus, we have the picture of an elaborate upper body covering, fastened to each shoulder and tied to the waist, with an impressive gold chain from shoulder to shoulder bearing the two onyx stones finely engraved with the names of the twelve patriarchs of Israel.

The breastplate, another costly and precious article, is described in Exod. 28:15–30. It was to be made of the same materials as the ephod. It was to be about nine inches square, folded in double thickness and attached to the ephod over Aaron's heart, presumably just below the gold chain with the onyx stones. On this nine-inch square were to be mounted, in gold filigree, twelve precious gems, each of a different stone, and each inscribed with the name of one of the sons of Israel. Gold rings were to be made for each of the corners of the breastplate by which it was to be secured with gold chains tied with blue cord to the shoulders and the waistband of the ephod, to keep it from swinging out from the body of Aaron during his priestly functions. The final articles to be placed within the fold of the breastplate were the Urim and Thummim.

Unfortunately for us, while there are other references in Scripture to the Urim and Thummim, nowhere are they actually described. All we really know for certain is that they were objects used by a priest in some way to determine the will of God in difficult decisions. When Saul, after the death of Samuel, was having great difficulty trying to decide what to do when facing the Philistines at Gilboa, he sought God's will through dreams, through Urim, and through prophets, but all to no avail. In despair, he consulted the witch of Endor, leading to his ultimate defeat and self-destruction (1 Sam. 28:1–8ff). In this instance the Urim was consulted to determine direction from God. After the return of the exiles from Jerusalem, the governor would not allow anyone to eat the food of the offering until "a priest could consult with the Urim and Thummim" (Ezra 2:63).

The Hebrew words "Urim and Thummim" actually mean "lights and perfections," but beyond this we know nothing. Commentators are fond of referring to these two objects as "sacred dice" by which God's will was determined. They gave a positive, negative, or neutral reply. It does not appear that they were used often, and they apparently dropped out of use by postexilic times. The Urim and Thummim apparently are the reason for the designation of the breastplate as "the the breastplate of judgment," but it seems from Exod. 28:29–30 that the breastplate is most important because Aaron "shall bear the judgment of the children of Israel over his heart before the LORD continually." No explanation is given for the ephod and the breastplate bearing the names of the twelve tribes of Israel, but this certainly provides a strong, living memorial to the patriarchs to be carried continually at the center of their life and worship.

The details of the robe to be worn by Aaron are given in Exod. 28:31–35. It was to be entirely of blue cloth, like a cassock with a hole in the center to slip over the priest's head. The edge of the hole was to be woven like a collar to prevent tearing. The hem of the robe was to be adorned with embroidered pomegranates alternating with gold bells. Apparently the pomegranates pointed toward their settlement in the fruitful land of promise, as a symbol of God's abundant provisions.

The pomegranate was highly visible in Solomon's temple. At the entrance were two massive bronze pillars (twenty-seven feet high and eighteen feet in circumference) topped with cast bronze capitals seven and one-half feet high. The dominant decoration on each of these capitals was "two hundred such pomegranates in rows on each of the capitals all around" (1 Kings 7:15–22; cf. Jer. 52:22). The pillars, by the way, were named Jachin ("he establishes") and Boaz ("in him is strength"). In extolling the beauties of his love, the writer of the Song of Solomon twice uses the symbol of the pomegranate: "Your temples behind your veil are like a piece of pomegranate" (4:3 and 6:7). When Caleb and Joshua went with the representatives of each tribe to scout out the land of Canaan from their encampment in Paran, they returned with a pole on which they carried a cluster of grapes along with some pomegranates and figs, attesting to the fruitful abundance of Canaan (Num. 13:1–25). Indeed, the embroidered pomegranates around the hem of the priestly robe were a foretaste of things to come.

The alternating gold bells around the hem would sound an audible signal of Aaron's movements about the tabernacle. Their sound protected Aaron from death as he moved in and out of the Holy Place.

The turban that Aaron was to wear (Exod. 28:36–38) was to carry on the front a pure gold plate on which was to be engraved the inscription, "HOLINESS TO THE LORD." It was to be attached to the turban with a blue cord, apparently hanging before Aaron's forehead (v. 38). This turban was to be worn only by Aaron as the high priest and was the crown of all the garments. Its chief purpose was to carry the plate of gold on Aaron's forehead, proclaiming that holiness is the essence of God as well as the goal and purpose of all the worship of the people.

The tunics and the turban were to be made of fine linen, and the sash was to be made by an embroiderer (v. 39). Tunics, sashes, and headbands were to be made for Aaron's sons "for glory and beauty" (v. 40). We learn in Exod. 39:29 that the sashes were made of "fine linen and blue and purple and scarlet thread, woven as the Lord had commanded Moses." Only after they have been clothed in these garments were Aaron and his sons to be ordained and consecrated to their special ministries as priests (v. 41).

Finally, linen undergarments reaching from the thigh to the waist were to be worn by the priests whenever they ministered in the tabernacle and the Holy Place "that they do not incur iniquity and die." The gravity of the propriety of their attire and of their performance of their duties was profound, as we shall see in Leviticus 10 with the case of Nadab and Abihu. The permanence of these instructions concludes Exodus 28.

Now we are ready to interact with the text of Leviticus as the day has arrived for the ordination of Aaron and his sons. There's a beautiful note of grace as a backdrop for this ordination of Aaron and his four sons as priests. While Moses was on the mountain at Sinai, the people rebelled against Moses and called upon Aaron to make new gods for them (Exodus 32). While Aaron didn't initiate the rebellion, he certainly led the process in the well-known incident of the making of the golden calf. With great anger, Moses confronted Aaron: "What did this people do to you that you have brought so great a sin upon them?" (Exod. 32:21). In a classic cop-out, Aaron replied: "Do not let the anger of my lord become hot. You know the people, that they are set on evil. For they said to me, 'Make us gods that shall go before us; as for this Moses, the man who brought us out of the land of Egypt, we do not know what has become of him.' And I said to them, 'Whoever has any gold, let them break it off.' So they gave it to me, and I cast it into the fire, and this calf came out." (Exod. 32:22–25). The chapter closes on a sad note: "So the Lord plagued the people because of what they did with the calf which Aaron made" (Exod. 32:35).

And that's where we left Aaron until he appears again in Leviticus 8. Was Aaron rejected because of his sin? Would someone else be appointed in his place? Can God's grace and forgiveness be given to Aaron? Can a sinner like Aaron be appointed to the highest religious office in the nation?   Leviticus 8 gives a resounding affirmation of God's grace in restoring Aaron to the place where God had called him to be. Again and again, throughout the Bible, God uses imperfect people to do His will. God uses people like Aaron in God's redemptive work in the world. God even uses people like us!

Verses 1–4 describe the celebrative gathering in the tabernacle before the entrance to the Holy Place. All is in readiness for this very special day that would mark the beginning of the priesthood, which, for us, will come to its fullest expression when Jesus dies on the cross, both as our High Priest and as the sacrificial lamb. Moses was told to gather the entire assembly, signifying this as an occasion of great and national significance.

Verses 5–9 describe the initial part of the ordination service, the clothing of Aaron with the special vestments. Aaron's sons will be clothed much more simply (8:13). The service began with the ceremonial washing of Aaron and his sons, the symbol of cleansing. No one can enter into God's presence or into God's service without being cleansed. Recall Isaiah's lament when he found himself in the presence of God: "Woe is me, for I am undone! Because I am a man of unclean lips, and I dwell in the midst of a people of unclean lips" (Isa. 6:5). In a day when we emphasize God's love and acceptance, we must also be aware of His holiness and our need for cleansing. We shall delve much more deeply into this matter of cleansing in Leviticus 11–15. Though they were to be priests because they were appointed by God, it was still necessary to observe the cleansing ritual, the outward washing being a symbol of inner cleansing. When the New Testament reminds believers that we are "a chosen people, a royal priesthood" (1 Pet. 2:9), the knowledge that God has chosen us and set us apart for God's service should be a source of overwhelming gratitude.

The importance of the office to which Aaron is being installed is symbolized, as we have learned, by the very special and colorful garments that have been made for him and are now to be donned for the first time. An appreciation of the beauty of these vestments adds to our awareness of the supreme importance of the priesthood in the life and worship of Israel. And the importance of the priesthood is a reminder of the importance of worship to the people of God in all times and places.

THE ANOINTING

10 Then Moses took the anointing oil, and anointed
the tabernacle and all that *was* in it, and sanctified
them.
11 He sprinkled some of it on the altar seven times,
anointed the altar and all its utensils, and the laver
and its base, to sanctify them.
12 And he poured some of the anointing oil on
Aaron's head and anointed him, to sanctify him.
13 Then Moses brought Aaron's sons and put
tunics on them, girded them with sashes, and put hats
on them, as the LORD had commanded Moses.

Lev. 8:10–13

Now that Aaron has been clothed with the magnificent garments of
the office of high priest, the service of ordination begins with the
anointing of everything in the tabernacle, along with Aaron himself,
and the clothing of Aaron's sons as priests.

For our enhancement in understanding the rich meaning of the
anointing ritual, we must again go to Exodus, now to 29:1–9, 30:22–
33, and 40:9–16. By anointing the tabernacle and everything in it, the
center of worship was set apart for the service of God. And by anointing Aaron and his sons with the special oil, they, too, were dedicated
to God. Anointing with oil thus became an ancient symbol of setting
things and people apart for special service to God.

The making of the anointing oil is carefully prescribed in Exod.
30:22–33. A large quantity is specified (vv. 23–24), consisting of more
than twelve pounds each of liquid myrrh and cassia, a little more than
six pounds each of fragrant cinnamon and cane, and about a gallon of
olive oil. This oil was to be used first for the anointing of everything in
the tabernacle (vv. 26–29) and then for the anointing of Aaron and his
sons (v. 30). It was to be retained thereafter for the subsequent anointing of future priests "throughout your generations." Any other use of
this oil was expressly forbidden (vv. 32–33), and no other oil was to
be made with the same formula (v. 32). Any deviation from these
rules would result in being cut off from one's people (v. 33). "It is
holy, and it shall be holy to you" (v. 32).

Both Exod. 29:1–9 and 40:9–16 give the instructions for the service of the anointing of everything in the tabernacle and of Aaron and his sons as carried out by Moses in Lev. 8:10–13. Only in Exod. 40:14–15 and 30:30 is it clearly stated that Aaron's sons are to be anointed with Aaron: "for their anointing shall surely be an everlasting priesthood throughout their generations" (40:15).

THE SACRIFICES

14 And he brought the bull for the sin offering. Then Aaron and his sons laid their hands on the head of the bull for the sin offering,

15 and Moses killed *it*. Then he took the blood, and put *some* on the horns of the altar all around with his finger, and purified the altar; and he poured the blood at the base of the altar, and sanctified it, to make atonement for it.

16 Then he took all the fat that *was* on the entrails, the fatty lobe *attached to* the liver, and the two kidneys with their fat, and Moses burned *them* on the altar.

17 But the bull, its hide, its flesh, and its offal, he burned with fire outside the camp, as the LORD had commanded Moses.

18 Then he brought the ram as the burnt offering. And Aaron and his sons laid their hands on the head of the ram,

19 and Moses killed *it*. Then he sprinkled the blood all around on the altar.

20 And he cut the ram into pieces; and Moses burned the head, the pieces, and the fat.

21 Then he washed the entrails and the legs in water. And Moses burned the whole ram on the altar. It *was* a burnt sacrifice for a sweet aroma, *and* an offering made by fire to the LORD, as the LORD had commanded Moses.

Lev. 8:14–21

There now follows, leading to the ordination service itself, two sacrifices: a sin offering (vv. 14–17) and a burnt offering (vv. 18–21) as prescribed in Exod. 29:10–18 and implemented here.

The ordination service begins with the sin offering (14–17), reminding us that one of the purposes of this offering was to cleanse the sins of the priest: "If the anointed priest sins, bringing guilt on the people, then let him offer to the LORD . . . a young bull without blemish as a sin offering" (Lev. 4:3). It is appropriate that the ordination begin with this particular sacrifice. It is performed in Lev. 4:3–12 as prescribed though no mention is made here of the required seven-fold sprinkling of the blood "in front of the veil of the sanctuary" (4:6). The offering actually follows each detail of the sin offering as set forth in Exod. 29:10–14. Throughout this service, Moses is acting as the priest in ordaining those to become priests. Thus, Moses, not Aaron, is actually the first priest. One wonders why at this point the blood was placed on the altar of burnt offerings (v. 15) rather than on the altar of incense within the Holy Place where the priests would be ministering. It would seem that this was because they were about to offer a sacrifice on the altar of burnt offering, thus necessitating the cleansing of it prior to what is to follow.

After the sin offering, Moses proceeds to a burnt offering (vv. 18–21). The offering follows with precision the instructions given in Exod. 29:15–18. One point of difference from the ritual as described in Lev. 1:1–9 occurs when Moses, not those making the offering, kills the animal. However, the essence of the service is the atonement for the sins of Aaron and his sons as their preparation for the assumption of the priesthood.

THE ORDINATION RITE

22 And he brought the second ram, the ram of consecration. Then Aaron and his sons laid their hands on the head of the ram,

23 and Moses killed *it*. And he took *some* of its blood and put it on the tip of Aaron's right ear, on the thumb of his right hand, and on the big toe of his right foot.

24 Then he brought Aaron's sons. And Moses put *some* of the blood on the tips of their right ears, on the thumbs of their right hands, and on the big toes of

their right feet. And Moses sprinkled the blood all
around on the altar.

25 Then he took the fat and the fat tail, all the fat
that *was* on the entrails, the fatty lobe *attached to* the
liver, the two kidneys and their fat, and the right
thigh;

26 and from the basket of unleavened bread that
was before the LORD he took one unleavened cake, a
cake of bread *anointed with* oil, and one wafer, and put
them on the fat and on the right thigh;

27 and he put all *these* in Aaron's hands and in his
sons' hands, and waved them *as* a wave offering
before the LORD.

28 Then Moses took them from their hands and
burned *them* on the altar, on the burnt offering. They
were consecration offerings for a sweet aroma. That
was an offering made by fire to the LORD.

29 And Moses took the breast and waved it *as* a
wave offering before the LORD. It was Moses' part of
the ram of consecration, as the LORD had commanded
Moses.

30 Then Moses took some of the anointing oil and
some of the blood which *was* on the altar, and
sprinkled *it* on Aaron, on his garments, on his sons,
and on the garments of his sons with him; and he
sanctified Aaron, his garments, his sons, and the
garments of his sons with him.

31 And Moses said to Aaron and his sons, "Boil the
flesh *at* the door of the tabernacle of meeting, and eat
it there with the bread that *is* in the basket of consecration offerings, as I commanded, saying, 'Aaron and
his sons shall eat it.'

32 "What remains of the flesh and of the bread you
shall burn with fire.

33 "And you shall not go outside the door of the
tabernacle of meeting *for* seven days, until the days of
your consecration are ended. For seven days he shall
consecrate you.

34 "As he has done this day, *so* the LORD has
commanded to do, to make atonement for you.

35 "Therefore you shall abide *at* the door of the
tabernacle of meeting day and night for seven days,

and keep the charge of the LORD, so that you may not
die; for so I have been commanded."
   36 So Aaron and his sons did all the things that the
LORD had commanded by the hand of Moses.

Lev. 8:22-36

I prefer to call this part of the service the ordination rite, rather than
regarding it as a continuation of the previous two sacrifices. To be
sure, the action itself is very much like the peace offering (Lev. 3:1-5),
but it has the unique feature of being the act by which Aaron and his
sons are set apart as priests for the service of God.

The opening sentence reminds us that, in addition to the priestly
garments, Moses was to bring the anointing oil, the bull for the sin
offering, two rams (one has been used for the burnt offering), and a
basket of unleavened bread (8:1). The service follows precisely the
instructions given in Exod. 29:19-37.

While the ordination sacrifice of the ram, including the part involving the breast and thigh of the ram and the bread and wafer, are akin
to the peace offering (Lev. 3:6-11), the distinguishing features of this
offering are the placing of the blood on Aaron and his sons (vv. 23-
24), and the sprinkling of the anointing oil and the blood on the
priests and their garments (v. 30). We will meet the practice of placing
some of the blood of the sacrificial animal *"on the tip of Aaron's right
ear, on the thumb of his right hand, and on the big toe of his right foot"* in
Lev. 14:14 and 25, in the cleansing ritual of one who has experienced
healing of a skin disease. Though the situations calling for this ritual
are dramatically different, the symbolism is intriguing in both. If one
considers the ear a symbol of hearing, the thumb a symbol of working, and the toe a symbol of walking, one can regard this action as
indicating that priests (and later cured "lepers") are now commissioned and established to listen to God, to work for God, and to walk
with God. I'm reminded of the meditation we sometimes use in our
worship service:

> God be in our minds and in our understanding.
> God be in our eyes and in our seeing.
> God be in our mouths and in our speaking.
> God be in our hearts and in our living.

God be in our ears and in our hearing.
God be in our hands and in our doing.
God be in our feet and in our walking.
God be with us now in our departing.

The drama comes to its climax in verse 30, with Moses taking some of the anointing oil and some of the blood from the altar and sprinkling it first on Aaron and his garments, and then upon Aaron's sons and their garments. "*And he sanctified Aaron, his garments, his sons, and the garments of his sons with him.*" This direct linkage of the altar, the priests, and their garments establishes the essential nature of the priesthood. Altars and priests are hereafter inseparable. The primary function of the priest is to preside at the altar where people are to bring their sacrificial offerings to God. Thus, the priest represents people before God. Yet all is of God's grace, for it is God who provides the altar and the priests by which atonement can be made for sin and the relationship with God maintained with integrity.

The instructions given to Aaron and his sons by Moses (vv. 31–35) are a condensed recapitulation of the instructions given Moses in Exod. 29:29–37. There, Moses is told "and you shall offer a bull every day as a sin offering for atonement. You shall cleanse the altar when you make atonement for it, and you shall anoint it to sanctify it. Seven days you shall make atonement for the altar and sanctify it. And the altar shall be most holy. Whatever touches the altar must be holy" (Exod. 29:36–37). We can assume that all of the details were carried out to the letter from the stern warning given to Moses: "*Therefore you shall abide at the door of the tabernacle of meeting day and night for seven days, and keep the charge of the LORD, so that you may not die; for so I have commanded*" (v. 35). Thus, the ordination service continued for seven days, with the offering of a bull for a sin offering each day along with the daily anointing of the altar. At the conclusion of these seven days, the altar is rendered holy. The idea of a period of seven days to observe special events was not uncommon, as, for example, after birth (Lev. 12), wedding feasts (Gen. 29:27; Judg. 14:12), and deaths (Gen. 50:10).

We cannot leave this chapter without recognizing that it points to a week of extreme importance in the entire Biblical record. What was begun through Moses with Aaron and his sons at this point in time will be continued down through the centuries, and presumably throughout history. The priesthood became central to the life and worship of the people of Israel, essential to their identity and self-understanding. The central meaning of the saving work of Christ on the cross can be understood and accepted only in the light of the priesthood. And Christian tradition has continued, in virtually all of its expressions, with the recognition that God calls and sets apart by ordination particular men and women to serve and lead the people in their worship and life together.

THE PRIESTS BEGIN THEIR MINISTRY

9:1 It came to pass on the eighth day that Moses called Aaron and his sons and the elders of Israel.

2 And he said to Aaron, "Take for yourself a young bull as a sin offering and a ram as a burnt offering, without blemish, and offer *them* before the LORD.

3 "And to the children of Israel you shall speak, saying, 'Take a kid of the goats as a sin offering, and a calf and a lamb, *both* of the first year, without blemish, as a burnt offering,

4 'also a bull and a ram as peace offerings, to sacrifice before the LORD, and a grain offering mixed with oil; for today the LORD will appear to you.'"

5 So they brought what Moses commanded before the tabernacle of meeting. And all the congregation drew near and stood before the LORD.

6 Then Moses said, "This *is* the thing which the LORD commanded you to do, and the glory of the LORD will appear to you."

7 And Moses said to Aaron, "Go to the altar, offer your sin offering and your burnt offering, and make atonement for yourself and for the people. Offer the offering of the people, and make atonement for them, as the LORD commanded."

8 Aaron therefore went to the altar and killed the calf of the sin offering, which *was* for himself.

9 Then the sons of Aaron brought the blood to him. And he dipped his finger in the blood, put *it* on

the horns of the altar, and poured the blood at the base of the altar.

10 But the fat, the kidneys, and the fatty lobe from the liver of the sin offering he burned on the altar, as the LORD had commanded Moses.

11 The flesh and the hide he burned with fire outside the camp.

12 And he killed the burnt offering; and Aaron's sons presented to him the blood, which he sprinkled all around on the altar.

13 Then they presented the burnt offering to him, with its pieces and head, and he burned *them* on the altar.

14 And he washed the entrails and the legs, and burned *them* with the burnt offering on the altar.

15 Then he brought the people's offering, and took the goat, which *was* the sin offering for the people, and killed it and offered it for sin, like the first one.

16 And he brought the burnt offering and offered it according to the prescribed manner.

17 Then he brought the grain offering, took a handful of it, and burned *it* on the altar, besides the burnt sacrifice of the morning.

18 He also killed the bull and the ram *as* sacrifices of peace offerings, which *were* for the people. And Aaron's sons presented to him the blood, which he sprinkled all around on the altar,

19 and the fat from the bull and the ram — the fatty tail, what covers *the entrails* and the kidneys, and the fatty lobe *attached to* the liver;

20 and they put the fat on the breasts. Then he burned the fat on the altar;

21 but the breasts and the right thigh Aaron waved *as* a wave offering before the LORD, as Moses had commanded.

22 Then Aaron lifted his hand toward the people, blessed them, and came down from offering the sin offering, the burnt offering, and peace offerings.

23 And Moses and Aaron went into the tabernacle of meeting, and came out and blessed the people. Then the glory of the LORD appeared to all the people,

24 and fire came out from before the LORD and
consumed the burnt offering and the fat on the altar.
When all the people saw *it,* they shouted and fell on
their faces.

Lev. 9:1–24

For an entire week the anticipation has been building! The colorful
vestments for Aaron and his sons have been placed upon them, the
ordination celebration has continued at the entrance to the Holy Place
for seven days, and now the moment has arrived for Aaron and his
sons to perform their very first priestly acts. To enter into the sense of
joy and gratitude that they must have felt, recall that after the initial
instructions for the building of the tabernacle and the making of the
priestly garments, there had followed the episode with the golden calf
and the shattering of the two tablets by Moses. With the replacement
of the tablets, the instructions were reiterated (Exodus 34–40) and the
liturgy for the sacrifices was given (Leviticus 1–7). Finally, after what
must have seemed to be interminable delays, the worship is to begin!

While many scholars suggest that this chapter either stands in
conflict with or does not presuppose the existence of chapter 8, I do
not find that such a reading is necessary. To be sure, there is a repetition of the sin and burnt offerings for Aaron and his sons (9:2), but
could that not be expected in the light of such daily offerings over a
period of seven days? And specific differences have been pointed out,
such as the difference in the language of 4:3 and 9:2 regarding the
young bull (a difference not indicated in our translation), but it seems
to me that this is almost straining at gnats to substantiate a specific
overview. Reading chapter 9 as a sequel to chapter 8 is not ruled out
by the text itself. The bottom line is that the sacrifices are regarded as
the basis, as given by God, for the maintenance of the relationship
between God and the people, the means by which sin is atoned for,
the dwelling place of God is cleansed, and the people are accepted by
God.

It seems best to read this chapter as a unity. Though Aaron and his
sons are now to begin their priestly functions, Moses is still the com-
manding figure (v. 1). The orders are given both to Aaron (v. 2) and,
through Aaron, to the people as a whole (v. 3). Aaron is to bring a
young bull and a ram as a sin and a burnt offering for himself, and the

people are to bring a young goat for a sin offering; a calf and a lamb for a burnt offering; a bull and a ram as peace offerings; and a grain offering. Thus, on this beginning day of the sacrifices, four of the five types of sacrifices are to be presented for the first time. After the instructions (vv. 1–6), Moses commands Aaron to begin the worship (v. 7). The acts of sacrifice are described in the rest of the chapter. Aaron's own sin offering (vv. 8–11), his own burnt offering (vv. 12–14), the sin offering for the people (v. 15), the burnt offering for the people (v. 16), and the grain offering for the people (v. 17) follow in succession. The peace offerings for the people are then offered, with the wave offering (vv. 18–21). Then Aaron gives the blessing to the people (v. 22) and enters the Holy Place with Moses, before coming out again to bless the people (v. 23). The chapter ends on the high note: *"Then the glory of the LORD appeared to all the people, and fire came out from before the LORD and consumed the burnt offering and the fat on the altar. When all the people saw it, they shouted and fell on their faces"* (9:23–24).

The heart of this chapter is to be found in the series of statements found in verses 4, 6, and 23-24 — *"today the LORD will appear to you . . . the glory of the LORD will appear to you . . . then the glory of the LORD appeared to all the people, and fire came out from before the LORD. . . ."* We do well to pause for a moment to reflect upon the meaning of "the glory of the LORD " (Hebrew, *kabod*). The word occurs only here in Leviticus, ten times in Exodus (chaps. 16–40), numerous times in Psalms, Isaiah, and Ezekiel, and occasionally in other parts of the Old Testament. Its root meaning is generally given as "weight," "heaviness," "honor," or "glory."

The first use of *kabod* with relationship to God is in Exodus 16:1–10. The children of Israel are engaged in complaining against Moses for having brought them out into the wilderness, longing for "the good old days" back in slavery in Egypt. God reassures Moses and Aaron that He is with them, and that He will provide meat in the evening and bread in the morning in abundance for them. Moses and Aaron announce to the grumbling gathering: "At evening you shall know that the LORD has brought you out of the land of Egypt. And in the morning you shall see the glory of the LORD "(Exod. 16:6–7). The passage continues, "Now it came to pass, as Aaron spoke to the whole congregation of the children of Israel, that they looked toward the wilderness, and behold, the glory of the LORD appeared in the cloud. And the LORD spoke to Moses" (Exod. 16:10, 11).

We next meet *kabod* in Exodus 24, when Moses, with Joshua, is on Mount Sinai with the Lord, leaving Aaron and Hur in charge of the people. "Then Moses went up into the mountain, and a cloud covered the mountain. Now the glory of the LORD rested on Mount Sinai, and the cloud covered it six days. And on the seventh day He called to Moses out of the midst of the cloud. The sight of the glory of the LORD was like a consuming fire on the top of the mountain in the eyes of the children of Israel" (Exod. 24:15–17).

In Exodus 29:43, we have already seen that "the tabernacle shall be sanctified by My glory." In Exodus 40, noting the completion of the building of the tabernacle:

> "Then the cloud covered the tabernacle of meeting, and the glory of the Lord filled the tabernacle. And Moses was not able to enter the tabernacle of meeting, because the cloud rested above it, and the glory of the LORD filled the tabernacle. When the cloud was taken up from above the tabernacle, the children of Israel went onward in all their journeys. But if the cloud was not taken up, then they did not journey till the day that it was taken up. For the cloud of the LORD was above the tabernacle by day, and fire was over it by night, in the sight of all the house of Israel, through-out all their journeys.
>
> *Exod. 40:34–38*

On another occasion, we meet *kabod* when Moses is pleading with God: "Please, show me Your glory." God is recorded as replying, "I will make all My goodness pass before you, and I will proclaim the name of the LORD before you. . . . " But, He said, "You cannot see My face; for no man shall see Me, and live. . . . Here is a place by Me, and you shall stand on the rock. So shall it be, while My glory passes by, that I will put you in the cleft of the rock, and will cover you with My hand while I pass by. Then I will take away My hand, and you shall see My back; but My face shall not be seen" (Exod. 33:18–23).

We meet *kabod* in the story of the return of the spies from Canaan, when most of them insisted that they could not hope to best the "giants" in Canaan. When Joshua and Caleb stood against the rest and urged movement directly into Canaan, the congregation was calling for their stoning. But "the glory of the LORD appeared in the tabernacle of meeting before all the children of Israel" (Num. 14:10), threatening the people with pestilence because of their cowardly disobedience. As Moses pleaded with the Lord to pardon the people, the Lord said: "I have pardoned, according to your word; but truly, as I live, all the earth shall be filled with the glory of the LORD" (14:20).

When Ezekiel prophesied his vision of the restoration of the temple, he proclaimed, "And behold, the glory of the God of Israel came from the way of the east. His voice was like the sound of many waters; and the earth shone with His glory. . . . And the glory of the LORD came into the temple by way of the gate which faces toward the east. The Spirit lifted me up and brought me into the inner court; and behold, the glory of the LORD filled the temple" (Ezek. 43:2–5).

From these passages, a clear meaning of "the glory of the LORD" emerges. The glory of the Lord obviously refers to the presence of God. God's presence among them was accompanied by visible manifestations, such as the cloud and the fire over the tabernacle and the cloud and fire over Mount Sinai. But the manifestations were not the glory. The "glory" is God's presence. It would seem to me that we would not miss the mark if we were to translate *kabod* in relationship to God as "presence."

And may we not justly envy them? How often I have wished that God would give us some cloud or pillar of fire by which we might be certain, beyond any doubt, of God's presence. I think of a young mother who came to me for help. Subsequent to the birth of her second child, she was gripped with serious, deep depressions accompanied by terrifying anxiety attacks. Just labeling it postpartum experience did not bring relief to her. We brought in medical and psychological help, but many of the symptoms continued. She was a person with deep faith in God's love and care and had lived out that faith dynamically throughout her life. Her question repeatedly was, "Where is God? Why doesn't God help me with these terrible feelings?" Every pastor knows that these are not moments for the rehearsal of platitudes and easy answers. There are no sure shortcuts to healing and wholeness. How often in those pastoral moments I think of the ancient Hebrews who could see the cloud and the fire and be assured that God was present with them. We don't have the visible assurances of God's presence as they did. But we do have the promise of the Holy Spirit, the continuing presence of Jesus Himself. In what is often called the High Priestly prayer of Jesus, His prayer for His disciples just prior to His betrayal and arrest in Gethsemane, He requested: "Father, I desire that they also whom You gave Me may be with Me where I am, *that they may behold My glory* which You have given Me; for You loved Me before the foundation of the world" (John 17:24). Earlier, Jesus had said to His disciples: "It is to your advantage that I go away; for if I do not go away, the Helper will not come to you; but if I depart, I will send Him to you" (John 16:7). It was this promise of God's presence that became to this young woman a growing source of strength and healing. She continues to have occasional bouts with depression, and she continues to use the help available through psychological and medical resources. But she tells me that her communion with God in prayer and worship is her underlying help and strength.

The sense of God's presence, the "glory" of God, can be known by us in the daily walk of prayer and faith in Jesus Christ. The desire for visible signs of that presence is always with us, but happy are those who learn what David learned when he was in the wilderness of Judea, a barren waste where it is difficult even to imagine God's presence. In Psalm 63 he expresses his thirst and hunger for God:

> O God, You are my God;
> Early will I seek You;
> My soul thirsts for You;
> My flesh longs for You
> In a dry and thirsty land
> Where there is no water.
> So I have looked for You in the sanctuary,
> To see Your power and Your glory.

vv. 1, 2

But from the Judean wilderness, as in our wildernesses, God's glory in the sanctuary cannot be seen. So David turned to reflection upon God's loving-kindness and to the praise of God in his present pain and fear, and then could proclaim:

> When I remember You on my bed,
> I meditate on You in the night watches.
> Because You have been my help,
> Therefore in the shadow of Your wings I will rejoice.
> My soul follows close behind You;
> Your right hand upholds me.

vv. 6–8

It is this kind of growing faith that can say:

> Yea, though I walk through the valley
> of the shadow of death,
> I will fear no evil;
> For You are with me;
> Your rod and Your staff, they comfort me.

Ps. 23:4

There is another moment in Leviticus 9 that we must not miss. After offering four of the five kinds of sacrifices in this beginning of priestly worship, a great moment arrives: *"Then Aaron lifted his hand toward the people, blessed them. . . . And Moses and Aaron went into the tabernacle of meeting, and came out and blessed the people"* (vv. 22–23).

The tradition of the blessing is as old as Israel itself and is continued with our tradition of the benediction at the close of our services of worship. It seems that the meaning of blessing begins with creation. In the Genesis narrative, there is no mention of blessing until the creation of living beings. After the creation of living creatures in the waters and the birds, "God blessed them, saying, 'Be fruitful and multiply'" (Gen. 1:22). Again, after the creation of the man and the woman, "God blessed them, and God said to them, 'Be fruitful and multiply; . . . have dominion over the fish of the sea, over the birds of the air, and over every living thing that moves on the earth'" (1:28). Finally, upon the completion of the creation, God rested on the seventh day, "Then God blessed the seventh day and sanctified it, because in it He rested from all His work which God had created and made" (2:3). The blessings of God upon Adam's descendants and upon Noah and his sons are articulated in Gen. 5:2 and 9:1. These blessings of the animals, the people, and the Sabbath might best be described as a commissioning. They are assigned specific places, tasks, and meanings. And certainly, with the blessings God gives the power to accomplish them.

The blessing theme is crucial in the call of Abraham:

> "Get out of your country,
> from your kindred
> and from your father's house,
> to a land that I will show you.

> I will make you a great nation;
> I will bless you
> and make your name great;
> and you shall be a blessing.
> I will bless those who bless you,
> and I will curse him who curses you;
> and in you all the families
> of the earth shall be blessed."
>
> *Gen. 12:1-3*

Here we have both God's blessing to Abraham and the promise that God's blessing shall be transmitted to all of the peoples of the earth through Abraham. Again, the idea of commissioning to specific tasks and purposes is paramount in the blessing. When Abraham meets the priest-king Melchizedek, he receives a blessing in which Melchizedek blesses both Abraham and God Most High (Gen. 14:18). Here, the blessing to God is obviously an ascription of praise to God.

Perhaps the most dramatic story in the Bible involving the blessing is that of Jacob and Esau in their striving over the blessing of their father, Isaac, from his deathbed. The intense rivalry between the twin brothers is portrayed as having begun while they were still within Rebekah's womb (Gen. 25:21-28). Esau, the firstborn, received the birthright, giving him the privileged position in the family and the right of inheritance. Esau was portrayed as the outdoorsman, "a man of the field," while Jacob was the crafty one, always the opportunist. The conflict between the brothers was heightened by the continuing favoritism of Isaac for Esau and Rebekah for Jacob. Esau even sold his birthright to Jacob, in a hungry moment, for some bread and a stew of lentils (Gen. 25:29-34). On his death bed, after much scheming and deception by Rebekah and Jacob, Isaac was tricked into giving the paternal blessing, intended for Esau, to Jacob:

> "Surely, the smell of my son
> is like the smell of a field
> which the LORD has blessed.
> Therefore may God give you
> of the dew of heaven,
> of the fatness of the earth,
> and plenty of grain and wine.
> Let peoples serve you

and nations bow down to you.
Be master of your brethren,
and let your mother's sons bow down to you.
Cursed be everyone who curses you,
and blessed be those who bless you.

Gen. 27:27–29

Even after Isaac discovered that he had been tricked by Rebekah and Jacob, he was powerless to rescind or change the blessing. In a poignant moment "Esau said to his father, 'Have you only one blessing, my father? Bless me, even me also, O my father!' And Esau lifted up his voice and wept" (27:38). To which Isaac replied with his blessing for Jacob:

"Behold, your dwelling shall be of the fatness of the earth, and of the dew of heaven from above. By your sword you shall live, and you shall serve your brother; and it shall come to pass, when you become restless, that you shall break his yoke from your neck."

vv. 39–40

Here again, the blessing is in the form of a commission, accompanied with binding authority. We know from subsequent history that the blessings to Jacob and Esau were, indeed, lived out as given. The blessing of the father was regarded as having continuing force. Years later, we meet Jacob as he is trying to meet with Esau in a conciliatory effort. When he heard that Esau was coming to meet him with four hundred men, his guilt and fear took over, and, in his crafty way, he initiated a strategy designed to appease what he assumed would be Esau's wrath (Gen. 32:1–21). During the night, he was engaged in the wrestling match at the Jabbok river with the mysterious man, whom Jacob assumed to be a messenger from God (32:30). In the height of the struggle, Jacob cried out, "I will not let You go unless You bless me!" The blessing came with the changing of Jacob's name, "he deceives," to Israel, "he struggles with God." Again, the blessing is really a commissioning to a ministry. The concept of blessing is found throughout the Bible as integral to the life of the people of God.

I believe that we do well to carry this sense of the blessing into the Sermon on the Mount. It certainly seems to me that Jesus is transmitting the blessing to His disciples, commissioning them to a new way of life, when He says:

> Blessed are the poor in spirit,
>   for theirs is the kingdom of heaven.
> Blessed are those who mourn,
>   for they shall be comforted.
> Blessed are the meek,
>   for they shall inherit the earth.
> Blessed are those who hunger and
>   thirst for righteousness,
>   for they shall be filled.
> Blessed are the merciful,
>   for they shall obtain mercy.
> Blessed are the pure in heart,
>   for they shall see God.
> Blessed are the peacemakers,
>   for they shall be called sons of God.
> Blessed are those who are persecuted
>   for righteousness' sake,
>   for theirs is the kingdom of heaven."

Matt. 5:3–10

Must we not recover the hunger for the blessing of God to rest upon us? And may we not see ourselves as the representatives of God's blessing to one another? God has chosen men and women to be conductors of His blessing. I must confess to a sense of awe, when I lift my hands over the congregation at the conclusion of a service of worship and realize that, through no power of my own, by the grace of God, the blessing is transmitted again, as it was in the days of Aaron. For Aaron had been instructed by Moses to bless the people by saying to them:

> The Lord bless you and keep you;
> the Lord make His face shine upon you,
> and be gracious to you;
> the Lord lift up His countenance upon you,
> and give you peace.

Num. 6:24–26

101

THE DEATH OF NADAB AND ABIHU

10:1 Then Nadab and Abihu, the sons of Aaron, each took his censer and put fire in it, put incense on it, and offered profane fire before the LORD, which He had not commanded them.

2 So fire went out from the LORD and devoured them, and they died before the LORD.

3 Then Moses said to Aaron, "This is what the LORD spoke, saying:

'By those who come near Me
I must be regarded as holy;
And before all the people
I must be glorified.'"

So Aaron held his peace.

4 And Moses called Mishael and Elzaphan, the sons of Uzziel the uncle of Aaron, and said to them, "Come near, carry your brethren from before the sanctuary out of the camp."

5 So they went near and carried them by their tunics out of the camp, as Moses had said.

6 And Moses said to Aaron, and to Eleazar and Ithamar, his sons, "Do not uncover your heads nor tear your clothes, lest you die, and wrath come upon all the people. But let your brethren, the whole house of Israel, bewail the burning which the LORD has kindled.

7 "You shall not go out from the door of the tabernacle of meeting, lest you die, for the anointing oil of the LORD *is* upon you." And they did according to the word of Moses.

8 Then the LORD spoke to Aaron, saying:

9 "Do not drink wine or intoxicating drink, you, nor your sons with you, when you go into the tabernacle of meeting, lest you die. *It shall be* a statute forever throughout your generations,

10 "that you may distinguish between holy and unholy, and between unclean and clean,

11 "and that you may teach the children of Israel all the statutes which the LORD has spoken to them by the hand of Moses."

12 Then Moses spoke to Aaron, and to Eleazar and Ithamar, his sons who were left: "Take the grain offering that remains of the offerings made by fire to the LORD, and eat it without leaven beside the altar; for it *is* most holy.

13 "And you shall eat it in a holy place, because it *is* your due and your sons' due, of the sacrifices made by fire to the LORD; for so I have been commanded.

14 "The breast of the wave offering and the thigh of the heave offering you shall eat in a clean place, you, your sons, and your daughters with you; for *they are* your due and your sons' due, *which* are given from the sacrifices of peace offerings of the children of Israel.

15 "The thigh of the heave offering and the breast of the wave offering they shall bring with the offerings of fat made by fire, to offer *as* a wave offering before the LORD. And it shall be yours and your sons' with you, by a statute forever, as the LORD has commanded."

16 Then Moses diligently made inquiry about the goat of the sin offering, and there it was, burned up. And he was angry with Eleazar and Ithamar, the sons of Aaron *who were* left, saying,

17 "Why have you not eaten the sin offering in a holy place, since it *is* most holy, and *God* has given it to you to bear the guilt of the congregation, to make atonement for them before the LORD?

18 "See! Its blood was not brought inside the holy *place;* indeed you should have eaten it in a holy *place,* as I commanded."

19 And Aaron said to Moses, "Look, this day they have offered their sin offering and their burnt offering before the LORD, and such things have befallen me! *If* I had eaten the sin offering today, would it have been accepted in the sigh of the LORD?"

20 So when Moses heard *that,* he was content.

Lev. 10: 1–20

This story is likely to puzzle us if we read it as we would a contemporary news report. But this story was written to dramatize the reality that in matters of public worship, for the people of God, things must be done precisely as prescribed by God. Read this story, then, as a statement defending the authority of the priesthood established by God through Moses. Chapter 9 ended on the high note of God's fire coming down from the presence of the Lord, a confirmation that God's acceptance and approval had been granted in response to their worship. What a contrast to the beginning of chapter 10! Again, fire comes down from the presence of God, but this time in fatal judgment upon two disobedient priests.

The chapter consists of two sections. In verses 1–7, we have the narrative of the "profane fire" of two of the newly ordained priests, followed by a series of instructions from the Lord to Aaron (8–11), and from Moses to Aaron and his remaining two sons (12–20).

Nadab and Abihu were the two oldest sons of Aaron, the other two being Eleazar and Ithamar. It was Nadab and Abihu who had accompanied Aaron, Moses, and the seventy elders "up to the Lord" on Mount Sinai (Exod. 24:1). Now, in one moment, the priesthood was reduced from five to three, presumably on the first day of their ordination! All we know of their sin is that *"each took his censer and put fire in it, put incense on it, and offered profane fire before the LORD, which He had not commanded them"* (v. 1). What did they do that was so grievous? We really don't know. But if we go back to Exod. 30:1–10 we recall that the altar of incense played a significant role, both in the daily ministrations of the priests and on the Day of Atonement. It was located inside the Holy Place in front of the veil of the Holy of Holies. As a daily ritual, sweet incense was to be burned upon this altar each day by Aaron when tending the lamps and again when the lamps were lighted at twilight. It was called "a perpetual incense before the LORD" (Exod. 30:8). Specifically prohibited was the offering of "strange incense" upon the golden incense altar (Exod. 30:9), and one explanation of the "profane fire" of Nadab and Abihu could be that they had done just that. We still don't know what "strange incense" might be; some have suggested this is a reference to burning incense at a time other than that prescribed. Others suggest that the incense was tainted with impurities, reflecting carelessness by the priests. I've wondered if the simplest reading of the text might be that they were burning the incense in their censers, rather than on the golden altar of incense. Whatever we assume, the seriousness of their action is indicated by the closing words of the sentence, *"which He had not commanded them"* (v. 1). Whatever else the priests learn, they must learn to conduct the worship *exactly* as God had prescribed through Moses. They were not to improvise. To carry this to the extreme by suggesting that these particular worship practices must be observed throughout history cannot be supported by subsequent history in the unfolding drama of God's redemption. Thus, in time, the prophet Micah will say:

> With what shall I come before the LORD,
> and bow myself before the High God?
> Shall I come before Him with burnt offerings,
> with calves a year old?
> Will the LORD be pleased with thousands of rams
> or ten thousand rivers of oil?
> Shall I give my firstborn for my transgression,
> the fruit of my body for the sin of my soul?
> He has shown you, O man, what is good;
> and what does the LORD require of you
> but to do justly,
> to love mercy,
> and to walk humbly with your God?
>
> *Mic. 6:6–8*

But for now, strict adherence to the instructions given by God is the order of the day for Aaron and his sons. Just as the fire had come down from before the Lord to consume the burnt offering and the fat on the altar (9:24), so now *"the fire went out from the LORD and devoured them, and they died before the LORD "* (v. 2). The same fire is both an evidence of God's blessing and of God's displeasure. Moses has the first word for Aaron in this time of shock and grief (v. 3), and it is a brief couplet reiterating the central theme of all of Leviticus: the holiness of God. Aaron's anger and grief were assuaged by this word from Moses, *"So Aaron held his peace"* (v. 3).

Since priests were prohibited from going near the dead, since even inadvertent contact with the dead would contract ceremonial uncleanness and prohibit them from their priestly ministrations (Lev. 21:1–4), Moses called upon their cousins to remove their bodies from the tabernacle *"out of the camp."* Notice their own efforts to avoid contact with the bodies as they carried them out *"by their tunics"* (v. 5). The final word from Moses to Aaron, Eleazar, and Ithamar was a strict prohibition of their joining in any outward signs of mourning. Messing up the hair and tearing one's clothing were customary ways of showing grief (Gen. 37:29; Lev. 13:45, e.g.), and this was not allowed for the three remaining priests. Such mourning was not precluded for the rest of the people, but, presumably, outward mourning by Aaron and his remaining sons might appear to be a questioning of God's judgment. At this point, their solidarity with God was of the essence. Later, it was because of their disobedience at Kadesh that Moses and Aaron were denied the privilege of leading the children of Israel into the promised land of Canaan (Num. 20:1–13).

This incident certainly has something to say to those of us who have accepted responsibility to serve as "ministers of the Word and sacraments." The acceptance of the responsibilities which we take in our ordination vows requires of us higher standards in representing and affirming the holiness of God. This is undoubtedly what James had in mind when he said, "My brethren, let not many of you become teachers, knowing that we shall receive a stricter judgment" (James 3:1).

This devastating incident calls forth a word from the Lord directly to Aaron (vv. 8–11) expressly forbidding him and his sons from the consumption of wine or intoxicating drink "when you go into the tabernacle of meeting" (10:9). Because the consumption of alcohol is a matter requiring serious consideration by pastors and lay leaders, it is important to pause a moment here to reflect upon what this passage says, as well as what it doesn't say. It is clearly a prohibition to the priests from drinking while "on duty," implying that the sins of Nadab and Abihu were committed "under the influence" of alcohol. This prohibition obviously stresses the need for the priests to be clearheaded when leading in worship. Some suggest that it was a reminder not to indulge in the worship of the religions around them, in which alcohol was often used as a stimulus to false worship.

The passage does not ban their consumption of wine or intoxicating drink at all other times. The question always present to contemporary leaders in the church is the choice between moderation and abstinence from alcoholic beverages. In our culture, this must now include all substances that alter human behavior. Whether one likes it or not, a church leader will have to reckon with the general expectations of the immediate community of faith. The most direct passages relating to this question in the New Testament are found in Paul's discussion of Christian liberty in Romans 14 and 1 Corinthians 8. One of the obvious convictions of Paul is that the general concern for the well-being of others is always a priority for Christian leaders. Thus, it may well be that abstinence is the best option in some situations for the sake of the accepted norms of the community.

Yet, in these passages, Paul also strikes a blow for the responsible exercise of freedom, asserting one's right not to be bound by the scruples of those who deny the right of the leader to make free and responsible decisions regarding one's personal conduct. Obviously, intoxication is always out of the question, for that is to relinquish control of one's body to someone or something other than God. But drinking in moderation is never flatly ruled out, as long as it is not disruptive of the general well-being of the community. Paul's fundamental appeal is to maintain the unity of the community. He thus places the responsibility upon both parties in such conflicts not to "destroy the work of God for the sake of food" (Rom. 14:20).

We know, as perhaps Paul did not, that there are some folks for whom moderation is not an option. Whatever theory of alcoholism you may hold, the reality is that there are many people who simply must adopt a strict, unwavering pattern of total abstinence in order to maintain their continuing sobriety. They refer to themselves with rightful pride as "recovering alcoholics." I have yet to meet one of them who attempts to force their pattern of total abstinence upon others. The only people who have ever tried to force their view of abstinence on me are those who seem to have a greater concern for controlling my behavior than they do for my well-being. Pastors in many churches will find themselves in tension between their right to exercise responsible freedom in every aspect of personal behavior and the expectations of others who insist upon their right to control the behaviors of their pastors. I wish I could point to an easy way to keep everybody happy in these matters. I can't, because I haven't found one.

One of the assumptions worth questioning in this whole matter, in my judgment, is the virtual deification of consistency. Why is one forced to maintain identical conduct, say with regard to moderate drinking, in every cultural or personal situation? Standards and needs vary from place to place and from person to person. If I have friends for whom my having a glass of wine with dinner when dining with them is going to ruin the whole evening, I will obviously decide not to order my wine for the sake of our community. But I find other occasions when the glass of wine seems to add to the enjoyment of the evening's sharing. I'm prepared to argue that consistency is not in itself a virtue.

In verses 12–15, as priestly order is being restored, Moses checks to be certain that Eleazar and Ithamar have completed the sacrifices mentioned in chapter 9 with propriety. It was important that the grain offering accompanying the burnt offering be properly consumed by the priests, as well as *"the breast of the wave offering and the thigh of the heave offering"* (10:14).

Moses then discovered (10:16–20), to his anger, that they had not properly eaten the goat of the sin offering, the second offering in chapter 9 (v. 15), which was the sin offering for the people. Since the blood had not been brought into the tabernacle of meeting but had been sprinkled on the altar of burnt offering, the priests should have eaten the meat of the offering. Aaron pointed out to Moses that their error had not been because they were careless, but because they had been overly cautious. Aaron exclaims, *"such things have befallen me!"* (10:19).
In other words, "after the divine fire of judgment that fell on Nadab and Abihu, I wasn't about to risk eating the meat of that sacrifice!" Moses accepted Aaron's explanation, suggesting that to err on the side of caution is something quite other than the audacity of Nadab and Abihu. Here is grace in action.

The essence of this chapter, nowhere referred to in the New Testament writings, is found in verses 10–11: *"that you may distinguish between holy and unholy, and between unclean and clean, and that you may teach the children of Israel all the statutes which the LORD has spoken to them by the hand of Moses."*

The Priesthood and Us

There's a tendency to view these matters of the priesthood as little more than ancient history. But to relegate these chapters to the dustbin of history is to handle the Scriptures wrongly.

Whatever else speaks out clearly from these Scriptures, the reality and negative power of sin are clearly stated. Sin is universal and all pervasive. The place of worship must be cleansed, the priests and their clothing must be cleansed, and the people must be cleansed in order to enter into the presence of God for fellowship with Him. And this cleansing must be continually repeated throughout the Old Testament period.

The writer of the book of Hebrews develops the theme of Christ as the High Priest superior to Aaron in every way. It was not necessary for Christ to make sacrifices for His own sin (Heb. 7:27). Neither was His sacrifice in need of continual repetition, but His sacrifice was "once for all when He offered up Himself" (Heb. 7:27; 10:1–14). This would be a good place to read and study Hebrews 5–10. Beginning with a review of the qualifications of the priests, the writer of Hebrews establishes Christ as "a priest forever according to the order of Melchizedek" (Heb. 5:6). The writer makes clear that the old priesthood could never make a complete atonement for all of the sins of the world, but, at best, could limp along with all of its human inadequacies. Then Christ is presented as the fulfillment of all of the potential of the priestly system, "so Christ was offered once to bear the sins of many" (Heb. 9:28). "And every priest stands ministering daily and offering repeatedly the same sacrifices, which can never take away sins. But this Man, after He had offered one sacrifice for sins forever, sat down at the right hand of God. . . . For by one offering He has perfected forever those who are being sanctified" (Heb. 10:11–14).

It is here that we begin to appreciate the way in which Leviticus shapes and enriches our understanding of the meaning of the life, death, and resurrection of Jesus. In His life, Jesus can be seen as a priest in the long tradition of Israel, going back to the mysterious figure of Melchizedek to whom Abraham paid tithes. In His death, Jesus can be seen as John the Baptist saw Him: "Behold the Lamb of God!" (John 1:36). On the cross of Calvary, Jesus died not merely as a man dedicated to truth and justice, but as the one, full, and final sacrifice making atonement for all of the sins of all of the people in all of the world. In His resurrection, we see the final stamp of God's acceptance of the sacrifice, God's gracious provision of forgiveness for all. "And if Christ is not risen, then our preaching is vain and your faith is also vain. If in this life only we have hope in Christ, we are of all men the most pitiable" (1 Cor. 15:15–19).

Yet another lesson for us from these chapters is the dynamic role of formal worship in experiencing the glory of God. In a day of expansive and expressive individualism, we need to be drawn back to the reality of the covenant people of God, called to faithful, corporate worship. And that worship must be faithful to the formation of a people of God who "worship Him . . . in spirit and in truth" (John 4:24).

109

We obviously are not expected to return to the particulars of the priestly worship of the tabernacle or the temple. The ancient liturgy need not be restored. But must we not struggle with questions regarding the form and intent of our services of worship? Does anything that makes people feel "good" qualify as desirable for worship? Is it possible that some or much of what we call "contemporary" worship is really designed to produce effects within people rather than to worship God? Are some of our worship experiences more akin to the priestly tradition or to the arrogant spirits of Nadab and Abihu?

Pastors and the laity who are responsible for the planning and leading of worship must struggle regularly and painfully with these kinds of questions. Mere trendiness or relevance cannot be allowed to become the final criterion for our patterns and styles of worship. It seems to me that we do well to approach our worship planning with the awareness that there is a rich and vast diversity in styles and forms of worship, all of which have significant meaning to remarkably diverse groups of Christian worshipers throughout the world. Any thought that would claim universality would border on idolatry.

As a pastor, I'm convinced that we do best to work and rework our own tradition to try to achieve the highest worship experience within the parameters of our particular heritage. There have been times when people have come to me with some "new" experience that they have shared in a conference or meeting from another tradition. In their enthusiasm with a new experience, they have urged that we immediately move into the "new" way of doing things. I remind them, first of all, that this is not necessarily "new" just because it is new to them. And then I must remind them that there are likely to be a number of people within our congregation who came to us because they preferred our basic style and tradition over and above some of the aspects of this "new" style of worship. It has always seemed to me that we will bring confusion to our people if we keep emulating every "new" style that comes to our attention.

If we are Episcopalians, our people have every right to expect their worship to be within a certain framework. If Baptist, the same expectations are reasonable. And so with every possible variation from Pentecostal to Orthodox. Within each basic tradition there is certainly room for some latitude, but always within the framework of the tradition.

The danger is that we get locked into a too narrow interpretation of a particular tradition. And here is where the challenge to our creativity really comes into play. Merely transporting another tradition into our setting is not creative. Drawing upon other traditions to enrich our own is the hallmark of creativity.

And there are certain basics for corporate worship that seem to be held in common by most of our traditions. We do well to keep focused upon them. In the tradition with which I am most familiar, our basic elements of corporate worship are prayer, confession, Scripture read and proclaimed, baptism, communion, offering, and commitment. The invitation to respond to Jesus Christ is encouraged as a regular part of the worship. Within this framework is a wide variety of opportunities for diverse music and expression, encouraging the active involvement of the worshipers.

And let us always celebrate the universal priesthood of all believers in our life and worship. With the completeness of Christ's sacrificial offering, the repetitious acts of the descendants of Aaron are no longer needed. Each of us, and all of us, in Christ, "are a chosen generation, a royal priesthood, a holy nation, His own special people, that you may proclaim the praises of Him who called you out of darkness into His marvelous light; who once were not a people but are now the people of God, who had not obtained mercy but now have obtained mercy" (1 Peter 2:9–10).

I can't conceive of a church, this side of heaven, that will not find it essential to set aside some folks as "ordained" leaders, chosen by virtue of their gifts and calling, for leadership and special functions in the ongoing life of their church. For the most part, these people will be called "clergy" in contrast to the "laity." But in reality *all* of the people are the *laos*, the people of God. In this sense, I celebrate what Calvin called "the universal priesthood of all believers." While clergy may continue in most of our traditions with special authority and functions, especially with relationship to the administration of the Sacraments and the preaching of the Word of God, in fact is the ministries of the church in the world are the ministries of the *laos*, the whole people of God. The clergy function best when they are "equipping the saints for the work of ministry, for the edifying of the body of Christ" (Eph. 4:12).
It has been wisely suggested that we learn to distinguish between "church work" and "the work of the church." It is in the work of the church that all of us are called to ministry.

Welcome to the priesthood!

CHAPTER THREE

THE CLEAN AND THE UNCLEAN

LEVITICUS 11:1–15:33

The casual, modern reader of Leviticus is most likely to skim through this section and leave it with a sigh of gratitude that we are no longer bound by such regulations nor held captive to such beliefs. These five chapters deal with the means by which people may avoid or be cleansed from various kinds of uncleanness.

Since these ideas of uncleanness are foreign to our ways of thinking, and since some of them are declared no longer valid in the New Testament, we are in danger of ignoring them as irrelevant or as merely antiquarian. But we owe it to our commitment to the Scriptures to try to discover what meaning these matters had in the lives of the ancient people of God in order to discover both why some of them were later changed and what meaning, if any, they might have for us today.

The foundational principle for the entire life of Israel is found in 11:44–47, "For I am the LORD your God. You shall therefore sanctify yourselves, and you shall be holy; for I am holy. Neither shall you defile yourselves with any creeping thing that creeps upon the earth. For I am the LORD who brings you up out of the land of Egypt, to be your God. You shall therefore be holy, for I am holy. This is the law of the beasts and the birds and every living creature that moves in the waters, and of every creature that creeps on the earth, to distinguish between the unclean and the clean, and between the animal that may be eaten and the animal that may not be eaten." This principle had already been articulated in Lev. 10:10, "that you may distinguish between holy and unholy, and between unclean and clean."

Perhaps nowhere in the Scriptures do we have articulated more clearly the belief that God is omnipresent. God is present, not only in the tabernacle of meeting and in the sacrifices, but in every thought,

word, and deed of daily life. We have a popular saying in our fitness-
and nutrition-focused generation: "you are what you eat." This is
certainly demonstrable. A diet high in fat and low in fiber ultimately
produces a diseased and troubled body, and a diseased and troubled
body results in a troubled person. We have long since learned that
diet is inseparably linked to personal and social well-being. And in
this section, three additional areas of personal hygiene are also included. We cannot read these chapters without the awareness that to
the ancient Hebrew, every aspect of daily life was seen as intimately
linked with the presence of God.

We do well to observe that even with their keen sense of the
presence of God in every aspect of their lives, they did not fall into the
thinking of the religions and cultures of the people around them.
Seeing God's presence in all of life and nature was not unique to the
children of Israel. They lived in a world of pantheism, a world in
which people recognized gods everywhere and in everything. All
around them, in Egypt, in Canaan, and in the Transjordan kingdoms
all the way to Babylon and Persia, there was a near universal belief
that divine and magical powers were present in certain natural or
human-made objects and that people could control or activate these
powers through knowledge of the mysteries, with incantations, or
through certain rituals.

Pantheism, in its many diverse forms, has a remarkable tenacity to
this very day. Much of what is now known as the New Age movement is nothing more than an extension of pantheism. And this, the
Hebrews carefully and passionately avoided. They saw God present
and active in all of life while at the same time always affirming and
experiencing God as "wholly other."

Herein lies the essential difference between the pantheism of the
pagan world and the monotheism of the Hebrews. In every form of
pantheism (including our contemporary versions) there is a pronounced tendency to regard humans as able to save themselves by
their own devices. Thus, the vision of salvation becomes a reality by
enlisting men and women into the struggle with evil as cosaviors with
the gods, or developing systems of rites and prayers giving them
authority and power over evil, or introducing them into the knowledge of the secrets of being and nonbeing, of life and death, in which
they are ultimately liberated through mind and spirit from the prison
of the body and the dreary cycle of death and rebirth. The highest

form of salvation is the Platonic ideal in which the individual is redeemed through absorption into or attachment to the realm of ideals.

I find this section of Leviticus on the clean and the unclean a remarkably fascinating statement of their understanding of the holiness of God and of life in the light of the pantheism so endemic to the world around them. The idea of holiness is much more than differentiating between moral and immoral, good and bad. Holiness is a concept of being set apart, of being different, of being very special. The word for holy, both in the Old and New Testaments, always has the root meaning of "different" and "separate." God is supremely holy because God is totally different from all else in creation and is always to be regarded as separate from every aspect of the created order. The Sabbath is called holy because it is different from the other six days, and it is to be treated separately as a special day. The temple was holy because it was different from all other buildings and was used only for special and separate functions. A sacrificial animal was regarded as holy because it was different from other animals and was set apart separately for the worship of God. A priest was holy because he was born to be different from all of the others and was separated from them.

It has become painfully clear to me that the Book of Leviticus seems difficult and foreign to us because we have lost that ancient sense of the holiness of God and of life. There is a stark contrast between the early Christians and the contemporary church at this point. The Christians in the apostolic era were well aware that they were called to be different and separate, so much so that they would most likely be held in disdain by those around them and perhaps even martyred for their unique beliefs. But we have chosen an entirely different route. If anything, we have tried to minimize the ideas of difference and separateness. We have stressed the importance of being identified with the world in order to make the Christian faith more attractive to the world. Church membership is offered and encouraged with little or no demands to be different from others and separated to God.

I'm convinced that renewal is not going to be experienced among today's Christians and within our churches until we recover some sense of holiness. I know what you're thinking at this point. You're having some of the thoughts that come to me whenever I spend some time in the Amish sections of Pennsylvania. Seeing those folks moving down the side of the highway in their uniform horse-drawn carts, observing their uniformity of dress for the women as well as the men, and observing their commitment to being different and separate by refusing to utilize many of the products of modern technology (such as the internal combustion engine) has never portrayed a model of viable holiness to me.

Isn't it time, however, while rejecting such stilted forms of outward holiness, to intentionally seek the meaning of holiness as difference and separateness in ways that are rooted in the history of the people of God and appropriate to our own time and place? I don't see much evidence that Christ took people out of the world, but I do witness His call to His followers to be different within the world and to separate themselves from those powers and patterns in the world which lead to injustice, selfishness, and destruction. Isn't it time for Christians to be recognized as Christians by virtue of the values for which they stand in an increasingly valueless society? Shouldn't Christians be identifiable as disciples of Christ, not through mere cultural respectability but through their commitment to love, to peace, and to justice? Is it not time for Christians to be known as stewards of Christ, not because they profess God's blessing in the accumulation of wealth but because they use their wealth (or lack of it) for the well-being and benefit of others? The call to holiness was never expressed more clearly than when Jesus said, "If anyone desires to come after Me, let him deny himself, and take up his cross daily, and follow Me. For whoever desires to save his life will lose it, but whoever loses his life for My sake will save it" (Luke 9:23–24). It is past time for us to develop intentional strategies for the renewal of our understanding of and commitment to authentic holiness.

In this section, we have again a movement from the narrative form to a codification of regulations, just as we had in the movement from the end of Exodus to the opening seven chapters of Leviticus, returning to narrative in Leviticus 8–10. Chapter 11 deals with foods that may or may not be eaten and with the issues involved when an unclean carcass has been contacted. Chapter 12 deals with matters related to the birth of a child. Chapters 13–14 deal with various skin diseases and funguses. Chapter 15 deals with bodily discharges. There are things in these chapters that we are not likely to incorporate in our normal Sunday preaching, at least not in the children's sermon, but we must wrestle seriously with them to heighten our own sense of the concepts of clean/unclean and holy/unholy. And then we must turn to Jesus and the New Testament to interact with His application of these principles.

CLEAN AND UNCLEAN FOODS

11:1   And the LORD spoke to Moses and Aaron, saying to them,

2   "Speak to the children of Israel, saying, 'These *are* the animals which you may eat among all the beasts that are on the earth:

3   'Among the beasts, whatever divides the hoof, having cloven hooves *and* chewing the cud — that you may eat.

4   'Nevertheless these you shall not eat among those that chew the cud or those that have cloven hooves: the camel, because it chews the cud but does not have cloven hooves, is unclean to you;

5   'the rock hyrax, because it chews the cud but does not have cloven hooves, *is* unclean to you;

6   'the hare, because it chews the cud but does not have cloven hooves, *is* unclean to you;

7   'and the swine, though it divides the hoof, having cloven hooves, yet does not chew the cud, *is* unclean to you.

8   'Their flesh you shall not eat, and their carcasses you shall not touch. They *are* unclean to you.

9   'These you may eat of all that *are* in the water: whatever in the water has fins and scales, whether in the seas or in the rivers — that you may eat.

10   'But all in the seas or in the rivers that do not have fins and scales, all that move in the water or any living thing which *is* in the water, they *are* an abomination to you.

11   'They shall be an abomination to you; you shall not eat their flesh, but you shall regard their carcasses as an abomination.

12   'Whatever in the water does not have fins or scales — that *shall be* an abomination to you.

13   'And these you shall regard as an abomination among the birds; they shall not be eaten, they *are* an abomination: the eagle, the vulture, the buzzard,

14   'the kite, and the falcon after its kind;

15   'every raven after its kind,

16   'the ostrich, the short-eared owl, the seagull, and the hawk after its kind;

17 'the little owl, the fisher owl, and the screech
owl;
18 'the white owl, the jackdaw, and the carrion
vulture;
19 'the stork, the heron after its kind, the hoopoe,
and the bat.
20 'All flying insects that creep on *all* fours *shall be*
an abomination to you.
21 'Yet these you may eat of every flying insect that
creeps on *all* fours: those which have jointed legs
above their feet with which to leap on the earth.
22 'These you may eat: the locust after its kind, the
destroying locust after its kind, the cricket after its
kind, and the grasshopper after its kind.
23 'But all *other* flying insects which have four feet
shall be an abomination to you.

41 "And every creeping thing that creeps on the
earth *shall be* an abomination. It shall not be eaten.
42 'Whatever crawls on its belly, whatever goes on
all fours, or whatever has many feet among all
creeping things that creep on the earth—these you
shall not eat, for they *are* an abomination.
43 'You shall not make yourselves abominable
with any creeping thing that creeps; nor shall you
make yourselves unclean with them, lest you be
defiled by them.
44 'For I *am* the LORD your God. You shall therefore
sanctify yourselves, and you shall be holy; for I *am*
holy. Neither shall you defile yourselves with any
creeping thing that creeps on the earth.
45 'For I *am* the LORD who brings you up out of the
land of Egypt, to be your God. You shall therefore be
holy, for I *am* holy.

Lev. 11:1–23; 41–45

We must realize the difficulties in identifying accurately the birds
and reptiles that are pronounced fit or unfit for eating in Leviticus 11.
Some scholars feel that less than half of them can be named with
certainty. For example, in verse 16, the "ostrich" in our translation is
translated by the RSV as "seagull," while the NEB and NIV translate it as

"the horned owl." Accuracy in identifying most of the birds and reptiles is not possible, making any attempt to carry these dietary regulations specifically and accurately into present practice an impossibility. And, at least to us Western moderns, the underlying rationale for calling one animal clean and another unclean can be surmised but not with certainty in every case.

The regulations are divided into two parts: dietary matters (vv. 1–23, 41–45) and problems resulting from contact with animal carcasses (vv. 24–40).

With regard to the dietary matters, there are four categories of animals given consideration: animals that live on land ("the beasts," v. 2); fresh and saltwater creatures ("all that are in the water," v. 9); flying animals ("the birds," v. 13); and what our youngsters might call "creepy crawlers" ("all flying insects that creep on all fours," v. 13).

As to "the beasts" (vv. 4–8), only those which *both* have cloven hooves ("a split hoof completely divided," NIV) *and* chew the cud are fit for their consumption. This definition thus includes sheep, goats, oxen, and cows, which indeed were the most commonly domesticated animals. The Hebrew definition of "chewing the cud" seems to differ from our Western understanding based upon our knowledge that the cud-chewing animal swallows its food rather quickly, storing it in a stomach compartment for subsequent recall and rechewing. Here, the camel, the rock hyrax, and the hare are said to "chew the cud." In fact they chew their food in a "normal" manner before swallowing it. The underlying criteria are that an animal have split hooves and chew its food thoroughly. Most of us are well aware that the pig has always been regarded as unclean in Hebrew law, and here is the fundamental reason—it has divided hooves but does not chew its food. I recall my grandmother admonishing me when, in her judgment, I was eating my food too fast: "Don't eat like a pig!" I might have responded more favorably if she had just said, "It is better to chew your food more thoroughly."

The distinction between clean and unclean animals from the water (vv. 9–12) is solely based upon whether they have fins and scales. Those without fins or scales are declared to be *"an abomination"* to those eating them. Unlike the other categories, no identification of any particular species is articulated. While some have attempted to interpret this distinction hygienically, a more appealing interpretation recognizes that only fish with scales and fins are swimmers, the "normal" means of propulsion for creatures that live in the water.

Water creatures that don't swim are suspect, just as are land creatures that don't walk and eat "normally."

As for the birds (vv. 13–19), a list is given of those that may not be eaten, and they are declared to be an abomination to those who might eat them. It appears that the language of abomination as applied to fish, birds, and insects is stronger than the language of uncleanness applied to the land animals. There are many problems in identifying the actual species from this list, but the general consensus is that the prohibited birds are generally birds of prey which, among other things, break the fundamental law prohibiting the eating or drinking of blood, thus becoming unclean.

The fourth and final category relates to "all flying insects that creep on all fours" (vv. 20–23 and 41–43). Only four kinds of such creatures may be eaten, each of which has *"jointed legs above their feet with which to leap on the earth"* (v. 21). To me, the most appealing rationale for this distinction is in the idea of "normal" locomotion. Insects that creep and swarm have no direction, whereas those that hop are more like animals that walk, birds that fly, and fish that swim. Whether this whets your appetite for locusts, crickets, and grasshoppers is your decision, but at least they weren't prohibited. And some folks from the Middle East will tell you that locusts have long been a regular part of their diet. Don't forget that John the Baptist lived out in the Judean wilderness on a diet of "locusts and wild honey" (Mark 1:6).

We can't go any further in this chapter without examining the rationale underlying the distinctions between clean and unclean animals, fish, birds, and insects. Numerous and wide-ranging interpretations have been given, based upon different assumptions. The simplest approach simply affirms the sovereignty of God. God can do whatever God wishes to do, and it is never our right to question God's decrees. While such a view may constitute good theology, it's not likely to satisfy those of us who believe that it is our responsibility and privilege to use the minds God has given us to understand and apply the revelation given to us.

Another approach begins with the assumption that the animals labeled unclean were those used in pagan cults or identified with other gods. Avoidance of such animals was a matter of breaking all possible connections with all other gods and religions. The major problem with this thesis is that some of the other religions used the same animals as the Israelites for their sacrifices. The bull, for example, was used by both Canaanites and Egyptians in their sacrifices. But it was not considered unclean for that reason.

Another line of thought is that the animals were declared unclean for reasons of health and hygiene. Clean animals are safe to eat; unclean animals are likely to create health problems. We all know that pork can be a source of trichinosis and that uncooked shellfish can carry contamination from polluted water. And most recently we oyster and shrimp lovers have been warned about the dangers of such epicurean delights because of increasing pollution in our coastal waters. While there is no question that hygienic questions are related to some of the animals declared unclean, not all of them are demonstrably health threatening. Nor are all of the animals declared edible fully without some hygienic risk. But the greater problem with holding the hygienic view is that the Old Testament never suggests this connection. Health considerations are never mentioned. The issue is always the difference between the clean and the unclean in the context of what is holy. Later we will look at the changes that Jesus made in our understanding of the clean and the unclean, but here we must observe that he did not do so on the grounds of an advanced understanding of health and hygiene.

There is a fourth major avenue of interpretation which emphasizes the symbolic. Citing specifically the works of social anthropologist Mary Douglas, G. J. Wenham, in *The New International Commentary on the Old Testament* (*Leviticus*, pp. 168–70ff), develops this approach in a most appealing way. The underlying motif of the symbolic interpretation is that the habits of the clean animals are living illustrations of the ideal behavior of the people of God, while those of the unclean animals are illustrative of the way sinners live. This approach has its roots in pre-Christian rabbinic writers and has been present throughout the history of Christian interpreters. Even at its best, this school of thought is only partial. Neither it, nor any other school, can be made to fit all of the material and classifications given us. At its worst, it moves into absurd allegory, such as with an early Christian interpreter who avowed that a cud-chewing animal was clean because it reminded us to meditate on the law of God, or a later interpreter who taught that sheep were clean because they served as a reminder to the ancient Hebrew that the Lord was his shepherd, while the pig's dirty habits demonstrated clearly "the filth of iniquity."

Wenham feels that the works of Mary Douglas, however, avoid most of the pitfalls of the older symbolic interpretations. Referring to her three major works, *Purity and Danger* (London: Routledge and Kegan Paul, 1966), *Natural Symbols* (London: Barrie and Rockliff, 1970), and *Implicit Meanings* (London: Routledge and Kegan Paul, 1975), Wenham affirms her thorough and comprehensive reading of the Leviticus material from the perspective of ancient Israel, rather than from that of the whim of the modern reader. Recognizing the basic division of animal life into three spheres — flying in the sky, walking on the land, and swimming in the waters — the symbolic interpretation begins with the view that clean animals are those that conform to the basic types to which they belong. Unclean animals, in one way or another, do not conform to their "normal" type.

We still wonder why sheep and goats are labeled clean, while pigs are called unclean. Here Douglas's argument turns to the social background of the giving of the laws. Since sheep and goats had long been domesticated and used for food by the Hebrews, it was natural to regard them as clean. Pigs and camels, however, behaved strangely when compared to sheep and goats and were therefore regarded as unclean. If one grants that each sphere of the animal world has its particular structure, then it follows that some division between the clean and the unclean based upon some criteria of what is normal to the created order is likely to be recognized.

The next step is the recognition that to the ancient Hebrew the animal world and the human world were closely linked. In Gen. 1:29–30, the herbs and trees are given to humankind *and* to the animal world for food. Their solidarity is seen in Exod. 13:2, "Sanctify to Me all the firstborn, whatever opens the womb among the children of Israel, both of man and animal; it is Mine." And again in Exod. 13:13, "But every firstling of a donkey you shall redeem with a lamb; and if you will not redeem it, then you shall break its neck. And all the firstborn of man among your sons you shall redeem." The same principle stands at the center of the Sabbath law: "Six days you shall labor and do all your work, but the seventh day is the Sabbath of the LORD your God. In it you shall do no work: you, nor your son, nor your daughter, nor your manservant, nor your maidservant, nor your cattle, nor your stranger who is within your gates" (Exod. 20:9–10). In the laws pertaining to oxen which gore people, both the animal and the owner are held to certain accountabilities and penalties (Exod. 21:28–36).

It is this symbolic linkage between the animal world and the human world that supports Douglas's conclusions that the division between the clean and the unclean in the animal world was symbolic of the division between the Hebrew world and the gentile world. And as there were a few types of clean animals that could be sacrificed to God, so there were a few men within Israel who could make sacrifices to God, the line of Levi of the house of Aaron. Thus, through their symbolic understanding of the clean and the unclean, they were reminded in every act of eating that they were called to be a holy nation, the clean in the midst of the unclean.

While each of these schools of thought has its own logic, none of them fully accounts for all of the facts. It seems best to recognize that we have no all-encompassing, single principle which explains all of the distinctions made between the clean and the unclean animals. And yet these ancient laws point us to our need to recover some sense of the holy and to grow in our understanding of God's eternal call to us to be separate and different: *"You shall be holy; for I am holy"* (11:44, 45).

While on a flight from New York to Amsterdam recently, I was seated next to two Muslims. How did I know they were Muslim? First of all, by their head covering, the traditional woven "skull cap." Then, when the meal was served, they reminded the flight attendant that they had ordered special meals, meals prepared to their religious dietary requirements. And then, at the appointed hour, they rose from their seats, went into the space by the door of the aircraft, placed their prayer mats down, and prayed their prayers facing to the east. Some of the folks in the immediate vicinity were looking bemused or perplexed, but I thought of Leviticus 11 and longed for some appropriate ways to demonstrate openly my own devotion to the living God.

I knew that my traveling companions were followers of Allah, not because they handed me a tract or preached a sermon, but because of the way they dressed and ate and prayed. And I mused, "What is there about me that says to them that I am a follower of Jesus?"

CONTACT WITH ANIMAL CARCASSES

24 'By these you shall become unclean; whoever touches the carcass of any of them shall be unclean until evening;

25 'whoever carries part of the carcass of any of them shall wash his clothes and be unclean until evening:

26 *'The carcass* of any beast which divides the foot, but is not cloven-hoofed or does not chew the cud, *is* unclean to you. Everyone who touches it shall be unclean.

27 'And whatever goes on its paws, among all kinds of animals that go on *all* fours, those *are* unclean to you. Whoever touches any such carcass shall be unclean until evening.

28 'Whoever carries *any such* carcass shall wash his clothes and be unclean until evening. It *is* unclean to you.

29 'These also *shall be* unclean to you among the creeping things that creep on the earth: the mole, the mouse, and the large lizard after its kind;

30 'the gecko, the monitor lizard, the sand reptile, the sand lizard, and the chameleon.

31 'These *are* unclean to you among all that creep. Whoever touches them when they are dead shall be unclean until evening.

32 'Anything on which *any* of them falls, when they are dead shall be unclean, whether *it is* any item of wood or clothing or skin or sack, whatever item *it is,* in which *any* work is done, it must be put in water. And it shall be unclean until evening; then it shall be clean.

33 'Any earthen vessel into which *any* of them falls you shall break; and whatever *is* in it shall be unclean:

34 'in such a vessel, any edible food upon which water falls becomes unclean, and any drink that may be drunk from it becomes unclean.

35 'And everything on which *a part* of *any such* carcass falls shall be unclean; *whether it is* an oven or cooking stove, it shall be broken down; *for they are* unclean, and shall be unclean to you.

36 'Nevertheless a spring or cistern, *in which there is* plenty of water, shall be clean, but whatever touches any such carcass becomes unclean.

37 'And if a part of *any such* carcass falls on any planting seed which is to be sown, it *remains* clean.

38 'But if *any* water is put on the seed, and if *a part*
of *any such* carcass falls on it, it *becomes* unclean to you.
39 'And if any beast which you may eat dies, he
who touches its carcass shall be unclean until evening.
40 'He who eats of its carcass shall wash his clothes
and be unclean until evening. He also who carries its
carcass shall wash his clothes and be unclean until
evening.

Lev. 11:24–40

This second section of chapter 11 is perhaps even more difficult for
us moderns to appreciate and apply. It deals with the effects upon
people or things that have come in contact with animal carcasses,
intentionally or accidentally. My grandmother elevated the maxim
"cleanliness is next to godliness" to the level of canonical Scripture. In
fact, I was surprised to discover it wasn't in the Bible. Thus, the idea
that one's hands should be washed after touching a dead animal
would never have seemed unusual to me. But here we are dealing
with something quite different from physical uncleanness and matters of hygiene. To the Hebrew, any contact with a dead animal
caused ceremonial uncleanness, which meant that the person was
banned from entering the central place of worship, be it the tabernacle
or later the temple or synagogue, until the prescribed cleansing ritual
had been completed. Ceremonial uncleanness, foreign to our thinking, was of critical importance to the Hebrew because disqualification
from the right to worship was separation from God, feared as much as
death itself.

Rites of purification for all kinds of uncleanness abounded in virtually
all ancient religions. Archaeological discoveries, such as those of the
Qumran community near the Dead Sea and the more recent developments in the fascinating excavations below the southern wall of the
Temple Mount in Jerusalem, have established the fact that small pools
for ritual bathing abounded in houses and communities at the time of
Jesus and before. These pools, for the most part, were just large
enough and deep enough for one person to bathe in a manner in
which the entire body and head could be immersed without any parts
of the body contacting each other. Ritual cleansing was a normal and
essential part of life in the ancient world, and the Hebrews were no
exception.

Verses 24–31 spell out the effect of a person making any kind of contact, by touching or carrying, with the carcass of an unclean animal. That person becomes ceremonially unclean for the rest of the day. Recall that the Hebrew day begins with sundown, not at midnight or sunrise, as is customary to our thinking. That tradition is grounded in the creation narrative in Genesis 1 with the recurring statement, "So the evening and the morning were the first . . . second . . . third . . . day" (Gen. 1:5, 8, 13, 19, 23, 31). How fitting that the day *begin* with the time for rest and renewal!

The only washing required in these cases was of the clothing, though it seems fair to assume that a ritual washing of the person would also be involved. The point of washing the clothing would be the necessity of removing the uncleanness of the garments, lest in touching them unwashed one would again be contaminated. Interestingly, verses 29–30 expand the list of unclean creeping things to include moles and mice, to which the female members of my household would give hearty assent!

Verses 32–38 deal with different situations in which the carcasses fall upon an item of wood, clothing, skin, or sack (v. 32); an earthen vessel (v. 33); food or drink in such a vessel (v. 34); anything in an oven or cooking stove (v. 35); into a spring or cistern (v. 36); or on a seed that is to be planted (vv. 37–38). Different treatments are mandated. The items of wood, clothing, skin, or sack are to be soaked in water and considered unclean for the rest of the day. The earthen vessel, however, must be destroyed, and the food or drink in it is declared unfit for consumption. Ovens and cooking stoves are, likewise, to be destroyed. But if a dead animal falls into a spring or cistern, only the person fishing it out becomes unclean. This may strike us as strange, indeed, but we must remember that there was always a severe shortage of water, and to declare a large quantity of water unclean would be unthinkable. Why dry seed touched by a carcass remains clean, while wet seed so touched becomes unclean leaves room for question. Perhaps the wet seed is being readied for cooking and thus closer to human consumption.

Verses 39–40 complete the section, dealing with the question of the effects of contact with the carcasses of clean animals by touching, eating, or carrying. Presumably, one could eat the clean animal which had just been killed in the appropriate manner, but not without becoming unclean for the rest of the day. The cleansing required in these instances, as with the others, requires the washing of the clothing.

We began our look at this chapter by highlighting the twofold appeal in verses 44–45: "*You shall therefore be holy, for I am holy*" as one of the keys to the entire book of Leviticus. The command will occur again in 19:2, 20:7, and 20:26. Is this not the theme that Jesus must have had in mind when he said, "Therefore you shall be perfect, just as your Father in heaven is perfect" (Matt. 5:48). Certainly, at first hearing, this is a command impossible for us to obey. Hopefully, none of us would believe for a moment that we could achieve the perfection of God. But we can now see this command of Jesus in the light of our growing understanding of the holy. Holiness is not a matter of achieving some abstract ideal of perfection. Holiness is a matter of being set apart for God, different and separate. That which is set apart for God, ready to be offered to God, can be said to be perfect in this sense.

It must have been with this same sense of the holy that Peter wrote: "Coming to Him as to a living stone, rejected by men, but chosen by God and precious, you also, as living stones, are being built up a spiritual house, a holy priesthood, to offer up spiritual sacrifices acceptable to God through Jesus Christ" (1 Pet. 2:4–5). And then he added: "But you are a chosen generation, a royal priesthood, a holy nation, His own special people" (1 Pet. 2:9). We are to be holy because God is holy.

The Dietary Laws and Us

We must not leave Leviticus 11 without asking ourselves what role these laws should have in our lives. For us, the obvious place to begin shaping our answer to that question is to wrestle with some key passages in the New Testament relating specifically to them. They were certainly a major source of controversy in the early Christian community. At least three New Testament passages make this clear: Mark. 7:1–23; Matt. 5:17–20; and Acts 10.

The controversy began with Jesus himself. Without question, the most controversial and shocking encounter Jesus ever had with the Pharisees and scribes was that recorded in Mark 7:1–23, and we must examine it carefully:

> 7:1 Then the Pharisees and some of the scribes came together to Him, having come from Jerusalem.

2 Now when they saw some of His disciples eat bread with defiled, that is, with unwashed hands, they found fault.

3 For the Pharisees and all the Jews do not eat unless they wash *their* hands in a special way, holding the tradition of the elders.

4 *When they come* from the marketplace, they do not eat unless they wash. And there are many other things which they have received and hold, *like* the washing of cups, pitchers, copper vessels, and couches.

5 Then the Pharisees and scribes asked Him, "Why do Your disciples not walk according to the tradition of the elders, but eat bread with unwashed hands?"

6 He answered and said to them, "Well did Isaiah prophesy of you hypocrites, as it is written:

> *'This people honors Me with their lips,*
> *But their heart is far from Me.*
> 7   *And in vain they worship Me,*
>   Teaching as doctrines the
>   *commandments of men.'*

8 "For laying aside the commandment of God, you hold the tradition of men—the washing of pitchers and cups, and many other such things you do."

9 And He said to them, "All too well you reject the commandment of God, that you may keep your tradition.

10 "For Moses said, 'Honor your father and your mother'; and, 'He who curses father or mother, let him be put to death.'

11 "But you say, 'If a man says to his father or mother, "Whatever profit you might have received from me is Corban (that is, dedicated tto the temple)";

12 "and you no longer let him do anything for his father or his mother,

13 "making the word of God of no effect through your tradition which you have handed down. And many such things you do."

Mark 7:1–13

127

To those who took the ritual and dietary laws that we are studying most seriously, Jesus had become a terrifying threat. The radical differences between Jesus and the orthodoxy of his time are nowhere more dramatically articulated than in this passage. By the time of Jesus, the laws of Leviticus, along with those of the entire Pentateuch, had been amplified, expanded, and revised into literally thousands of rules and regulations relating to every possible situation that could occur in anyone's life. This expansion had begun in earnest in the fifth and fourth centuries before Christ with the emergence of the legal experts called the scribes. In the time of Jesus, these rules and regulations were not in written form, but were referred to as "the tradition of the elders." By elders was not meant a specific group of people, but the great legal experts of the old days such as Hillel and Shammai. This oral tradition was regarded as sacred and binding by the religious leaders of Jesus' day. Around the third century after Christ, these rules and regulations were reduced into written, summary form and called the Mishnah.

David McKenna (*Mark*, The Communicator's Commentary, vol. 2, pp.152–54) traces the steps by which God's laws had become distorted and perverted. The law begins with the representation of spiritual truth with a meaningful symbol. In this case, the issue centered on the law that required priests to wash their hands and feet in the bronze laver when entering the tabernacle to perform their duties in the worship service (Exod. 30:17–21). Failure to do so before offering the burnt offering would result in death. The symbolism was obvious; God was to be approached by priests whose clean hands and feet represented a pure heart in worship.

Such meaningful symbols and rites, however, became ritualized and required as a spiritual exercise, required of everyone who would seek holiness. By the time of Jesus, there were elaborate and rigid rules for the washing of hands before every meal, not just as a hygienic measure, but as an act of repeated ceremonial cleansing. The hand washing was required, not only before the meal, but between every course of the meal. The hands had, first of all, to be cleansed from external impurities such as dirt or sand. The water for washing was kept in special jars, which themselves were maintained in a condition of ceremonial cleanness, as we have seen in part in this chapter of Leviticus. With the fingers pointing upwards, about a quarter of a cup of water was poured over the hands with the requirement that it run at least down to the wrist. Then the fist of each hand was used to cleanse the palm of the other. Now the water had become unclean, so it was neccesary to point the fingers downward, and from the wrists pour water down over the hands and fingers to cleanse away the unclean water. Only after this ritual could one eat any food without being in danger of severe judgment by God or of attacks by demons. William Barclay's discussion (*Mark*, Daily Bible Study Series, 1975, pp. 163–67) of the elaborate cleansing processes that had been institutionalized by the time of Jesus gives us a clear picture of the enormity of the issue with which Jesus was dealing at this moment.

The third step of the corruption of the law as originally given is in the making of the ritual an end in itself. Up to this point, the symbolic ritual can be of significant value in spiritual growth. But when the ritual becomes the end in itself, the relationship with God that it is intended to symbolize becomes secondary to the correct performance of the rite. This is exactly what Jesus confronts, quoting Isaiah, "This people honors Me with their lips, But their heart is far from Me. And in vain they worship Me, teaching as doctrines the commandments of men" (Mark. 7:6–7). And Jesus adds, "For laying aside the commandments of God, you hold the traditions of men — the washing of pitchers and cups, and many other such things you do."

The final step in the corruption of the law is the use of ritual to justify and validate sinful behavior. This is the point that Jesus makes in Mark 7:9–13. The law of Corban, in its purest sense, had become a way of dedicating something wholly to God. By pronouncing Corban over money, or any object, it could never again be used for anything other than the service of God. In itself, the idea of Corban is very positive. What could be better than having a means by which to declare something wholly set apart for God? Would that we could recover this concept in our financial stewardship today. But the distortion of Corban can take place all too easily. This is what Jesus attacks. Here is a situation in which a person avoids responsibility to parents by declaring the financial resources that could and should have been used to help them as Corban, belonging to God. Even as I write, I'm preparing to settle my accounts with the Internal Revenue Service for the capital gains on the sale of our house this year. Wouldn't it be wonderful if I could just inform them that I have placed all of my assets in Corban?

The sting of Jesus on their hypocrisy in corrupting the intention of good laws had to arouse their defensive anger and stir their hostility. And then He threw down the final gauntlet, shocking and revolutionary:

> 14 And when He had called all the multitude *to Him,* He said to them, "Hear Me, everyone, and understand:
> 15 "There is nothing that enters a man from outside which can defile him; but the things which come out of him, those are the things that defile a man.
> 16 "If anyone has ears to hear, let him hear!"
> 17 And when He had entered a house away from the crowd, His disciples asked Him concerning the parable.
> 18 So He said to them, "Are you thus without understanding also? Do you not perceive that whatever enters a man from outside cannot defile him,
> 19 "because it does not enter his heart but his stomach, and is eliminated, *thus* purifying all foods?"
> 20 And He said, "What comes out of a man, that defiles a man.
> 21 "For from within, out of the heart of fornications, murders,
> 22 "thefts, covetousness, wickedness, deceit, licentiousness, and evil eye, blasphemy, pride, foolishness.
> 23 "All these evil things come from within and defile a man."

Mark 7:14–23

I'm not sure it's possible for us to realize fully what shock waves were sent out by this declaration. The very opening words, "Hear me, everyone, and understand," give a signal that Jesus was completely aware of what He was about to say. And what He said establishes the irreversible course toward His absolute rejection by the scribes and Pharisees. He had just established the irrelevance of their elaborate hand-washing rituals, and he had exposed the ways in which they had perverted otherwise good and beneficial laws. But now comes the most startling thing He could possibly say, an unmistakable rejection and repudiation of the dietary laws that they had held sacred for centuries!

Barclay, in commenting on this passage, cites an incident during the Maccabean period when the Syrian king, Antiochus Epiphanes, in his determination to extinguish the Hebrews, required that they eat pork. By the hundreds, they chose death rather than violate the dietary laws declaring pigs unclean. "Howbeit many in Israel were fully resolved and confirmed in themselves not to eat any unclean thing. Wherefore they chose rather to die, that they may not be defiled with meats, and that they might not profane the holy covenant; so then they died" (1 Macc. 1:62–63). To them, violation of the dietary laws was as much a violation of the covenant of God as murder or adultery. Even His disciples requested further amplification of such a radical statement, and He replied with the same insistence.

In one stroke, Jesus has rejected that which had become unquestionable in their understanding and practice. Don't miss the impact of this! He is rejecting the idea of things, animals in particular, as being clean or unclean. He is rejecting what they held to be the word of God! Only persons can be unclean, and what makes them unclean is not what they eat or touch, but what they do proceeding from their innermost being. He lists thirteen attitudes and behaviors (we would call all of them destructive behaviors) that are not produced by what one eats or touches, but by what one shapes in the counsels of one's inner thoughts. Thus, the issue is not what goes into a person by way of physical ingestion, but what comes out of a person in the give and take of daily life.

You would do well to work through each of the thirteen attitudes and resultant behaviors articulated here by Jesus, but allow me to single out one which may be a root cause of much of the personal and social disintegration running rampant about us. It is, in the language of the New Testament, *pleonexiai*, translated as "covetousness" (Mark 7:22). It made the cover of *Time* magazine recently, and was declared to be the central motive of millions of Americans. *Pleonexia* comes from two Greek words meaning "the desire to have more." How much is enough? We seem to have no way of answering that question. And it's not just the Trumps, the Helmsleys, and the Bakkers who get hooked on this addiction; it's just plain folks like you and me. When greed is the driving force, be it the greed for more money, power, pleasure, or comfort, the stench of uncleanness and decay is the inevitable product.

With this radical rejection of the dietary laws, Jesus has signed His ticket for rejection and crucifixion. But He has opened the door to a new quality and style of life. Is this possibly what He meant when He said in the Sermon on the Mount, "Do not think that I came to destroy the Law or the Prophets. I did not come to destroy but to fulfill. For assuredly, I say to you, till heaven and earth pass away, one jot or one tittle will by no means pass from the law till all is fulfilled. Whoever therefore breaks one of the least of these commandments, and teaches men so, shall be called least in the kingdom of heaven; but whoever does and teaches them, he shall be called great in the kingdom of heaven. For I say to you, that unless your righteousness exceeds the righteousness of the scribes and Pharisees, you will by no means enter the kingdom of heaven" (Matt. 5:17–20). Or is this a contradiction of what he said in Mark 7?

Two questions are critical in our interpretation of this saying, and in our relating it to the entire Book of Leviticus, as well as to the entire Pentateuch. The questions are (1) What did Jesus mean by the law, from which not one jot or tittle (the smallest parts of letters) shall pass away? (2) What did Jesus mean by the fulfilling of the law?

As we have seen, by the time of Jesus the general meaning of the law among the religious was the scribal tradition, later embodied in the Mishnah and expanded upon in the Talmud. But the more focused meaning of the law related most precisely to the Torah, the Ten Commandments, and more widely to the Pentateuch. Since, in the exposition of this saying that follows through the rest of Matthew 5, Jesus deals with matters not only relating to the Ten Commandments but to laws from other parts of the Pentateuch (as in 5:31, 33, 38, and 43), we must conclude that by the law, Jesus means the Pentateuch. Thus, He declares that He is not bound by the scribal traditions growing out of the Pentateuch, but only by the Pentateuch itself. But how, then, can He turn right around and reject many of the laws set forth in the Pentateuch, such as the dietary laws of Leviticus 11?

The key at this point is in what he meant by the fulfilling of the law. When he was pressed to name the greatest of the commandments in the law, he linked two commandments, one from the Torah and one from Lev. 19:18. "'You shall love the LORD your God with all your heart, with all your soul, and with all your mind.' This is the first and great commandment. And the second is like it: 'You shall love your neighbor as yourself.' On these commandments hang all the Law and the Prophets" (Matt. 22:37–40). Here, His view of the law is crystal clear. The law is no longer to be regarded merely or primarily as a set of rules and regulations to be slavishly followed, but it is a principle by which every word and action is to be shaped out of sheer love for God and for people.

Certainly we can say that, to Jesus, the fulfilling of the law did not consist of keeping rules and regulations. It was, rather, the filling of the law full of meaning through love for God and for people. Here are certainly echoes of the prophet Micah: "He has shown you, O man, what is good; and what does the Lord require of you but to do justly, to love mercy, and to walk humbly with your God?" (Mic. 6:8).

Should we then throw out Leviticus and all of the other rules and regulations of the Pentateuch? By no means! They are the word of God to us, as well as to the ancient Hebrews. But now we are to read them through the eyes of Jesus, no longer merely as rules to be slavishly obeyed, but as principles lived out by the Hebrews in their situation that now become to us, in the words of the Westminster Confession, "the only infallible rule of faith and practice." It is my conviction that our task in fulfilling the law of love will not lend itself to re-establishing rules and regulations because Jesus has taken us beyond that once and for all, and also because our world is becoming increasingly complex, certainly more than the ancient Hebrews could have imagined. That we can and should seek guidance from the Scriptures' every jot and tittle goes without saying. But the fulfilling of the law will only come in bold and creative actions based upon love for God and love for people. Those actions will be shaped by the experiences of all of our brothers and sisters of the people of God. Though what may have been specific for them may become symbolic to us, ours is the privilege and the resonsibility of living out that same love for God and for all around us. This was the joyous admonition of the writer of Hebrews: "Therefore we also, since we are surrounded by so great a cloud of witnesses, let us lay aside every weight, and the sin which so easily ensnares us, and let us run with endurance the race that is set before us, looking unto Jesus, the author and finisher of our faith, who for the joy that was set before Him endured the cross, despising the shame, and has sat down at the right hand of the throne of God" (Heb. 12:1–2). He never said it would be easy or comfortable, but there will always be meaning and fulfillment.

The early Christian community continued to struggle with this rejection of the dietary laws of the Old Testament by Jesus. Peter struggled with this when he had the vision that prepared him to respond to the need of the Gentile, Cornelius (Acts 10). While hungry, he saw something "like a great sheet bound at the four corners, descending to him and let down to the earth. In it were all kinds of four-footed animals of the earth, wild beasts, creeping things, and birds of the air. And a voice came to him, 'Rise, Peter; kill and eat'" (Acts 10:11–13). Peter remonstrated, "Not so, Lord! For I have never eaten anything common or unclean." Then came the voice from heaven, "What God has cleansed you must not call unclean" (10:15). This became the crucial event in Acts which caused the extension of the ministry and fellowship of the Jewish Christian church, including baptism, to the Gentiles without requiring adherence to the ceremonial laws of cleansing.

But there was still difficulty in this abandonment of the ancient practices and principles. So much so that a sharp controversy arose among the early Christians regarding whether circumcision and the observance of the laws should be required of gentile converts. A formal council was held in Jerusalem (Acts 15) to settle these matters once and for all. Peter played a key role in the decision of the council, reciting his vision and experience with Cornelius. At the same time, Paul and Barnabas witnessed to what God had been doing among the Gentiles through them. The decision was made to require nothing other than the abstinence "from things offered to idols, from blood, from things strangled, and from sexual immorality" (Acts 15:29). With that landmark decision, the ancient dietary laws were no longer operative in the Christian community.

This made a crucial difference in the missionary outreach of the church. It is possible for certain distinctives to become unnecessary hindrances to the communication of the gospel. As important as the dietary laws had become as a badge of separation to God, requiring that of Gentiles would have built an unnecessary and inseparable barrier between the people and the gospel of God's grace in Jesus Christ. There's always a fine line between those distinctives necessary to maintain the integrity of our walk with God and those which can become artificial barriers to the inclusion of all in the Kingdom of God.

CLEANSING AFTER CHILDBIRTH

12:1   Then the LORD spoke to Moses, saying,

2   "Speak to the children of Israel, saying: 'If a woman has conceived, and borne a male child, then she shall be unclean seven days; as in the days of her customary impurity she shall be unclean.

3   'And on the eighth day the flesh of his foreskin shall be circumcised.

4   'She shall then continue in the blood of *her* purification thirty-three days. She shall not touch any hallowed thing, nor come into the sanctuary until the days of her purification are fulfilled.

5   'But if she bears a female child, then she shall be unclean two weeks, as in her customary impurity, and she shall continue in the blood of *her* purification sixty-six days.

6   'When the days of her purification are fulfilled, whether for a son or a daughter, she shall bring to the priest a lamb of the first year as a burnt offering, and a young pigeon or a turtledove as a sin offering, to the door of the tabernacle of meeting.

7   'Then he shall offer it before the LORD, and make atonement for her. And she shall be clean from the flow of her blood. This *is* the law for her who has borne a male or a female.

8   'And if she is not able to bring a lamb, then she may bring two turtledoves or two young pigeons — one as a burnt offering and the other as a sin offering. So the priest shall make atonement for her, and she will be clean.'"

Lev. 12:1–8

Though this is surely the shortest chapter in Leviticus, it raises a number of questions. Since God commanded us to be fruitful and multiply (Gen. 8:7), why should the birth of a child render the mother "unclean"? Why is the circumcision of a male child to be on the eighth day? Why does the purification period last for a total of forty days? Why does the birth of a female child cause twice the period of uncleanness as a male child? When the final purification offering is brought to the priest, what is being atoned for?

The tradition of the eighth day for the circumcision of the male child goes back to the earliest part of Hebrew history with the birth of Isaac to Abraham. "Then Abraham circumcised his son Isaac when he was eight days old, as God had commanded him" (Gen. 21:4). The command was formalized in Genesis 17: "This is My covenant which you shall keep, between Me and you and your descendants after you: Every male child among you shall be circumcised; and you shall be circumcised in the flesh of your foreskins, and it shall be a sign of the Covenant between Me and you. He who is eight days old among you shall be circumcised, every male child in your generations, he who is born in your house or bought with money from any stranger who is not your descendant . . . and My covenant shall be in your flesh for an everlasting covenant" (Gen. 17:10–14).

Ishmael was thirteen years old when he was circumcised, and the Ishmaelites maintained that age for circumcision. Circumcision seems to have been an ancient custom, not practiced exclusively by the Hebrews. There are records of its practice near Syria in the third millenium before Christ, and it was practiced in Egypt, with the age set at fourteen. Paul seemed to be making it clear that he was not an Ishmaelite or a stranger brought into Israel when he emphasized that he had been "circumcised the eighth day, of the stock of Israel, of the tribe of Benjamin, a Hebrew of the Hebrews" (Phil. 3:5).

Jesus used an interesting aspect of the rite of circumcision on an occasion of intense conflict in a confrontation with people in Jerusalem at the time of the Feast of Tabernacles (John 7:14–24). Jesus had been accused of breaking the Sabbath law, having healed a man on the Sabbath at the pool of Bethesda (John 5:1–18). In this heated exchange, Jesus sets out to justify his action, even though it had been on the Sabbath. With a very wise and clever bit of logic, he made his point in a tense situation. He pointed out that in their practice of circumcison, always on the eighth day after birth, not infrequently the circumcision would be performed on the Sabbath. To say that no work could be done on the Sabbath while, at the same time, performing the work of circumcision on the Sabbath was contradictory, for the only medical work allowed by their Sabbath laws was that essential to saving life. If, indeed, it was standard practice to perform circumcisions on the Sabbath, work technically in violation of their own laws, why should they come down on him for making a sick man well? Here we see the mind of Jesus at its best. And his final appeal is consistent with what we have seen of his view of the law: "Do not judge according to appearance, but judge with righteous judgment" (John 7:24).

The questions relating to the uncleanness of the mother after giving birth, the lengthy period of that uncleanness, and the necessity of both a burnt offering and a sin offering remain matters of speculation. It is not clear why the woman should be unclean by bearing children, since this is what God commanded her to do (Gen. 1:28). Even a husband and wife having intercourse within marriage become unclean for the remainder of the day (Lev. 15:18). And yet childlessness was regarded as a great misfortune, and a large family was seen as a sign of God's blessing.

The reason for the period of uncleanness being twice as long for the birth of a girl (eighty days) remains an enigma to the contemporary interpreter. Theories abound, some believing that in this law we have a residue from pre-Israelite practice, others that women after childbirth were prone to attack by demons, but no interpretation seems to give a convincing rationale.

Most likely the doubling of the time of uncleanness after the birth of a girl is an expression of the Hebrew view of the relative value of women, such as is expressed by the redemption price for women being half of that for men (Lev. 27:2-7).

According to the law, it is not the baby that makes the mother unclean but the discharge of blood that follows childbirth. This seems to relate to the whole issue of various bodily discharges as sources of uncleanness, which we shall confront in Leviticus 15.

Luke (2:21-24) indicates that these customs of circumcision and purification were followed by Mary and Joseph after the birth of Jesus, and we get a further insight into their economic condition, for the provision to bring two turtledoves or young pigeons was given to those who could not afford to bring the standard offering of a lamb for the burnt offering (12:6, 8).

There is no evidence that this law for purification after childbirth was questioned by the early Christian community, though the destruction of the temple in A.D. 70 certainly ended its observance.

Laws Concerning Skin Diseases

Chapters 13 and 14 form a unit dealing with the effect of serious skin diseases on persons, clothing, and houses. In such matters, the priests are called to double or triple duty, serving also as doctors and public health officers. Rituals for the cleansing of healed lepers are also provided. The older English translations use the word "leprosy" throughout these chapters, but it is now generally agreed that none of the skin diseases named here are the same as leprosy (which we call Hansen's disease). There are twenty-four different types of diseases delineated, a veritable dermatological catalog!

We must appreciate that the diagnostic precision of the ancient Hebrews is not to be compared with ours. While we would not use the same name for mildew and psoriasis, the Hebrew naming system was based upon similarities in appearances, and thus easily becomes confusing to us. But the ultimate purpose of these chapters is not to provide a medical manual for modern dermatologists but to provide ways for the recognition and treatment of skin diseases as they experienced them, with special attention to the issues of cleanness and uncleanness.

The primary interest of these chapters for us is their picture of the meaning of holiness as physical wholeness. Anyone experiencing the symptoms described was obviously not whole. And such diseases were considered infectious, capable of contaminating even clothing and buildings. For the people of God, wholeness that witnessed to God's design in creation was tantamount to holiness. Only perfect animals, without blemish, could be brought to the tabernacle for offering to God. Wholeness was required of the priests. All abnormalities must be dealt with.

Skin Diseases in People

13:1 And the LORD spoke to Moses and Aaron, saying:
2 "When a man has on the skin of his body a swelling, a scab, or a bright spot, and it becomes on the skin of his body *like* a leprous sore, then he shall be brought to Aaron the priest or to one of his sons the priests.

3 "The priest shall look at the sore on the skin of the body; and if the hair on the sore has turned white, and the sore appears *to be* deeper than the skin of his body, it *is* a leprous sore. Then the priest shall look at him, and pronounce him unclean.

4 "But if the bright spot *is* white on the skin of his body, and does not appear *to be* deeper than the skin, and its hair has not turned white, then the priest shall isolate *the one who has* the sore seven days.

5 "And the priest shall look at him on the seventh day; and indeed *if* the sore appears to be as it was, *and* the sore has not spread on the skin, then the priest shall isolate him another seven days.

6 "Then the priest shall look at him again on the seventh day; and indeed *if* the sore has darkened, *and* the sore has not spread on the skin, then the priest shall pronounce him clean; it *is only* a scab, and he shall wash his clothes and be clean.

7 "But if the scab should at all spread over the skin, after he has been seen by the priest for his cleansing, he shall be seen by the priest again.

8 "And *if* the priest sees that the scab has indeed spread on the skin, then the priest shall pronounce him unclean. It *is* leprosy.

9 "When the leprous sore is on a person, then he shall be brought to the priest.

10 "And the priest shall look *at him;* and indeed *if* the swelling on the skin *is* white, and it has turned the hair white, and *there is* a spot of raw flesh in the swelling,

11 "it *is* an old leprosy on the skin of his body. The priest shall pronounce him unclean, and shall not isolate him, for he *is* unclean.

12 "And if leprosy breaks out all over the skin, and the leprosy covers all the skin of *the one who has* the sore, from his head to his foot, wherever the priest looks,

13 "then the priest shall consider; and indeed *if* the leprosy has covered all his body, he shall pronounce *him* clean *who has* the sore. It has all turned white. He *is* clean.

14 "But when raw flesh appears on him, he shall be unclean.

139

15 "And the priest shall look at the raw flesh and pronounce him to be unclean; *for* the raw flesh *is* unclean. It *is* leprosy.

16 "Or if the raw flesh changes and turns white again, he shall come to the priest.

17 "And the priest shall look at him; and indeed *if* the sore has turned white, then the priest shall pronounce *him* clean *who has* the sore. He *is* clean.

18 "If the body develops a boil in the skin, and it is healed,

19 "and in the place of the boil there comes a white swelling or a bright spot, reddish-white, then it shall be shown to the priest;

20 "and *if,* when the priest sees it, it indeed *appears* deeper than the skin, and its hair has turned white, the priest shall pronounce him unclean. It *is* a leprous sore which has broken out of the boil.

21 "But if the priest looks at it, and indeed *there are* no white hairs in it, and *if* it *is* not deeper than the skin, but has faded, then the priest shall isolate him seven days;

22 "and if it should at all spread over the skin, then the priest shall pronounce him unclean. It *is* a leprous sore.

23 "But if the bright spot stays in one place, *and* has not spread, it *is* the scar of the boil; and the priest shall pronounce him clean.

24 "Or if the body receives a burn on its skin by fire, and the raw *flesh* of the burn becomes a bright spot, reddish-white or white,

25 "then the priest shall look at it; and indeed *if* the hair of the bright spot has turned white, and it appears deeper than the skin, it *is* leprosy broken out in the burn. Therefore the priest shall pronounce him unclean. It *is* a leprous sore.

26 "But if the priest looks at it, and indeed *there are* no white hairs in the bright spot, and it *is* not deeper than the skin, but has faded, then the priest shall isolate him seven days.

27 "And the priest shall look at him on the seventh day. If it has at all spread over the skin, then the priest shall pronounce him unclean. It *is* a leprous sore.

28 "But if the bright spot stays in one place, *and* has not spread on the skin, but has faded, it *is* a swelling from the burn. The priest shall pronounce him clean, for it *is* the scar from the burn.

29 "If a man or woman has a sore on the head or the beard,

30 "then the priest shall look at the sore; and indeed if it appears deeper than the skin, *and there is* in it thin yellow hair, then the priest shall pronounce him unclean. It *is* a scall, a leprosy of the head or beard.

31 "But if the priest looks at the sore of the scall, and indeed it does not appear deeper than the skin, and *there is* no black hair in it, then the priest shall isolate *the one who has the sore* of the scall seven days.

32 "And on the seventh day the priest shall look at the sore; and indeed *if* the scall has not spread, and there is no yellow hair in it, and the scall does not appear deeper than the skin,

33 "he shall shave himself, but the scall he shall not shave. And the priest shall isolate *the one who has* the scall another seven days.

34 "On the seventh day the priest shall look at the scall; and indeed *if* the scall has not spread over the skin, and does not appear deeper than the skin, then the priest shall pronounce him clean. He shall wash his clothes and be clean.

35 "But if the scall should at all spread over the skin after his cleansing,

36 "then the priest shall look at him; and indeed if the scall has spread over the skin, the priest need not seek for yellow hair. He *is* unclean.

37 "But if the scall appears to be at a standstill, and there is black hair grown up in it, the scall has healed. He *is* clean, and the priest shall pronounce him clean.

38 "If a man or a woman has bright spots on the skin of the body, *specifically* white bright spots,

39 "then the priest shall look; and indeed *if* the bright spots on the skin of the body *are* dull white, it *is* a white spot *that* grows on the skin. He *is* clean.

40 "As for the man whose hair has fallen from his head, he *is* bald , *but* he *is* clean.

41 "He whose hair has fallen from his forehead, he
is bald on the forehead, *but* he *is* clean.

42 "And if there is on the bald head or bald forehead a reddish-white sore, it *is* leprosy breaking out
on his bald head or his bald forehead.

43 "Then the priest shall look at it; and indeed *if*
the swelling of the sore *is* reddish-white on his bald
head or on his bald forehead, as the appearance of
leprosy on the skin of the body,

44 "he is a leprous man. He *is* unclean. The priest shall
surely pronounce him unclean; his sore *is* on his head.

45 "Now the leper on whom the sore *is,* his clothes
shall be torn and his head bare; and he shall cover his
mustache, and cry, 'Unclean! Unclean!'

46 "He shall be unclean. All the days he has the
sore he shall be unclean. He *is* unclean, and he shall
dwell alone; his habitation *shall be* outside the camp.

Lev. 13:1–46

This part of chapter 13 deals with the diagnosis and treatment of
various diseases of the skin, twenty-one to be exact. Until recent
years, the Hebrew *tsara'ath,* following the Greek translation *lepra,* has
generally been translated "leprosy," as in our translation. But
Wenham points out that modern medical opinion is agreed that true
leprosy (Hansen's disease) is not one of the diseases described here.
Archaeological evidence from Egypt does not indicate people having
leprosy prior to the fifth century A.D. Though records show that leprosy had been identified before then, it was certainly rare in Palestine
prior to the time of Christ. Further, medical authorities affirm that the
signs and symptoms of Hansen's disease are not those indicated in
any of the biblical references to *tsara'ath.* True leprosy was designated
by the Greek word *elephantiasis,* not by *lepra.* Medical efforts to identify the actual disease(s) indicated by *tsara'ath,* the "leprous sore" of
13:2 and throughout the chapter, point to scaly skin disease(s) of some
kind. Wenham cites medical authorities who point to psoriasis, favus,
leucoderma, and extreme eczema. Wenham has an excellent, brief
discussion of the nature of these skin diseases (pp. 195–97).

The general pattern of each section (vv. 2–8, 9–17, 18–23, 24–28,
29–37, 38–39, and 40–44). begins with a preliminary statement of the
symptoms followed by an inspection by one of the priests, Aaron or

one of his sons. Then there is a statement of the symptoms upon which the diagnosis is to be based, such as the color of a hair or a scab, followed by the diagnosis by the priest and the prescription of clean or unclean. When the diagnosis was inconclusive on some occasions, a week or two weeks of further observation was stipulated. Full or partial baldness, though singled out, did not require priestly inspection and was declared clean (vv. 40-41). The dreadful fate of those diagnosed as infected and unclean is described in 45-46.

The first section (vv. 2-8) gives the criteria for differentiating between what we would call chronic and acute skin diseases. If the hair has turned white (perhaps a reference to the effect of the white scales of the skin disease clinging to the hair), the person is pronounced unclean and must tear one's clothes, bare one's head, cover his mustache (a sign of mourning), and from one's solitary dwelling outside the camp warn any who approach by crying out, "Unclean! Unclean!" (vv. 45-46). If, however, the symptoms are inconclusive, the person is confined for a week for further examination. If the scale has not spread, there is a confinement for one more week and another examination. The person is declared clean if the affected area has remained static. Imagine the release that would come after two weeks of intense anxiety!

In the second section (vv. 9-17), the diagnosis is based upon the presence of "raw flesh" within the swelling. This presumably refers to bleeding scales, indicating a patchy condition such as advanced psoriasis. In this case, there was to be no isolation for further diagnosis (v. 11), but an immediate declaration of unclean. If, however, the skin has turned white, indicating healing, the patient is declared clean.

Verses 18-28 deal with inflammations relating to boils or burns. White hair and deep infection are sure signs of serious disease. When doubtful, a seven-day diagnostic period is again operative. Medical opinion suggests that these cases appear to be psoriasis, favus, or patchy eczema. If active, they are declared unclean, with the sentencing of verses 45-46.

Infections of the scalp or beard of "a man or woman" (v. 29) are the subject of verses 29-37. A different word, netek, is used in verse 30 to describe the disease. The priest is told to look for yellow, thin hair rather than white hair as before, and medical opinion favors the diagnosis here of favus rather than psoriasis. A quarantine of up to two weeks is prescribed for the diagnostic period, along with possible shaving of the infected area. A black hair in the infected area war-ranted a diagnosis of clean.

There is general agreement that the disease in verses 38–39 is vitiligo or leucoderma, in which patches of skin turn completely white, without scaling. It is declared clean.

Finally, the section in verses 40–44 deals with further diseases of the scalp. The same diagnostic tests are operative, and if the presence of what is likely to have been psoriasis is indicated, the person is declared unclean.

The horrible fate of all those declared unclean due to serious skin diseases is prescribed in verses 45–46. The victim was required to live outside the camp, for it was within the camp that God lived with the people, and uncleanness had no place within the community. As we shall see in chapter 14, provision is made to end the banishment and restore the person to the community when the healing of the skin disease had taken place. Thus, this separation of the diseased person must not be seen as a punishment but as a means of preserving the health and purity of the community in its relationship with the God who is holy.

But we must not minimize the dehumanization experienced by the victims of these dreaded skin diseases. Living alone outside the camp would be the ultimate dread of any Hebrew. Unlike us modern West-ern individualists, the Hebrew lived and breathed for the community of God's people. We shall deal in greater depth with the meaning of being outside the camp in the next chapter of this commentary, when we study the Great Day of Atonement in Leviticus 16. To be outside the camp was to be separated from God and one's family. To be outside the camp was to be removed from the worship of the living God, for the tabernacle was in the midst of the camp. To be outside the camp was to be cut off from one's people and from God's covenant. Nothing could be worse.

Banishment evoked the symbols of grief and mourning in the tear-ing of the clothes, the baring of the head (probably the messing up of the hair), and the covering of the upper lip. All of these were visible expressions of grief and sorrow, found in other parts of the Bible. As we have seen, Aaron and his sons were not permitted to enter into outwardly grieving for the deaths of Nadab and Abihu who had profaned the Lord's altar: "Do not uncover your heads nor tear your clothes" (Lev. 10:6). The high priest was not allowed to share in public mourning by uncovering his head or tearing his clothes (Lev. 21:10). David mourned the deaths of Saul and Jonathan by tearing his clothes along with the men who were with him (2 Sam. 1:11). Ezekiel was not allowed to mourn over the death of his wife and was told not to cover his lips (as a sign of mourning) (Ezek. 24:17, 22). To be banished to live outside the camp was to live a life of continual mourning, along with the degrading and debasing requirement of shouting to anyone approaching, "*Unclean! Unclean!*"

Only when we can begin to feel the pathos and utter dehumanization of anyone doomed to live outside the camp as a "leper," can we appreciate the compassion and love of Jesus when he healed the "leper," an event recorded in all three of the synoptic gospels (Mark 1:40–45; Matt. 8:2–4; Luke 5:12–14). The drama is intense in Mark's account for two reasons. In the first place, the man came to Jesus, "imploring Him, kneeling down to Him and saying to Him, 'If You are willing, You can make me clean'" (Mark 1:40). There must have been something very special about Jesus for this diseased and ostracized man to dare to approach Jesus and initiate a conversation. We know that he was entitled to say nothing other than "Unclean! Unclean!" In approaching Jesus, the man had clearly broken the law for lepers, but Jesus accepted him, listened to him, and responded to him, thus breaking the law Himself. And would not this encounter have taken place outside the camp? Here was Jesus, out where "lepers" were, open and available.

But even more awesome, "Jesus . . . put out His hand and *touched* him" (Mark 1:41). Immediately, the man was healed. In reaching out and touching the man, Jesus entered into the man's uncleanness.

Here is the powerful and moving picture of the One who enters into our suffering and brokenness with us. He does not offer a word of encouragement from a distance. No! He touches the untouchable. He loves the unlovable. He heals the incurable. Is there anyone like Him in all of heaven or earth?

And yet, while Jesus broke the law in touching the man, he instructed the man, "But go your way, show yourself to the priest, and offer for your cleansing those things which Moses commanded, as a testimony to them" (Mark 1:44). Barclay sees this as Jesus telling the man to avail himself of the treatment that was available. He suggests that the lesson is that we should use every human means available for healing as well as seeking God's direct intervention. It seems better to me to read this in the light of what we are learning from Leviticus. The cleansing ritual that we are about to study in Leviticus 14 was not a ritual for healing but rather a ritual for ceremonial cleansing after the diseased person had been cured. Here, then, is a lesson in the ambiguity of Jesus in relationship to the laws of Moses. He ignores the law when it comes to the healing of the "leper." And then He submits to the law when it is in the best interests of the healed man for his restoration into the community—another validation of Jesus' claim that He came not to abolish the law but to fulfill it.

SKIN DISEASES IN CLOTHING

47 "Also, if a garment has a leprous plague in it, *whether it is* a woolen garment or a linen garment,

48 "whether *it is* in the warp or woof of linen or wool, whether in leather or in anything made of leather,

49 "and if the plague is greenish or reddish in the garment or in the leather, whether in the warp or in the woof, or in anything made of leather, it *is* a leprous plague and shall be shown to the priest.

50 "The priest shall look at the plague and isolate *that which has* the plague seven days.

51 "And he shall look at the plague on the seventh day. If the plague has spread in the garment, either in the warp or in the woof, in the leather *or* in anything made of leather, the plague *is* an active leprosy. It *is* unclean.

52 "He shall therefore burn that garment in which is the plague, whether warp or woof, in wool or in linen, or anything of leather, for it *is* an active leprosy, it shall be burned in the fire.

53 "But if the priest looks, and indeed the plague has not spread in the garment, either in the warp or in the woof, or in anything made of leather,

54 "then the priest shall command that they wash *the thing* in which *is* the plague; and he shall isolate it another seven days.

55 "Then the priest shall look at the plague after it has been washed; and indeed *if* the plague has not changed its color, though the plague has not spread, it

is unclean, and you shall burn it in the fire; it continues eating away, *whether* the damage *is* outside or inside.

56 "If the priest looks, and indeed the plague has faded after washing it, then he shall tear it out of the garment, whether out of the warp or out of the woof, or out of the leather.

57 "But if it appears again in the garment, either in the warp or in the woof, or in anything made of leather, it *is* a spreading *plague;* you shall burn with fire that in which is the plague.

58 "And if you wash the garment, either warp or woof, or whatever is made of leather, if the plague has disappeared from it, then it shall be washed a second time, and shall be clean.

59 "This *is* the law of the leprous plague in a garment of wool or linen, either in the warp or woof, or in anything made of leather, to pronounce it clean or to pronounce it unclean."

Lev. 13:47–59

To our way of thinking, linking skin diseases to mold or mildew on wool or leather clothing doesn't make much sense. Not so with the ancient Hebrews. For in this passage the same word is used to describe mold on a garment as has just been used to describe skin diseases (*tsara'ath*). And a similar diagnostic procedure for such irregularities is prescribed.

If a person notices a green or red mold or fungus on a garment of linen, wool, or leather, it is to be brought to the priest for a seven-day observation period. If the mold has spread, the garment is declared unclean and must be burned (vv. 51–52). If, however, the mold does not appear to be spreading, the garment is to be washed and then observed for another seven days. If the mold has not changed color, even though not spreading, the garment is declared unclean and burned (vv. 53–55). But if the mold has faded after the washing, it is to be removed from the garment, but the garment may be kept (v. 56). If it should appear again, the garment is to be burned (v. 57), and if, after washing, the mold is no longer apparent, the garment shall be declared clean after one more washing.

This passage, obviously, must be read in the context of chapters 11–15, or it would have no significance other than an ancient recollection of one aspect of maintaining one's wardrobe. The issue continues to be the maintenance of holiness throughout the community. A garment with a mildew or fungus is not whole, and, presumably, such garments should not be worn during the worship of God. Just as the animals to be sacrificed were to be without defects, the priests offering the sacrifices were to be without physical deformities. The worshiper also should be ceremonially clean, so the clothing worn by the worshipers was to be free of foreign growths.

We gain from this section a growing sense of the importance that wholeness and purity in every dimension of life and existence had for the Hebrews of old. To be sure, these matters seem strange to those of us for whom worship is nothing more than an optional decision to attend a church service.

We shouldn't leave this section without recognizing this theme in the often overlooked and somewhat enigmatic Book of Jude. Toward the close of the brief letter, Jude writes: "And on some have compassion, making a distinction; but others save with fear, pulling them out of the fire, hating even the garment defiled by the flesh" (vv. 22–23). Jude must have had the Levitical law in mind when he referred to "the garment defiled by the flesh." And the preferred translation of the opening phrase of verse 23, as footnoted in our text is "on some have mercy with fear." Thus the ancient understanding that a person could be made unclean by contact with an unclean garment is applied to warn of the risk involved in evangelistic outreach to some folks. When Jesus reached out and touched the leper, he took the uncleanness upon himself. Perhaps we need to take some risks ourselves in reaching out and touching others for Christ, but we must be aware of the need to approach them with mercy *and* with fear. As Dr. Sam Shoemaker used to say to us, "we must hate the sin but love the sinner."

THE CLEANSING RITUAL FOR HEALED "LEPERS"

14:1 Then the LORD spoke to Moses, saying,
    2 "This shall be the law of the leper for the day of his cleansing: He shall be brought to the priest.

3 "And the priest shall go out of the camp, and the priest shall look; and indeed, *if* the leprosy is healed in the leper,

4 "then the priest shall command to take for him who is to be cleansed two living *and* clean birds, cedar wood, scarlet, and hyssop.

5 "And the priest shall command that one of the birds be killed in an earthen vessel over running water.

6 "As for the living bird, he shall take it, the cedar wood and the scarlet and the hyssop, and dip them and the living bird in the blood of the bird *that was* killed over the running water.

7 "And he shall sprinkle it seven times on him who is to be cleansed from the leprosy, and shall pronounce him clean, and shall let the living bird loose in the open field.

8 "He who is to be cleansed shall wash his clothes, shave off all his hair, and wash himself in water, that he may be clean. After that he shall come into the camp, and shall stay outside his tent seven days.

9 "But on the seventh day he shall shave all the hair off his head and his beard and his eyebrows — all his hair he shall shave off. He shall wash his clothes and wash his body in water, and he shall be clean.

10 "And on the eighth day he shall take two male lambs without blemish, one ewe lamb of the first year without blemish, three-tenths *of an ephah* of fine flour mixed with oil as a grain offering, and one log of oil.

11 "Then the priest who makes *him* clean shall present the man who is to be made clean, and those things, before the LORD, *at* the door of the tabernacle of meeting.

12 "And the priest shall take one male lamb and offer it as a trespass offering, and the log of oil, and wave them as a wave offering before the LORD.

13 "Then he shall kill the lamb in the place where he kills the sin offering and the burnt offering, in a holy place; for as the sin offering *is* the priest's, so *is* the trespass offering. It *is* most holy.

14 "The priest shall take *some* of the blood of the trespass offering, and the priest shall put *it* on the tip

149

of the right ear of him who is to be cleansed, on the thumb of his right hand, and on the big toe of his right foot.

15 "And the priest shall take *some* of the log of oil, and pour *it* into the palm of his own left hand.

16 "Then the priest shall dip his right finger in the oil that *is* in his left hand, and shall sprinkle some of the oil with his finger seven times before the LORD.

17 "And of the rest of the oil in his hand, the priest shall put *some* on the tip of the right ear of him who is to be cleansed, on the thumb of his right hand, and on the big toe of his right foot, on the blood of the trespass offering.

18 "The rest of the oil that *is* in the priest's hand he shall put on the head of him who is to be cleansed. So the priest shall make atonement for him before the LORD.

19 "Then the priest shall offer the sin offering, and make atonement for him who is to be cleansed from his uncleanness. Afterward he shall kill the burnt offering.

20 "And the priest shall offer the burnt offering and the grain offering on the altar. So the priest shall make atonement for him, and he shall be clean.

21 "But if he *is* poor and cannot afford it, then he shall take one male lamb *as* a trespass offering to be waved, to make atonement for him, one-tenth *of an ephah* of fine flour mixed with oil as a grain offering, a log of oil,

22 "and two turtledoves or two young pigeons, such as he is able to afford: one shall be a sin offering and the other a burnt offering.

23 "He shall bring them to the priest on the eighth day for his cleansing, to the door of the tabernacle of meeting, before the LORD.

24 "And the priest shall take the lamb of the trespass offering and the log of oil, and the priest shall wave them *as* a wave offering before the LORD.

25 "Then he shall kill the lamb of the trespass offering, and the priest shall take *some* of the blood of the trespass offering and put *it* on the tip of the right ear of him who is to be cleansed, on the thumb of his right hand, and on the big toe of his right foot.

26 "And the priest shall pour some of the oil into
the palm of his own left hand.

27 " Then the priest shall sprinkle with his right
finger *some* of the oil that *is* in his left hand seven
times before the LORD.

28 "And the priest shall put *some* of the oil that *is* in
his hand on the tip of the right ear of him who is to be
cleansed, on the thumb of the right hand, and on the
big toe of his right foot, on the place of the blood of
the trespass offering.

29 "The rest of the oil that *is* in the priest's hand he
shall put on the head of him who is to be cleansed, to
make atonement for him before the LORD.

30 "And he shall offer one of the turtledoves or
young pigeons, such as he can afford —

31 "such as he is able to afford, the one *as* a sin
offering and the other *as* a burnt offering, with the
grain offering. So the priest shall make atonement for
him who is to be cleansed before the LORD.

32 " This *is* the law *for one* who had a leprous sore,
who cannot afford the usual cleansing."

Lev. 14: 1–32

We must be careful not to misread this section as offering a ritual
for the healing of the skin diseases of chapter 13. The rites prescribed
in this chapter are for the cleansing of the person who has been healed
of the disease. After one had experienced the healing of the disease,
however that healing may have come, it was still necessary to restore
that person back into the worshiping community. Thus we are dealing with joyous ceremonies of the restoration of those who had been
outcasts because of their uncleanness.

Before the person who has experienced healing of the skin disease
can return from outside the camp to the community, there must be an
examination by the priest. And that examination is to be done outside
the camp for obvious reasons. If the priest confirms that the disease
has been cured, the first part of the cleansing ritual is celebrated while
still outside the camp (2–9). The service begins by bringing "*two living
and clean birds, cedar wood, scarlet, and hyssop.*" One of the birds is to be
killed and placed in a clay pot with fresh water. The living bird is
dipped in the blood in the pot, along with the cedar wood, the scarlet

thread, and the hyssop. Then the blood from the pot is sprinkled on the person to be cleansed and the living bird is released to fly away. The healed person then washes his or her clothing, shaves off all hair, and washes completely in water. At this point the person can return into the camp but must live outside his or her tent for seven days. Then there is to be another thorough washing of clothing and body and another shaving prior to the second phase of the cleansing service.

Most of the symbolism seems reasonably obvious. The ceremony with the birds presupposes an identification of the person being cleansed with the birds. We have already seen this principle of the identification of the worshiper with the sacrificial animal in the other offerings. The bird that dies portrays vicariously what would have happened to the person if God had not intervened. The bird that flys away may be symbolic of the new life now given to the cured person; or, perhaps, it conveys the picture of the skin disease being carried away by the bird. One cannot help but feel a parallel to the two goats used on the Great Day of Atonement (Leviticus 16). This, to me, is a dramatic moment. Imagine the sense of release and gratitude as the healed person watches the bird vanish from sight, never to return again! The sevenfold sprinkling of the blood on the person being cleansed is similar to the trespass offering of the poor (5:7–10). The use of cedar wood, scarlet yarn, and hyssop is not uncommon in purification rites as indicated in Num. 19:6, 18; Ps. 51:7, and Heb. 9:19. Cedar was a precious wood, regarded as the strongest and best for construction, but its symbolism here is not certain. The scarlet thread, though used a great deal in the tabernacle itself, has uncertain symbolism here. Perhaps we can anticipate the words of Isaiah, "Though your sins are like scarlet, they shall be as white as snow" (Isa. 1:18). Hyssop is a small bushy herb very common in Egypt and Palestine. Its thick, hairy leaves and branches were made into a bunch to hold liquids for sprinkling. It was a bunch of hyssop that was used for sprinkling the blood on the lintel and doorposts on the eve of their deliverance from Egypt (Exod. 12:22). All three were used in the sprinkling of the blood on the healed person.

Not until the eighth day, however, was the cured person fully cleansed and allowed to return to the home tent and bring sacrifices into the tabernacle. John Calvin drew a parallel between this and circumcision on the eighth day, suggesting that as the infant male was brought into the family of God on the eighth day, so now the restored outcast, who had been dead to the community, was born anew and restored to the family.

The scene now shifts to the court of the tabernacle (vv. 10–20). The healed person is ready for the second act of the cleansing celebration. Wenham points out that these rituals find their closest parallels in the covenant rituals in Exodus 24 and in the ordination service in Leviticus 8–9. The gravity of the occasion is made obvious by the need for all of the required sacrifices (burnt, grain, sin, and trespass) to be presented with this offering. Only the peace offering, which is almost always voluntary, is not required. The offering requires three lambs (two male and one female), about six quarts of fine flour mixed with oil, and less than a pint (a log) of oil. The priest begins with the sacrifice of one of the male lambs as a trespass offering (Leviticus 5), followed by the sin offering (Leviticus 4). Then follows the burnt offering and the grain offering (Leviticus 1, 2).

As always, provision is made for a less expensive alternative for one who is poor and cannot afford three lambs (vv. 21–32): one male lamb for the trespass offering, two quarts of fine flour mixed with oil (instead of six) for the grain offering, and two turtledoves (or two young pigeons) for the sin and burnt offerings. This gracious provision for the poor should speak loudly and clearly to us in all of our contemporary practices.

The presentation of the last three offerings is consistent with what we have learned of the basic meaning of the offerings in Leviticus 1–5. The grain offering was a pledge of renewed commitment and dedication to God. The sin offering was to cleanse the sanctuary of any uncleanness the disease may have caused, and the burnt offering was essential to the person's reconciliation and rededication to God. But the trespass offering calls for our attention.

As we learned in 5:14–6:7, there were three basic offenses requiring the trespass offering: "unintentionally in regard to the holy things of the LORD" (5:15), committing "any of these things which are forbidden to be done by the commandments of the LORD, though he does not know it" (5:17), and "lying to his neighbor . . . about a pledge . . . and swears falsely" (6:2–3). Why, then, is the trespass offering required for the cleansing of the person who has been cured from a skin disease? Perhaps the person would feel there had been some unintentional trespass against the things of the Lord or of the commandments, and such a cleansing rite would be designed to free the person from such feelings. Certainly, the four offerings combined would bring a full sense of cleansing and restoration to the cured person.

Of particular interest in this cleansing ritual is the use of some of the blood of the trespass offering. It is to be put *"on the tip of the right ear of him who is to be cleansed, on the thumb of his right hand, and on the big toe of his right foot"* (vv. 14, 25). Then follows the ritual in which some of the oil is poured into the palm of the priest's left hand so that with his right finger he can then "sprinkle some of the oil with his finger seven times before the LORD" (vv. 16, 27). Then he is to repeat, with the oil, what he had done with the blood on the right ear, the right thumb, and the right big toe (vv. 17, 28). The ritual concludes when the priest pours the remaining oil from his left hand onto the head of the one being cleansed.

The anointing with the blood and the oil on the ear, the thumb, and the big toe reminds us of the same anointing of Aaron and his sons when they were ordained to the priesthood (8:22–24). Just as the priests were ordained to a ministry in which their ears, hands, and feet were consecrated to hearing, serving, and walking with the Lord, so this person, brought back from outside the camp into fellowship again with the people of God, is now dedicated again to hearing, serving, and walking with the living God.

This passage has come to have special meaning for me by reading it through the eyes and feelings of the one being cleansed. Imagine what it must have felt like to watch that lesion growing on your skin and to experience dread and helplessness as the symptoms persist. Feel the total despair as the priest diagnoses the condition as "unclean." You say goodbye, you must assume for the last time ever, to your family, friends, and loved ones. For now you must live outside the camp — cut off from all but other "lepers," removed from all of the normal aspects of daily life, and becoming, literally, God-forsaken. From now on, you awake every morning with no reason to get up, nothing to do, unneeded and uncared for by anyone. And then, beyond your wildest hopes and dreams, healing comes, the disease is arrested! Imagine the joy of returning to the camp, and now being restored to all the rights and privileges of being human again, to the high privilege of worshiping the living God again in the tabernacle with your friends and family. Renewed! Restored! What a celebration those services of cleansing must have been.

Can we not see the same picture for those who come to salvation by grace through faith in Jesus Christ? One of the strongest motivations I have experienced for witnessing to our faith with people "outside the camp" and for inviting them to faith and life in Christ is the belief that in doing so I am truly a messenger of good news to them. If we really believe that people are lost in sin and darkness, alienated from God and from each other, and if we have a message of redemption and reconciliation that will enable them to become fully human and fully alive, what greater joy can there be than sharing that good news? Imagine the joy that Jesus must have felt when he touched the "leper," bringing wholeness and restoration to him. You and I have the same opportunities every day of our lives to extend the touch of Jesus to every person we know, sometimes through an appropriate word of witness, sometimes through an act of loving kindness, sometimes by entering into his or her pain. And wouldn't our churches come alive with new vitality if we were having more celebrations of people being cleansed and restored by the power of Christ's atoning sacrifice on the cross at Calvary?

THE CLEANSING OF CONTAMINATED HOUSES

33 And the LORD spoke to Moses and Aaron, saying:

34 "When you have come into the land of Canaan, which I give you as a possession, and I put the leprous plague in a house in the land of your possession,

35 "and he who owns the house comes and tells the priest, saying, 'It seems to me that *there is* some plague in the house,'

36 "then the priest shall command that they empty the house, before the priest goes *into it* to look at the plague, that all that *is* in the house may not be made unclean; and afterward the priest shall go in to look at the house.

37 "And he shall look at the plague; and indeed *if* the plague *is* on the walls of the house with ingrained streaks, greenish or reddish, which appear to be deep in the wall,

38 "then the priest shall go out of the house, to the door of the house, and shut up the house seven days.

39 "And the priest shall come again on the seventh day and look; and indeed *if* the plague has spread on the walls of the house,

40 "then the priest shall command that they take away the stones in which *is* the plague, and they shall cast them into an unclean place outside the city.

41 "And he shall cause the house to be scraped inside, all around, and the dust that they scrape off they shall pour out in an unclean place outside the city.

42 "Then they shall take other stones and put *them* in the place of *those* stones, and he shall take other mortar and plaster the house.

43 "And if the plague comes back and breaks out in the house, after he has taken away the stones, after he has scraped the house, and after it is plastered,

44 "then the priest shall come and look; and indeed *if* the plague has spread in the house, it *is* an active leprosy in the house. It *is* unclean.

45 "And he shall break down the house, its stones, its timber, and all the plaster of the house, and he shall carry *them* outside the city to an unclean place.

46 "Moreover he who goes into the house at all while it is shut up shall be unclean until evening.

47 "And he who lies down in the house shall wash his clothes, and he who eats in the house shall wash his clothes.

48 "But if the priest comes in and looks *at it*, and indeed the plague has not spread in the house after the house was plastered, then the priest shall pronounce the house clean, because the plague is healed.

49 "And he shall take, to cleanse the house, two birds, cedar wood, scarlet, and hyssop.

50 "Then he shall kill one of the birds in an earthen vessel over running water;

51 "and he shall take the cedar wood, the hyssop, the scarlet, and the living bird, and dip them in the blood of the slain bird and in the running water, and sprinkle the house seven times.

52 "And he shall cleanse the house with the blood of the bird and the running water and the living bird, with the cedar wood, the hyssop, and the scarlet.

53 "Then he shall let the living bird loose outside
the city in the open field, and make atonement for the
house, and it shall be clean.
54 "This *is* the law for any leprous sore and scall,
55 "for the leprosy of a garment and of a house,
56 "for a swelling and a scab and a bright spot,
57 "to teach when *it is* unclean and when *it is* clean.
This *is* the law of leprosy."

Lev. 14:33–57

Our section on the clean and the unclean continues with a provision for the cleansing of houses that have been declared unclean. Like clothing, houses can become involved in decay through mold, mildew, dry rot, and other things. Notice that this passage looks ahead to a time when the Hebrews shall live in houses in Canaan, and thus speaks of stone houses built in cities. Prior to their arrival in Canaan after Joshua's conquests, they lived in tents and camps, and the provisions we have seen in chapters 13 and 14 are applicable to life in the desert camp. Here, the principles by which they dealt with uncleanness in garments and tents are applied to a later time when they would live in houses and cities.

An interesting aspect of the diagnostic process described is that which allows them to remove everything from the house before the priestly diagnosis and decision. By doing so, the occupants would escape total economic disaster, for if the house was declared unclean, then everything in it would also become unclean. While this was certainly a technical matter, it was a gracious privilege extended to the owner.

The process of diagnosis is the same as with people and garments, including a seven-day waiting period before the final judgment is made by the priest. Every effort is made to save the house by beginning with the removal of the portion of the structure affected by the fungus, mold, or whatever, and the replacement of the diseased members with new stones, mortar, and plaster (vv. 39–42). If the "renovation" fails to cure the malady, then, as a last resort, the entire structure is to be demolished, with careful disposal to be made outside of the city (vv. 43–47). If the "renovation" was successful, the same kind of cleansing ceremony as the initial ceremony for the cured leper outside the camp shall be performed by the priest. The house shall then be declared clean and may be lived in again. No sacrifices are required for the cleansing of the house, since houses do not relate to God and the tabernacle. The summary (vv. 54–57) concludes chapters 13 and 14.

This lengthy section on skin diseases seems to indicate that this was a serious problem for the ancient Hebrews. We need to keep in mind that their concept of holiness was akin to wholeness, and thus serious skin disease was regarded as a barrier between the person with the disease and God as well as the community. Apart from a cure, separation (uncleanness) was the only option they had.

What a contrast with the ministry and message of Jesus. Here is good news indeed — especially to "lepers." While the community may isolate them, along with others, such as prostitutes and tax collectors, Jesus came "to seek and to save that which was lost" (Luke 19:10). He went to them, and they came to him. He touched them, loved them, healed them, and brought them back to God. He rejected those laws that insisted on isolation and introduced a new law of love, which is committed to seeking, to caring, to healing, and to restoring.

Our communities (and we might add churches) have many ways of isolating those who are different from us or unacceptable to us. We in the church must constantly reexamine our biases and our prejudices by which we justify our indifference to and avoidance of those who are not "our kind." Some who specialize in the field of church membership growth hold that most churches that are growing can be characterized by "the homogeneous unit principle." This is to say that growing churches are churches that bring together the same kind of people, ethnically, economically, culturally, etc. If the conclusion is valid, it may be a sad commentary on what some growing churches are doing. If the church is just another enclave in the community that maintains the status quo of the separation of groups, races, and classes from each other, it may well be "successful," but it may not be the church of Jesus Christ.

UNCLEAN GENITAL DISCHARGES

15:1 And the LORD spoke to Moses and Aaron, saying,
2 "Speak to the children of Israel, and say to them: 'When any man has a discharge from his body, his discharge is unclean.

3 'And this shall be his uncleanness in regard to his discharge — whether his body runs with his discharge, or his body is stopped up by his discharge, it *is* his uncleanness.

4 'Every bed is unclean on which he who has the discharge lies, and everything on which he sits shall be unclean.

5 'And whoever touches his bed shall wash his clothes and bathe in water, and be unclean until evening.

6 'He who sits on anything on which he who has the discharge sat shall wash his clothes and bathe in water, and be unclean until evening.

7 'And he who touches the body of him who has the discharge shall wash his clothes and bathe in water, and be unclean until evening.

8 'If he who has the discharge spits on him who is clean, then he shall wash his clothes and bathe in water, and be unclean until evening.

9 'Any saddle on which he who has the discharge rides shall be unclean.

10 'Whoever touches anything that was under him shall be unclean until evening. He who carries *any of* those things shall wash his clothes and bathe in water, and be unclean until evening.

11 'And whomever he who has the discharge touches, and has not rinsed his hands in water, he shall wash his clothes and bathe in water, and be unclean until evening.

12 'The vessel of earth that he who has the discharge touches shall be broken, and every vessel of wood shall be rinsed in water.

13 'And when he who has a discharge is cleansed of his discharge, then he shall count for himself seven days for his cleansing, wash his clothes, and bathe his body in running water; then he shall be clean.

14 'On the eighth day he shall take for himself two turtledoves or two young pigeons, and come before the LORD, to the door of the tabernacle of meeting, and give them to the priest.

15 'Then the priest shall offer them, the one *as* a sin offering and the other *as* a burnt offering. So the priest

shall make atonement for him before the LORD because of his discharge.

16 'If any man has an emission of semen, then he
shall wash all his body in water, and be unclean until
evening.

17 'And any garment and any leather on which
there is semen, it shall be washed with water, and be
unclean until evening.

18 'Also, when a woman lies with a man, and *there
is* an emission of semen, they *both* shall bathe in
water, and be unclean until evening.

19 'If a woman has a discharge, *and* the discharge
from her body is blood, she shall be set apart seven
days; and whoever touches her shall be unclean until
evening.

20 'Everything that she lies on during her impurity
shall be unclean; also everything that she sits on shall
be unclean.

21 'Whoever touches her bed shall wash his clothes
and bathe in water, and be unclean until evening.

22 'And whoever touches anything that she sat on
shall wash his clothes and bathe in water, and be
unclean until evening.

23 'If *anything* is on *her* bed or on anything on which
she sits, when he touches it, he shall be unclean until
evening.

24 'And if any man lies with her at all, so that her
impurity is on him, he shall be unclean seven days;
and every bed on which he lies shall be unclean.

25 'If a woman has a discharge of blood for many
days, other than at the time of her *customary* impurity,
or if it runs beyond her *usual* time of impurity, all the
days of her unclean discharge shall be as the days of
her customary impurity. She *shall be* unclean.

26 'Every bed on which she lies all the days of her
discharge shall be to her as the bed of her impurity;
and whatever she sits on shall be unclean, as the
uncleanness of her impurity.

27 'Whoever touches those things shall be unclean;
he shall wash his clothes and bathe in water, and be
unclean until evening.

160

28 'But if she is cleansed of her discharge, then she shall count for herself seven days, and after that she shall be clean.

29 'And on the eighth day she shall take for herself two turtledoves or two young pigeons, and bring them to the priest, to the door of the tabernacle of meeting.

30 'Then the priest shall offer the one *as* a sin offering and the other *as* a burnt offering, and the priest shall make atonement for her before the LORD for the discharge of her uncleanness.

31 'Thus you shall separate the children of Israel from their uncleanness, lest they die in their uncleanness when they defile My tabernacle that *is* among them.

32 'This *is* the law for one who has a discharge, and *for him* who emits semen and is unclean thereby.

33 'and for her who is indisposed because of her customary impurity and for one who has a discharge, either man or woman, and for him who lies with her who is unclean.'"

Lev. 15:1–33

We come to the last chapter in this section on the clean and the unclean. The most controversial thing about it seems to be in giving it a title. Most commentaries use language such as "unclean discharges," "cleanliness and holiness," and "ceremonial uncleanness." No one wants to declare that the chapter deals specifically with normal and abnormal secretions from the male and the female genitals. I have no intention of preaching on this chapter unabashedly, but we may want to consider making this chapter a part of a wider study (outside of the pulpit) on sexuality, and on the theology of maleness and femaleness. Bailey suggests that such a study over a period of a few weeks would be edifying to men and women alike, and I have found this to be the case. Such a study might begin with the opening chapters of Genesis which make it clear that the female is in no way inferior or subordinate to the male, but is, rather, the crowning of creation. Our own translation rightly corrects the erroneous "helpmeet" of Gen. 2:18 to "I will make him a helper comparable to him." The story of the Fall does not blame the woman, even though

Adam tried to. It is, rather, the tragic story of us all. Such a study should affirm male and female, especially using the Psalms and Proverbs, and take a thorough look at both the teaching of Jesus and the relationships of Jesus with men and women. Leviticus 12 and 15 should also be included in this study, with special emphasis upon what these laws were trying to accomplish in their own time. This is difficult to do without imposing our own standards upon the passages, or by accepting too readily the conclusions of previous interpreters.

The structure of the chapter is carefully thought out. Two cases relate to men and two to women. Two cases relate to abnormal, continuing emissions, and two cases relate to normal emission. The structure seems designed to emphasize the unity of the two sexes through the use of chiasmus, a literary device found often in both Old and New Testaments. The chiastic structure is best described as A1-B1-C-B2-A2. So here, we have A1=abnormal, long-term male discharges (vv. 1–15); B1=normal, short-term male emissions (vv. 16–17); C=intercourse (v. 18); B2=normal, short-term female discharges (vv. 19–24); B1=abnormal, long-term female discharges (vv. 25–30). The pattern affirms the unity and interdependence of humankind in the two sexes, which is most significantly and intimately expressed in sexual intercourse, placed at the middle of the structure.

Though the text is not specific, it seems that all four of the cases in this chapter deal with emissions or secretions from the genital organs. This is not a discussion of runny noses or teary eyes.

It has long been assumed that the abnormal, male long-term discharge described here (2–15) is gonorrhea. Remember that the issue here is not the medical problem, but the issue of clean and unclean relating to the worship life of the covenant community. The abnormal, long-term discharge renders the man unclean. In other words, he is disqualified from full participation in the life of the community. Everything on which he sits (including saddles) and lies is rendered unclean (as is everyone on whom he spits!). Anyone who makes almost any contact with him or anything that he has touched also becomes unclean. That person must wash his or her clothes and bathe in water and be unclean until evening. There is no exclusion from the community as with serious skin diseases. Here again we understand the widespread prevalence of pools for ceremonial bathing being found by archaeologists.

For the infected man, after the discharge has been cured, a cleansing period of seven days is to be observed with prescribed washing of clothing and bathing in fresh water. On the eighth day, he is to bring to the priest in the tabernacle two turtledoves or two young pigeons (the least expensive sacrifices) for a sin offering and a burnt offering.

With regard to normal emissions of semen (vv. 16-17), ceremonial uncleanness exists only for the remainder of the day. The man is to bathe, and any garments or leather are to be washed as part of the cleansing rite.

When a man and woman have sexual intercourse with the emission of semen, they are both unclean until evening, and both are required to bathe (v. 18).

The normal menstrual cycle for the woman (vv. 19-24) renders her unclean for seven days, while those who touch her or anything she has sat or laid on are unclean only for the remainder of the day. If any man *"lies with her at all"* (presumably any kind of intimate contact), he becomes unclean for seven days. No rite of cleansing is required at the end of the seven days for the woman (or for the man who may have become unclean).

In the case of abnormal, long-term female discharges (vv. 25-30), the complications and the cleansing process are the same as for men.

Verse 31 is a terse statement of the purpose of these laws pertaining to normal and abnormal genital discharges and emissions: *"Thus you shall separate the children of Israel from their uncleanness, lest they die in their uncleanness when they defile My tabernacle that is among them."* The focus is upon the necessity of coming to God in worship with absolute purity of soul and body. To them, sexual activity and abnormalities of genital discharges could have no place in the worship of the community. When read in the context of the religions around them, which often emphasized fertility rites and temple prostitution and sometimes equated orgiastic frenzy with worship, these laws were not designed to curtail sexual activity within the parameters created by God but to avoid any appearance of the distortions around them. Recall their basic understanding of holiness as separateness and differentness. It should be obvious that, far from denigrating sex, these laws were trying to elevate it to a higher level than was the case in the world around them.

We must observe their belief that semen, the mysterious element in the process creating life, should not be wasted. It was held in high regard because it represented potential for life, belonging to God. Thus, even normal nocturnal emissions may well have elicited a sense of waste or misuse (especially when accompanied by dreams of sexual activity), and must, therefore, be separated from the tabernacle and its worship.

Menstruation, though always regarded as normal, was undoubtedly beyond their understanding and therefore something of a mystery, especially since it involved blood. And to the Hebrew, as we have already seen, blood was the essence of life, and blood belonged exclusively to God. As normal as the menstrual cycle is, it must have been held with a certain awe and wonder. Thus, the separation from the tabernacle and worship.

We cannot read this chapter without recalling the tender story of the woman who had "a flow of blood for twelve years" (Mark 5:25–34). For twelve years she had been ceremonially unclean, unable to worship in the temple, to some degree a social outcast, but not to the extent of those with serious skin diseases. She had heard of the power of Jesus and was among those who placed great hope in just touching Jesus and being healed (Mark 6:56). Imagine her joy as she reached out and touched His garment and experienced the healing for which she had prayed and hoped for twelve years! Jesus, sensing that "power had gone out of Him" asked the question, "Who touched My clothes?" With fear and trembling, the woman brought her admission to Him and then heard His gracious words, "Daughter, your faith has made you well. Go in peace, and be healed of your affliction." I've often wondered what it was that Jesus felt when the woman touched Him. I suspect that it wasn't the loss of power in whatever effected the healing but the loss in being touched by her uncleanness. I like to think of Him as absorbing her sickness and uncleanness, for it seems to me that's what is meant when we say that He took the sins of the world upon Himself. To touch Him is to be relieved of one's sins and to be restored to wholeness.

And What About Us?

Before we leave this section, we must ask ourselves again, "What does all of this have to do with us?" The casual reader might wish to move on very quickly with the assumption that this is only of antiquarian interest. But now we know better. We must always return to the idea on which all of these laws were based, the idea of *holiness*. God is holy! This means that God is "the wholly Other." God is completely different from all others and everything else. God is perfect in wisdom, power, goodness, purity, justice, and truth. And the Holy God calls the people of God to be holy, because God is holy.

As we have already seen, the root idea of holiness is *separateness*. This means that persons who are not holy are separated *from* God, for the holy are separated *to* God. In the imagery of Leviticus, the unholy — the unclean — cannot touch anything that is clean. That which is profane can in no way relate to the sacred.

Only as we begin to enter into this understanding of the holiness of God can we begin to comprehend the seriousness with which these ancient Hebrews approached the worship of God. The tabernacle, and later the temple, was the place where God was present for them. It was God's dwelling place, and no one could approach God without proper preparation. Every single detail — clothing, cleanliness, attitude — had to be right. Approaching God was a serious and awesome matter in which nothing was treated lightly or left to chance.

I can identify in a rather remote and partial way with how the priests and people might have felt when they approached the tabernacle. I was once invited to the White House for a meeting with the President and some of his staff to clarify our denomination's disagreements with some aspects of his foreign policy in Central America. We were deeply grateful for the privilege extended to us. I can assure you that in preparing for that meeting, no detail was overlooked, even down to the clothing I wore. Nothing was left to chance as I prepared for my visit with that very special person in that very special place.

As I read about the meticulous care for detail that was involved in their worship of God, and in reflecting on my anxiety as I prepared to go to the White House, I am reminded all the more of how essential it is for us to prepare properly for our worship of God, be it personally or with a congregation. But sadly, I'm aware that my own preparation for worship has, all too often, been casual and unthinking. I do believe that there is a great need for us to gain a deeper sense of the holiness of our Creator God, Almighty God, who loves us and truly cares for us.

I have urged our people to begin to prepare themselves for worship as early as Saturday afternoon. Scripture reading and prayer should be a vital exercise before retiring on Saturday night. Why can't we give our people the order of worship the week before, so that they might review the words of the hymns, read the Scriptures, and pray the prayers in preparation for the worship? I'm convinced this could make a vital difference in how we approach our services of worship. And, certainly, this places a strong resonsibility upon us who prepare the services to make them coherent, cohesive, and worthy of the time and energy of the worshipers. The most unthinkable thing in the church should be a dull and boring worship service!

Holiness for the Hebrews did not mean the attainment of sinless perfection, and it need not mean that for us. But it does mean that we are to be committed to reaching for that ideal of holiness for all who would enter into God's presence.

Hopefully, we now see that in reading this section of Leviticus, we need not get bogged down in the details of the dietary and health laws listed here. Nor do we need to duplicate the ceremonial and ritual laws. For the Hebrews, the entire system had obvious validity. Though the details have changed, the underlying principles are still active and valid, even though we still are not sure of all the facts.

One of these principles is the very close linkage between the physical and the spiritual. What we eat, how we take care of our bodies, personal cleanliness and sanitation, all are engaged in our relationships with God and with others. There is a strong emphasis among us on health and fitness, though our tendency toward careless nutrition and lack of exercise is all too apparent. If we are to be good stewards of all that God has given us, we will be as concerned with the physical as we must be with the spiritual. They go together.

Another principle basic to this section is that of "cleansing" as a continuing necessity. Cleansing was necessary in order to enter into the holy presence of God, as well as to maintain regular relationships in the community. And God made all of the provisions for the requisite cleansing. Too often, the Old Testament has been portrayed among Christians as teaching salvation by works. I disagree. The essence of everything we have studied in this section is the gracious provision of God for our needs. The Bible is the good news of God's grace from Genesis through Revelation.

Both the principle of the unity of the physical and spiritual and that of the necessity of cleansing are clearly enunciated in the New Testament as well. To the Corinthian Christians, who lived in a city widely known for its moral decadence, Paul wrote, "Or do you not know that your body is the temple of the Holy Spirit who is in you, whom you have from God, and you are not your own? For you were bought at a price; therefore glorify God in your body and in your spirit, which are God's" (1 Cor. 6:19). There is no separation between the physical and the spiritual for the person in Christ. And we are joyously reminded that "if we confess our sins, He is faithful and just to forgive us our sins and to cleanse us from all unrighteousness" (1 John 1:9). God has provided the means for our continual cleansing.

CHAPTER FOUR

THE GREAT DAY OF ATONEMENT

LEVITICUS 16:1-34

We come now to what, for us, may be the central chapter of the Book of Leviticus. Many contemporary scholars insist that chapter 16 must follow directly after chapter 10, since it begins with a solemn reminder of the death of the two sons of Aaron for either their carelessness or arrogance in the exercise of their priestly ministry. But a case can also be made for maintaining the given order of the chapters. The intervening chapters (11–15) teach the people the importance of carefully observing the differences between the clean and the unclean. Now they are better able to understand why the standards for the priests, in offering the sacrifices in the tabernacle, are so very strict.

God is not portrayed as a finicky pedant who kills priests because they make a simple mistake. God is the Holy One with whom sin and uncleanness have no correspondence. God's continuing presence with the people is only possible when the priests, the people, and the center of worship itself can be cleansed from all pollutions. There is always the underlying sense that God cannot dwell with uncleanness; therefore, uncleanness in the central place of worship will drive God out of the camp. He will no longer dwell there nor stroll among them.

The capstone of all of the sacrifices and worship of God's people came once each year on the Day of Atonement, Yom Kippur, the day called by many Rabbis across the centuries the Day. Interestingly, there is no other mention of Yom Kippur in any of the historical books of the Old Testament, leading many scholars to the conclusion that the ritual we encounter in Leviticus 16 did not mature into its fullness until after the return from exile toward the end of the sixth century. Without repeating my discussion of this in the Introduction, I simply state here that, in my judgment, this conclusion need not be drawn from the silence of the other historical sections of the Old Testament.

The rite was as integral to the tabernacle as it would later be to the temple. The basic elements of this very special day of worship may well have been in existence from Israel's earliest days. And the basic ritual, though only in symbolic form since the destruction of the temple in A.D. 70, is observed once each year in every Jewish synagogue throughout the world.

RITUAL FOR THE DAY OF ATONEMENT

16:1 Now the LORD spoke to Moses after the death of the two sons of Aaron, when they offered profane fire before the LORD and died;

2 and the LORD said to Moses: "Tell Aaron your brother not to come at *simply* any time into the Holy *Place* inside the veil, before the mercy seat which *is* on the ark, lest he die; for I will appear in the cloud above the mercy seat.

3 "Thus Aaron shall come into the Holy *Place*: with *the blood of* a young bull as a sin offering, and *of* a ram as a burnt offering.

4 "He shall put the holy linen tunic and the linen trousers on his body; he shall be girded with linen sash, and with the linen turban he shall be attired. These *are* holy garments. Therefore he shall wash his body in water, and put them on.

5 "And he shall take from the congregation of the children of Israel two kids of the goats as a sin offering, and one ram as a burnt offering.

6 "Aaron shall offer the bull as a sin offering, which *is* for himself, and make atonement for himself and for his house.

7 "He shall take the two goats and present them before the LORD *at* the door of the tabernacle of meeting.

8 "Then Aaron shall cast lots for the two goats: one lot for the LORD and the other lot for the scapegoat.

9 "And Aaron shall bring the goat on which the LORD's lot fell, and offer it *as* a sin offering.

10 "But the goat on which the lot fell to be the scapegoat shall be presented alive before the LORD, to make atonement upon it, *and* to let it go as the scapegoat into the wilderness.

11 "And Aaron shall bring the bull of the sin offering, which is for himself, and make atonement for himself and for his house and shall kill the bull as the sin offering which *is* for himself.

12 "Then he shall take a censer full of burning coals of fire from the altar before the Lord, with his hands full of sweet incense beaten fine, and bring *it* inside the veil.

13 "And he shall put the incense on the fire before the Lord, that the cloud of incense may cover the mercy seat that *is* on the Testimony, lest he die.

14 "He shall take some of the blood of the bull and sprinkle *it* with his finger on the mercy seat on the east *side*; and before the mercy seat he shall sprinkle some of the blood with his finger seven times.

15 "Then he shall kill the goat of the sin offering, which *is* for the people, bring its blood inside the veil, do with that blood as he did with the blood of the bull, and sprinkle it on the mercy seat and before the mercy seat.

16 "So he shall make atonement for the Holy *Place*, because of the uncleanness of the children of Israel, and because of their transgressions, for all their sins; and so he shall do for the tabernacle of meeting which remains among them in the midst of their uncleanness.

17 "There shall be no man in the tabernacle of meeting when he goes in to make atonement in the Holy *Place*, until he comes out, that he may make atonement for himself, for his household, and for all the congregation of Israel.

18 "And he shall go out to the altar that *is* before the LORD, and make atonement for it, and shall take some of the blood of the bull and some of the blood of the goat, and put it on the horns of the altar all around.

19 "Then he shall sprinkle some of the blood on it with his finger seven times, cleanse it, and sanctify it from the uncleanness of the children of Israel.

20 "And when he has made an end of atoning for the Holy *Place*, the tabernacle of meeting, and the altar, he shall bring the live goat;

21 "and Aaron shall lay both his hands on the head of the live goat, confess over it all the iniquities of the children of Israel, and all their transgressions, concerning all their sins, putting them on the head of the goat, and shall send *it* away into the wilderness by the hand of a suitable man.

22 "The goat shall bear on itself all their iniquities to an uninhabited land; and he shall release the goat in the wilderness.

23 "Then Aaron shall come into the tabernacle of meeting, shall take off the linen garments which he put on when he went into the Holy *Place*, and shall leave them there.

24 "And he shall wash his body with water in a holy place, put on his garments, come out and offer his burnt offering and the burnt offering of the people, and make atonement for himself and for the people.

25 "The fat of the sin offering he shall burn on the altar.

26 "And he who released the goat as the scapegoat shall wash his clothes and bathe his body in water, and afterward he may come into the camp.

27 "The bull *for* the sin offering and the goat *for* the sin offering, whose blood was brought in to make atonement in the Holy *Place*, shall be carried outside the camp. And they shall burn in the fire their skins, their flesh, and their offal.

28 "Then he who burns them shall wash his clothes and bathe his body in the water, and afterward he may come into the camp.

29 "*This* shall be a statute forever for you: In the seventh month, on the tenth *day* of the month, you shall afflict your souls, and do no work at all, *whether* a native of your own country or a stranger who sojourns among you.

30 "For on that day *the priest* shall make atonement for you, to cleanse you, *that* you may be clean from all your sins before the LORD.

31 "It *is* a sabbath of solemn rest for you, and you shall afflict your souls. *It is* a statute forever.

32 "And the priest, who is anointed and consecrated to minister as priest in his father's place, shall make atonement, and put on the linen clothes, the holy garments;

33 "then he shall make atonement for the Holy Sanctuary, and he shall make atonement for the tabernacle of meeting and for the altar, and he shall make atonement for the priests and for all the people of the congregation.

34 "This shall be an everlasting statute for you, to make atonement for the children of Israel, for all their sins, once a year." And he did as the LORD commanded Moses.

Lev. 16:1–34

The chapter begins with a solemn reminder of the deaths of Nadab and Abihu (Lev. 10:1–5), placing the giving of the rules for the Day of Atonement in the time of Moses and Aaron and providing a serious warning to all subsequent priests about the performance of their duties in the tabernacle. Note well that the instructions are not given to Aaron but to Moses. Throughout Leviticus, God addresses the people directly through Moses alone. The mystery and sanctity of the Most Holy Place (often called the Holy of Holies) is unequivocally articulated (v. 2). Aaron is to be instructed that he is not free to enter the Most Holy Place at any time other than that which is to be provided in what follows in this chapter. The reason given is that the mercy seat, the cover of the ark of the covenant, is the place where God chooses to appear. Thus, it came to be regarded as the place where God dwelt. Even the high priest is forbidden casual entrance into the presence of God, just as Moses had experienced on Mount Sinai. For those of us who grew up with popular songs such as "Have you talked to the Man upstairs?" or slogans such as "God is my co-pilot," some recovery of the holiness of God which regards access to God's presence with awe and wonder is of the essence.

In teaching or preaching from this chapter, I find it essential to review the basic scheme of the tabernacle, focusing upon the Most Holy Place in Exodus 25. The central feature was the ark of the covenant, a chest made of acacia wood and overlaid with pure gold inside and out, about 3' 9" long and 2' 3" wide and deep. It was to be carried on poles of acacia wood overlaid in gold, the poles to be inserted through two gold rings attached to the ark upon both sides. The poles were never to be removed from the ark . The tablets of the law given to Moses, the tangible symbol of the Covenant, were kept inside the ark . The cover of the ark was called the mercy seat (though no one was ever to sit on it), made of pure gold. Two gold cherubim with outstretched wings faced each other from either end of the mercy seat. There, above the cover of the ark, between the two cherubim, God promised to meet with Moses to give all of the commands for the people of Israel (Exod. 25:22). Only the ark was in the Most Holy Place. Outside, separated by the blue, purple, and scarlet curtain, were the table, overlaid with gold, the golden lampstand, and the altar of incense (Exod. 37:10–29). This was concealed behind the curtain separating the Holy Place from the court of the tabernacle. The utter mystery and awe surrounding the Most Holy Place cannot be overstated.

Special preparations were required for the ritual of the Day of Atonement (vv.3–5). Five animals were to be used in the worship: a bull for a sin offering and a ram for a burnt offering, to be the offering for Aaron and his family; and two male goats and a ram, to be the offering for the people. It is important to underscore that Aaron had to offer the initial sacrifice of the bull and the ram for his own sins and those of his family.

Of special interest is the preparation required of Aaron himself, first in bathing and then in the clothing that was to be worn. Bathing was a vivid symbol of the necessity of his cleansing before entering into God's presence. Even the high priest needed such cleansing. The writer of the Book of Hebrews will emphasize the dramatic difference between Christ's priestly work and Aaron's. "For such a High Priest was fitting for us, who is holy, harmless, undefiled, separate from sinners, and has become higher than the heavens; who does not need daily, as those high priests, to offer up sacrifices, first for His own sins and then for the people's, for this He did once for all when He offered up Himself" (Heb. 7:26–27). Christ is without sin, and thus fulfills the role both of the clean sacrificial animal and of the totally clean priest making the offering.

The clothing that Aaron was to wear on this special day was different from the normal priestly vestments described in Exodus 28. Those vestments were elaborate and regal, embellished with fine needle work, gold, and jewelry, making the high priest look like a king. On this day, he was to wear garments that were even simpler than those of an ordinary priest, as described in Exod. 39:27–29. He was dressed more like a slave on this occasion, a significant reminder that when the high priest enters the very presence of God he is nothing more than a simple servant.

In a day when we are prone to regard ourselves, somewhat casually, as partners with God, or to use prayer and spirituality to get what we want from God, we do well to ponder what it really means to enter into God's presence. The necessity of the cleansing rituals and the simplicity of the special clothing to be worn on this annual, special day might well point to some things we need to consider. There was an old Presbyterian tradition, now long abandoned, that came to America from Scotland. It was symbolized by "communion tokens," now found in some historical museums. The communion token was a small coin required of the parishioner in order to be served communion. It was the practice of the elders to visit the members of the congregation during the days immediately preceding communion, encouraging them to self-examination, confession of sin, and prayer as proper preparation for receiving the sacrament. After such sharing and prayer, the congregant would be given the communion token which, in turn, was to be given to the officiant at the communion service prior to being served the Lord's Supper. While such a custom has long been abandoned in our churches, have we not lost our sense of the need for special preparation for the worship of God? Should we not encourage one another to serious preparation for our community worship? I'm convinced that our worship services will take on new meaning and vitality for every worshiper who will make serious and intentional preparation for worship.

And perhaps we could extend this to the matter of attire as well. Timothy was urged to counsel the women, presumably in Ephesus, to dress modestly and without the ostentation of excessive fashion or jewelry when coming to the worship of God (1 Tim. 2:9–10). In our culture, we need not restrict this to women's attire. Ostentation in dress has become as much a part of masculine style. If a basic simplicity of dress was essential for the priests on this special day of worship long ago, why not give attention to simplicity of attire in our gatherings for worship? Rather than calling attention to ourselves by our fashionable (or unfashionable) clothing, we can do far better in focusing our attention on the worship of God by our own simplicity and moderation in attire.

Perhaps we pastors need to re-think our own attire as leaders of worship. For the high priest, there were occasions when the celebrative and more elaborate vestments were deemed appropriate, but on this day, simplicity was of the essence. Perhaps we should consider different attire for different worship occasions, always with the focus on how to help the worshiper focus upon the worship of God and not upon the leader(s) of worship.

In typical Hebrew form, the basic outline of the ritual for the day is given briefly in verses 6–10 and then expanded in more detail in 11–28. Perhaps the best way to fix the dramatic actions of this day in our minds is by enumeration:

1. First, Aaron had to make a sin offering as an atonement for his own sins and those of his household (vv. 6, 11). Just as he had to be cleansed by washing, so he must make the appropriate offering for himself and his household to God. We have already observed that the writer of the Book of Hebrews draws a sharp contrast between Christ's and Aaron's ministries at this point. In the making of this sin offering on this special day, he is to enter into the Most Holy Place and there light the incense. The smoke of the incense will conceal the mercy seat, lest he die in seeing it clearly (vv. 12, 13). Here, the interpreter must choose among three alternative explanations for the meaning of the smoke of the incense in protecting the high priest from death. One approach is to point out that incense is sometimes used to ameliorate God's wrath, such as in Num. 16:46–50, in which the burning of the incense by Aaron stopped the plague which had been initiated by God to destroy the Hebrews for their sin. Another possibility is that the smoke of the incense would keep God from seeing the sinner. The most appealing view to me is that the smoke would create a protective screen, keeping the high priest from seeing God, as had been the experience of Moses with the cloud covering on Mount Sinai (Exod. 24:15–18), and in his experience in the cleft of the rock (Exod. 33:18–21) when he was told by God, "You cannot see My face, for no man shall see Me, and live."

In the smoke-filled room, Aaron is to take some of the blood from the sin offering and sprinkle some of it onto the mercy seat seven times (v. 14). Having made the sin offering in the Most Holy Place for himself and his household, he is now to move back out with the people.

2. Aaron is now to cast lots (v. 8) to determine which of the two goats is to be sacrificed as a sin offering for the Lord and which is to become the "scapegoat" (Hebrew, "for Azazel," also in vv. 10, 26). We shall discuss this at greater length shortly.

3. Aaron is to sacrifice the first goat as a sin offering for the people (vv. 9, 15–19). He is to take some of the blood of the goat in to the Most Holy Place, as he had done with the previous offering. Then he is to come out and do the same for the Holy Place (vv. 16–17) and for the altar of the burnt offerings (vv. 18–19). The striking difference between this process and the normal offerings (cf. 4:6–7) is that here the blood is sprinkled on the mercy seat within the Holy of Holies rather than on the curtain that separates the Holy of Holies from the Holy Place. In this ritual the place of worship is cleansed annually, from the center out. Even the worship center was besmirched by the sins of the people. Not only do the priests and the people need cleansing, but the place of worship needs cleansing as well! This is a clear expression of their basic belief that God could not and would not dwell in an unclean place.

4. The fourth, and most striking, event on this special day was the sending of the scapegoat into the wilderness (vv. 20–22). The sacrifices for the sins of Aaron, his family, and the people have been made; the tabernacle has been purged from uncleanness incurred by the sins of the people; now there remains the live goat, previously chosen by lot to be the scapegoat. Aaron was to lay his hands upon the head of the goat while confessing all of the sins of the people for the past year (v. 21). Now the goat is the bearer of the sins of the people and is led out into the wilderness by a specially appointed man. The goat is never to be seen again, a rich and liberating symbolism. We will have much more to say about this moment in the Day of Atonement, but, from the outset, don't miss the drama here enacted as the people watch the scapegoat bearing all their sins out into the desert, never to be seen again!

5. Aaron is to go into the Holy Place (vv. 23–24a) and remove the special garments that he had donned for this occasion. He is then to bathe once more before putting on his regular garments. It is significant that the day begins and ends for Aaron with a ritual bath, purging him from all ceremonial uncleanness. While it is not stated, it

could be assumed that in the placing of his hands upon the head of the scapegoat, confessing over it all of the wickedness and rebellion of Israel, he could well have become ceremonially unclean.

6. Next Aaron is to sacrifice the burnt offerings for himself and for the people (vv. 24b–25), burning the fat of the sin offering on the altar in the usual manner.

7. Meanwhile, the man who had been chosen to escort the scapegoat out into the wilderness must wash his clothing and bathe ceremonially before returning to the camp (v. 26). This is fully consistent with what we have learned about cleanness and uncleanness in chapters 11–15.

8. In the eighth and final act of the day's drama (vv. 27–28), the remains of the bull and the goat used for the sin offering are to be disposed of outside the camp, as prescribed for the regular sacrifices. The man assigned this chore was required to wash his garments and bathe ritually for his own cleanness before returning to the camp.

Thus was completed the annual drama of Yom Kippur, the Day of Atonement, *the* Day. Surely, it came to be one of the most anticipated days of the entire year for the people of Israel. And for many, it still is! To me, Easter has the same potential for anticipation and celebration. Yet, as a pastor, I find myself with mixed feelings every Easter, knowing all too well how many folks come to worship casually and routinely, many for what seems to be an annual cultural exercise. I choose, however, to join with those who make this *the* Day for the Christian community, the special day each year when we celebrate our Day of Atonement, the day when Christ was our high priest, our sacrificial offerings, and our scapegoat rolled into one, once and for all!

The Day of Atonement is established for all time in verses 29–34. For strong emphasis, it is stated three times (vv. 29, 31, 34) that this is to be a perpetual ritual, an annual fast and Sabbath to be observed on the tenth day of the seventh month (Tishri). That month begins with the Feast of Trumpets (later called Rosh Hashanah, the Jewish New Year) and includes the Feast of Tabernacles from the fifteenth to the twenty-first. The Day of Sacred Assembly (Lev. 23:36b) was observed on the twenty-second of Tishri. Thus, the seventh month (i.e., September [October by our calendar]) was a very special month of festive worship and celebration. The other major festival month was the first month (Abib, our March-April), which included the Passover, the Feast of Unleavened Bread, and the celebration of Firstfruits.

With the perpetual establishment of the Day of Atonement is given specific instructions for what the people are to do: *"This shall be a statute forever for you: In the seventh month, on the tenth day of the month, you shall afflict your souls, and do no work at all, whether a native of your own country or a stranger who sojourns among you. For on that day the priest shall make atonement for you, to cleanse you, that you may be clean from all your sins before the* LORD*"* (vv. 29-31). The Day of Atonement was not just a day when the high priest did certain things. It called for full participation by all of the people, natives and foreigners alike. The exact meaning of the phrase *"afflict your souls"* probably has to do with fasting. It is used seldom, occurring elsewhere only in Lev. 23:27, 32; Num. 29:7; Ps. 35:13; and Isa. 58:3, 5. On this day, all of the people are to be deeply and intensely engaged in worship, prayer, and fasting.

We cannot leave our analysis of the text without dealing with the questions surrounding the meaning of the Hebrew phrase "for Azazel," in verses 8, 10, and 26. In our translation, it is simply translated "scapegoat," with no reference to the Hebrew *azazel*. In the Jerusalem Bible, the Revised Standard Version, and the New English Bible, the term *Azazel* is used in the text. In the Amplified Bible, the translation reads "for Azazel, or removal." The New International Version uses "scapegoat" with a footnote at verse 8, "That is, the goat of removal; Hebrew *azazel*; also in verses 10 and 26."

These variations indicate that there is less than universal agreement on the meaning of *azazel* and thus different interpretations of the meaning of the "scapegoat" ritual on the Day of Atonement. There have been three major schools of thought.   That favored by many contemporary Old Testament scholars holds that Azazel is the name of a demon who lived out in the desert. One of the strengths of this view is in the structure of verse 8 in which the casting of lots is set in contrast: "one lot for the Lord and the other lot for Azazel." The major problem with this view is the idea of a sacrifice designed to appease a desert demon, a practice strongly condemned in the very next chapter: "They shall no more offer their sacrifices to demons" (17:7). Linking sacrifice to a demon to the annual Day of Atonement raises serious questions.

An alternate view within this school of thought proposes that while the goat was indeed sent out to the desert demon Azazel, it was as a rebuke rather than an offering. The scapegoat was not sent to appease Azazel, but rather to confront the demon. The arrival of the goat, bearing the sins of the people, was a virtual mockery of Azazel, saying in effect, "Here are all of the sins you have engineered. You can have them back. They have power over us no longer."

A second major school of thought revolves around the uncertain etymology of *azazel*. Different meanings of this term, which occurs only here in the Old Testament, are suggested, such as "to drive away, remove," "dismissal," "entire removal," and "complete destruction." Here, the term refers to the result of the transfer of the sins of the people to the goat and the subsequent banishment of the goat to the wilderness. No purpose other than removal or destruction of the sins is intended.

Yet a third view of *azazel* translates it as "a rocky precipice." This is reflected in an ancient tradition which holds that the goat was taken out by the man assigned to the task to a rocky cliff outside the camp and pushed (in one version, backwards) over the cliff to its total destruction.

However one chooses to translate *azazel* the emphasis must remain upon what the goat was meant to accomplish. The common strand in each interpretation is that the goat carried away the sins of the people into the remote wilderness, never to return and never to be seen again. What a joyous celebration it must have been as the people watched the silhouette of the goat disappear over the horizon, etching indelibly upon their hearts and minds a profound insight into the nature of God!

It is probably best not to make too sharp a distinction between the two goats, since the two together are described as "a sin offering" in the singular in verse 5. It seems best to hold that the two goats represented a different aspect of the same sacrifice, one the means and the other the results.

Possibly, David was reflecting upon the ritual of the scapegoat when he wrote the stanza of the song:

> As far as the east is from the west,
> So far has he removed our transgressions from us.
>
> *Ps. 103: 12*

And Isaiah could well have had the picture of the scapegoat ceremony in mind in his dramatic affirmation:

> Surely He has borne our griefs
> and carried our sorrows; . . .
> All we like sheep have gone astray;
> we have turned, every one, to his own way;
> and the Lord has laid on Him the iniquity of us all.

Isa. 53:4, 6

Strangely, it seems to me, the writers of the New Testament make no direct reference to the scapegoat ritual of the Day of Atonement. I don't think this prevents us from developing the vivid imagery of this annual act in conjunction with our understanding of the rich meaning of Christ's death on the cross. The New Testament, of course, speaks often of Christ as the One who bears our sins on the cross, as in Heb. 9:28. I can't imagine a more dramatic picture of the grace and mercy of God than that of the lonely figure of the scapegoat carrying away our sins, surely a poignant picture of the work of Christ in His death and resurrection.

The Day of Atonement and Us

We cannot leave this remarkable chapter without developing some of the remarkable preaching and teaching values of the Day of Atonement for us as disciples of Christ.

Because of the dramatic parallels between the atoning death of Christ on the cross and the vivid ceremonies on the Great Day of Atonement, the contemporary reader of this chapter of Leviticus is in danger of falling into two grievous errors.

The first, and most common, is that of reading the ancient text altogether typologically. In this kind of reading, all that is seen in the ancient rites is the way in which they point to Christ's death on the cross for the sins of the world. The error here is in failing to pause long enough to enter into the meaning that this day must have had for the people of that and subsequent times. Shortly, we will celebrate the insights of the writer of the Book of Hebrews, forever linking Christ's death with the ritual of the Great Day of Atonement, but first we do well to reflect upon the ancient drama itself, and upon the meanings that it must have had to the people of Israel from the time of Moses and Aaron.

The Great Day of Atonement was the supreme statement of God's forgiving love by grace alone. How often have I heard it said that salvation in the Old Testament was by good works, while salvation in the New Testament is by grace alone. Such a statement reveals woeful ignorance of the Old Testament. Forgiveness is costly, to be sure, but it is always at the initiative of God. It is God who initiates the sacrificial system, God's way of providing a way for forgiveness and reconciliation. It is God who provides the priesthood and the rituals by which sin may be covered and removed.

Was the problem of the person with any sensitivity toward God and God's holiness any different then than for us now? What can be more devastating, then or now, than to be aware of the holiness and majesty of God and at the same time to be aware of one's constant proclivity to deception, selfishness, greed, lust, pride, and all the rest? How can such persons have any hope of fellowship with a holy and just God? In the most intimate of human relationships, do we not have to face the shadow side of ourselves with loathing and fear? How much more then in the relationship with God.

Imagine their joy in knowing that on the Great Day of Atonement, all the sins of all the people for the entire year were forgiven by God, symbolically cleansed with the offering of the sacrifices and the cleansing of the place of worship and sent out of sight on the head of the goat. What a release to know that the heavy accumulation of sins was atoned for! What a joy to know that God's dwelling place, cleansed anew, was a fit place for God to continue to dwell among them! What a cheering section they must have become as the goat was led off into the wilderness, never to be seen again!

Are we not much more fortunate than they? No longer must we anticipate an annual day, for to us has been given the joyous tradition of assembling each week on the Lord's day, the day commemorating Christ's triumph over sin and death, to bring our confession of sins, and to receive, especially in the bread and the cup of the sacrament, the assurance of God's gracious love and forgiveness. No less a person than John Calvin felt strongly that the Sacrament of Holy Communion should be celebrated as frequently as each Lord's Day. Where can we be closer to the essential meaning of the Day of Atonement than when we are gathered around the Lord's Supper?

And it surely seems to me that we in Christian worship, when celebrating the Lord's Supper, are closer to the meaning that the Day of Atonement had for the ancient Hebrews than we are in any other aspect of our worship. To be sure, there is less than universal agreement as to the actual meaning of the sacrament in our various traditions. Historically, there have been sharp contentions and divisions over this sacrament, and those conflicts continue. But whether one views the bread and the wine as actually becoming the body of Christ, or as becoming the real presence of Christ, or as simple symbols to be reminders, each view holds that the service of communion is the central act in our worship which affirms and celebrates the atoning death of Christ for us. I see nothing in church history to raise any hope that we shall ever be able to overcome our differences in our understandings of this important matter, but I am absolutely convinced that these differences need not separate us in our basic and common affirmation that the death of Jesus on Calvary brought to fulfillment all that had been set forth and practiced in the sacrificial system and worship of Israel.

In all of our differing views of the sacrament, we hold in common that it brings to us continuing spiritual nurture and strengthens us in our fellowship in the body of Christ. Each of its different names points to a particular aspect of its meaning. When we call it the Lord's Supper, we emphasize its historical origin in the upper room in Jerusalem, instituted on that night long ago as Jesus shared the Passover meal with his disciples. When called Holy Communion, the emphasis is upon the reality of the community of faith that shares in the living communion of believers with their Lord and with one another. It is sometimes called the Eucharist, which means thanksgiving, and here the emphasis is upon the gratitude with which we receive the gifts of God through the sacrifice of Christ. Some prefer to call it the breaking of bread with the memory of the way in which Jesus became known to the disciples at Emmaus as the risen Lord broke bread with them. In the act of worship designated by all of these names, regardless of the form of the service or the credentials of the officiants, everything points to the central fact that the Christian community is brought into being and sustained by the life, death, and resurrection of Jesus Christ. And thus it is that in receiving the bread and the cup, whether at an altar, at table, in a pew, or around a coffee table, we are celebrating the word of God that mediates to us grace, mercy, and forgiveness through the sacrifice of Christ, even as the Hebrews of old celebrated the grace, mercy, and forgiveness of God on the Day of Atonement long before Christ's coming. We do well to keep in touch with the meaning that *the* Day had for them as an enrichment for the meaning of our own worship today.

The second major error to be avoided is that of becoming so involved in reconstructing the history of the documentation that we fail to discover the meaning of their history for our experience. In recent years much of the scholarship on Leviticus has emphasized the historical questions (e.g., whether the ritual of the Great Day of Atonement was postexilic rather than Mosaic), to the exclusion of principles or parallels that might relate to us. Typically, one commentary concludes that this section "has little real homiletic material, except for the wonderful passage quoted by our Lord as the summation of all the law: 'You shall love your neighbor as yourself' (Lev. 19:18)." While the questions of authorship and dating are significant to our understanding of the text, they are not the entire matter. Once we have settled the basic questions of the reliability and the setting of the sources, we still must apply them to our own life situations. Without such application, through the presence and guidance of the Holy Spirit, we are dealing only with ancient documents, not with the word of God. To relate every part of the ancient story to our stories is the never-ending challenge to the teacher of the Bible. In teaching a Bible class on a weekly basis for many years, I've come to appreciate the tension between scholarship and application, and I've long since come to the conclusion that pastors and lay teachers are "brokers" between the scholars and the people. I'm afraid that all too many Bible teachers are negligent or careless when it comes to keeping abreast of the current scholarship around a given passage of Scripture. From time to time I read or hear sermons or lessons given as though nothing new had been developed in the scholarship on a passage or theme since the nineteenth century. At the same time, I also read or hear scholarly discussions that are so esoteric that only a handful of the very "learned" could possibly make any sense of them. For the most part, scholars talk to and with each other in ways that are not readily interpreted by those outside their disciplines. Thus, the need for "brokers," folks like us with reasonable ability and training to interact with the scholars, but to live with the people and interpret to them the growing edges of scholarly understanding in language and stories by which they can make creative and significant application of the truths of Scripture to their lives and relationships. Without this skilled combinaton of scholarship and application, we will never enable our people to come to a full understanding and appreciation of the rich meaning of the Day of Atonement, both in the experience of the people of Israel and in its relationship to the death of Christ on the cross.

ADDENDUM
THE DAY OF ATONEMENT AND THE CROSS OF CHRIST

Early in the development of this commentary, I became convinced that at some point we would need to do an overview study of the Book of Hebrews, recognizing it as the New Testament's commentary on Leviticus. Certainly, they are companion volumes, and one cannot be studied comprehensively apart from the other. I can think of no more significant place to link these two books than at this point of the Day of Atonement in Leviticus 16. All of the major streams of both books converge at this point.

The questions of the authorship and dating of the Book of Hebrews are not within the purview of our study. We must recognize, nevertheless, that the identification of a specific author for the epistle has never become a matter of consensus among New Testament scholars. Nor has the date of Hebrews been determined with certainty. There is universal agreement that the letter was written to Christians who were suffering intense persecution, but there were various times when such trials were the lot of the New Testament church, beginning in the early 60s and continuing through the first century. The crucial date is A.D. 70, when the second temple was destroyed by the Romans. Dating the epistle prior to that time allows that the sacrifices and the priesthood were still active at the time of its writing. If it had been written after A.D. 70 then, of course, the priesthood and the sacrifices were no longer existent. There has been no restoration of priesthood and sacrifice in Judaism subsequent to the destruction of the second temple. Whether the epistle is dated before or after the destruction of the temple, the early Christians had to deal with the fact that they did not have a central place of worship, a prescribed liturgy, a priesthood, or a system of sacrifices. Thus, there must have been a frequent and strong temptation to revert to the old traditions and time-honored customs, especially since they had come down to them from the time of Moses.

The writer of Hebrews thus makes strong appeals to them for faithfulness to Christ, for unswerving devotion and commitment in the midst of persecution, for joyful fidelity to the community in the midst of suffering. The appeals are grounded in the insistence that the earthly sanctuary was but a temporary copy of the heavenly, eternal sanctuary; that the death of Christ was the fulfillment of all of the sacrificial systems and offerings; that Christ was now our eternal High Priest, abrogating the need for any system of human priesthood; and that Christ was now at the right hand of God exercising His priestly ministry on our behalf. Even later, parts of the church would attempt to recover the human priesthood and restore the sacrificial system through the Mass, in spite of the clear development of these themes in Hebrews. Our understanding of the meaning of Leviticus, as well as of the meaning of Christ's death on the cross, will be enhanced by the development of these themes.

The letter begins with what is universally recognized as one of the most eloquent passages of Greek writing to be found in the New Testament. Here is the articulation of a sweeping overview of God's redemptive work in history. All of the bits and pieces of God's self-disclosure and redeeming activity are now brought together in Christ. "God, who at various times and in different ways spoke in time past to the fathers by the prophets, has in these last days spoken to us by His Son, whom He has appointed heir of all things, through whom also He made the worlds; who being the brightness of His glory and the express image of His person, and upholding all things by the word of His power, when He had by Himself purged our sins, sat down at the right hand of the Majesty on high" (Heb. 1:1–3). Here the uniqueness and finality of Christ are powerfully and eloquently penned. Jesus is portrayed as active in the creation of the universe, as the brightness of God's glory, and as the express image of God. The very phrase "the Son of God" assigns to Christ a unique and authoritative role in God's redemption, and this concept is crucial to all trinitarian theology. Central to the entire Book of Hebrews is this picture of Christ, both as the perfect priest and as the perfect sacrifice. The phrase "sat down at the right hand of the Majesty on high" portrays the priestly work as completed, for the priest did not sit down until the sacrifices were finished. But this priest, like no other priest, was given a position of supreme authority.

Of special significance to our studies in Leviticus is the phrase in verse 3, "when He had by Himself purged our sins." Here is the language of complete cleansing, the end result of the priestly and sacrificial ministry of Christ. It was this cleansing that was the central purpose and meaning of the Day of Atonement.

Having declared the unique superiority of Christ over the prophets, the author spends the rest of chapter 1 affirming the superiority of Christ over the angels. This passage certainly indicates the strong place that belief in angels had in the theology of the Hebrews of that period. To them, angels were intermediaries, bridging the gulf between themselves and God. While they held that there were millions of angels, some of whom they gave names, it was the intention of the author of Hebrews to insist that Jesus stood in a unique relationship to God and humankind as the sole mediator, a thought expressed in 1 Tim. 2:5–6, "For there is one God and one Mediator between God and men, the Man Christ Jesus, who gave Himself a ransom for all, to be testified in due time."

After a brief exhortation regarding the grave urgency of giving serious attention to this gospel of God's salvation (2:1–4), the writer now moves to a major theme of the Epistle, establishing the theme of the priesthood of Christ (2:5–7:28). In the first place, Christ is portrayed as a legitimate priest because of His full participation in our humanity (2:5–18). He shared in our sufferings, He called us his brothers and sisters, He shared in our very flesh and blood, and even in death, and He was tempted as are we. Paul's great passage to the Philippians comes to mind, stressing the humanity of Jesus in making "Himself of no reputation, taking the form of a servant, and coming in the likeness of men" (Phil. 2:7). Jesus could only be a priest by being truly human. This theme of Christ's identification with us in His humanity is further underscored in the appeal, "Seeing then that we have a great High Priest who has passed through the heavens, Jesus the Son of God, let us hold fast our confession. For we do not have a High Priest who cannot sympathize with our weaknesses, but was in all points tempted as we are, yet without sin. Let us therefore come boldly to the throne of grace, that we may obtain mercy and find grace to help in time of need" (Heb. 4:14–16). The true humanity of Christ is crucial to our access to God.

Another aspect of Christ as priest was His fidelity to the priestly ministry. No one would question the faithfulness of Moses, who really served as priest until the appointment of Aaron and his descendants. And yet, Moses was only faithful as a servant in God's house, while Jesus was faithful as "a Son over His own house" (Heb. 3:6).

Yet a third dimension of Christ's priesthood lies in the fact of divine appointment. As we know from Leviticus, one could not become a priest except by being born into the household and lineage of Aaron (Heb. 5:4). Of special interest to us in this section is the introduction of a theme that is critical to our understanding of Leviticus and Hebrews, "You are a priest forever according to the order of Melchizedek" (Heb. 5:6, quoting from Ps. 110:4). This theme is repeated in Heb. 5:10, 6:10, 7:17, and 7:21. It is so important to our understanding, not only of the Book of Hebrews, but of the meaning of Christ's death on the cross, that we must give it special attention. In fact, it is so important that we must have both of the passages in Hebrews pertaining to it before us. The first is Hebrews 5:1–10.

5:1 For every high priest taken from among men is appointed for men in things *pertaining* to God, that he may offer both gifts and sacrifices for sins.

2 He can have compassion on those who are ignorant and going astray, since he himself is also beset by weakness.

3 Because of this he is required as for the people, so also for himself, to offer for sins.

4 And no man takes this honor to himself, but he who is called by God, just as Aaron *was*.

A Priest Forever

5 So also Christ did not glorify Himself to become High Priest, *but it* was He who said to Him:
"You are My Son,
Today I have begotten You."

6 As *He* also *says* in another *place:*
"You *are* a priest forever
According to the order of
Melchizedek";

7 who, in the days of His flesh, when He had offered up prayers and supplications, with vehement

cries and tears to Him who was able to save Him
from death, and was heard because of His godly fear,

8 though He was a Son, *yet* He learned obedience
by the things which He suffered.

9 And having been perfected, He became the
author of eternal salvation to all who obey Him,

10 called by God as High Priest "according to the
order of Melchizedek,"

Heb. 5:1–10

The second passage on the Melchizedek priesthood of Christ is
Hebrews 7:1–28. The chapter division at the end of chapter 6 breaks
the thought of the passage. In a beautiful metaphor at the close of
chapter 6, Jesus is portrayed as the forerunner who has entered "behind the veil" of the Holy of Holies (6:19–20), a clear reference to the
entry of the high priest into that sacred place on the Day of Atonement. The word used for "forerunner" is used of an advance scout
who moves into an unknown area to determine whether it is safe for
the troops to follow. Thus Jesus is presented as the One who makes it
possible for us now to enter into the Holy of Holies, the very presence
of God. And in this He is said to have become "High Priest forever
according to the order of Melchizedek" (6:20). Then follows chapter 7:

7:1 For this Melchizedek, king of Salem, priest of the
Most High God, who met Abraham returning from
the slaughter of the kings and blessed him,

2 to whom also Abraham gave a tenth part of all,
first being translated "king of righteousness," and
then also king of Salem, meaning "king of peace,"

3 without father, without mother, without genealogy, having neither beginning of days nor end of life,
but made like the Son of God, remains a priest
continually.

4 Now consider how great this man *was*, to whom
even the patriarch Abraham gave a tenth of the spoils.

5 And indeed those who are of the sons of Levi,
who receive the priesthood, have a commandment to
receive tithes from the people according to the law,
that is, from their brethren, though they have come
from the loins of Abraham;

6 but he whose genealogy is not derived from them received tithes from Abraham and blessed him who had the promises.

7 Now beyond all contradiction the lesser is blessed by the better.

8 Here mortal men receive tithes, but there he *receives them,* of whom it is witnessed that he lives.

9 Even Levi, who receives tithes, paid tithes through Abraham, so to speak,

10 for he was still in the loins of his father when Melchizedek met him.

Need for a New Priesthood

11 Therefore, if perfection were through the Levitical priesthood (for under it the people received the law), what further need *was there* that another priest should rise according to the order of Melchizedek, and not be called according to the order of Aaron?

12 For the priesthood being changed, of necessity there is also a change of the law.

13 For He of whom these things are spoken belongs to another tribe, from which no man has officiated at the altar.

14 For *it is* evident that our Lord arose from Judah, of which tribe Moses spoke nothing concerning priesthood.

15 And it is yet far more evident if, in the likeness of Melchizedek, there arises another priest

16 who has come, not according to the law of a fleshly commandment, but according to the power of an endless life

17 For He testifies:
"You *are* a priest forever
According to the order of
  Melchizedek."

18 For on the one hand there is an annulling of the former commandment because of its weakness and unprofitableness,

19 for the law made nothing perfect; on the other hand, *there is the* bringing in of a better hope, through which we draw near to God.

Greatness of the New Priest

20 And inasmuch as *He was* not made *priest* without an oath

21 (for they have become priests without an oath, but He with an oath by Him who said to Him:

"The LORD has sworn
And will not relent,
'You *are* a priest forever
According to the order of
Melchizedek'"),

22 by so much more Jesus has become a surety of a better covenant.

23 And there were many priests, because they were prevented by death from continuing.

24 But He, because He continues forever, has an unchangeable priesthood.

25 Therefore He is also able to save to the uttermost those who come to God through Him, since He ever lives to make intercession for them.

26 For such a High Priest was fitting for us, *who is* holy, harmless, undefiled, separate from sinners, and has become higher than the heavens;

27 who does not need daily, as those high priests, to offer up sacrifices, first for His own sins and then for the people's, for this He did once for all when He offered up Himself.

28 For the law appoints as high priests men who have weakness, but the word of the oath, which came after the law, *appoints* the Son who has been perfected forever.

Heb. 7:1–28

Now, with the passages before us, let us attempt to enter into the meaning of this idea of a priesthood after the order of Melchizedek. The best place to begin is with the mysterious person, Melchizedek, who was both king and priest. The writer of Hebrews refers to him first by quoting from Ps. 110:4 in 5:6. The psalm is a messianic psalm, singing the announcement of God's coming *mashiah*, the One who had been promised to David as the Anointed One who would redeem His people. The psalm opens with the words: "The LORD said to my Lord,

'Sit at My right hand, Till I make Your enemies Your footstool.' The LORD shall send the rod of Your strength out of Zion. Rule in the midst of Your enemies!" (vv. 1–2). Verse 4 continues the theme: "You are a priest forever according to the order of Melchizedek." The psalmist has introduced the idea that the Messiah will be a priest of a different order from Aaron. While the opening words of the psalm were widely used in conjunction with the messianic role of Jesus, the use of verse 4 here, to the best of our knowledge, was unique to the writer of Hebrews. The linkage of Messiah with king and priest, as our author does here by using Ps. 2:7 in verse 5 and Ps. 110:4 in verse 6, gives the Messiahship of Jesus a broader focus. That the Messiah must be a king of the line of David was unquestionable. But if the Messiah is also to be high priest, He cannot be from the line of Aaron. Aaron came from the tribe of Levi, but David belonged to the tribe of Judah. Thus, if Jesus is to exercise a high priestly ministry, He cannot do so in the Aaronic line. Attempts to establish a Levitical relationship for Jesus through Mary's kinswoman Elizabeth, who was "of the daughters of Aaron" (Luke 1:5), have met with little acceptance. Thus, the use of Ps. 110:4 opens up a new direction—another priestly order besides that of Aaron, designating the Davidic King as a priest in this order.

We meet Melchizedek in Gen. 14:18–20 as "king of Salem" (identified by most as Jerusalem, *yer-salem*) and "priest of God Most High." Centuries later, David would capture the then Jebusite city of Jerusalem and make it the capital, calling it the City of David (2 Sam. 5:6–9). As he and his house became the successors to Melchizedek's kingship, so, it would seem, one could say that he also became successor to Melchizedek as the priest of God Most High. But during the period of the monarchy, the offices of king and priest were never combined. In fact, the chief priesthood in Jerusalem during and after the monarchy was held by the family of Zadok, not of the Davidic line and not of "the order of Melchizedek." When, much later, under the Hasmoneans, the offices of king and priest were combined, not only was such a merger strongly opposed, but the Hasmoneans had nothing to do with the idea of an order of Melchizedek. There is good reason to believe that the writer of Hebrews may have been the first to bring both the kingly and priestly aspects of the Messiahship of Jesus together by the use of these two psalms. And recall that in this section (5:1–10) our author is establishing two qualificatons for the priesthood: divine appointment and true obedience in suffering.

After an extended exhortation calling for deeper commitment to growing discipleship, the writer returns to the Melchizedek theme, this time by turning to Genesis 14, the only other place in the Bible where Melchizedek appears. In the Genesis story, Chedorlaomer, an Elamite king, with three allies, conducted raids in Transjordan and the Negeb, defeating some of the city-states in Jordan such as Sodom and Gomorrah. They carried off a number of captives including Lot, Abraham's nephew. Hearing of this in Mamre, near Hebron, Abraham enlisted 318 trained servants of his own household and pursued the invaders all the way past Damascus, defeating them and rescuing the captives and the loot. Returning home in triumph, he was met by the king of Sodom, who proposed that Abraham should release the captives to him but retain the material spoils. The latter Abraham declined because he had been met on the way by Melchizedek, to whom he had apparently given an oath to take nothing whatever of the spoils.

One of the remarkable aspects of this entire matter is that we know so little of Melchizedek from the narrative. All we have in the entire Bible is this brief narrative:

> Then Melchizidek king of Salem brought out bread and
> wine; he was the priest of God Most High.
> And he blessed him and said:
> "Blessed be Abram of God Most High,
> Possessor of heaven and earth;
> and blessed be God Most High,
> who has delivered your enemies into your hand."
> And he gave him a tithe of all.
>
> *Gen. 14:18–20*

In true Hebrew style, the writer of Hebrews finds as much significance in what was *not* said about Melchizedek as he does in what *was* said. Note that in the Genesis narrative Melchizedek is described as having brought bread and wine out to Abraham, but our writer makes no reference to it. Subsequent commentators, needless to say, have made much of this possible sacramental connection. Was this action of Melchizedek only a matter of bringing the basic staples of bread and wine for Abraham's refreshment, or did this action point toward the role that bread and wine would have sacramentally in worship? The writer of Hebrews chooses, rather, to emphasize

Abraham's payment of tithes to Melchizedek (Heb. 7:1-10). The logic of our writer is straightforward. Abraham was a great and special man, called by some "a prince of God" and called by God "my friend." Since Abraham pays tithes to Melchizedek, and since it is Melchizedek who blesses Abraham, Melchizedek is obviously even greater than Abraham. This being so, the priesthood of Melchizedek should be held in great honor. And lest there be any further doubt, even Levi, regarded as still in the loins of Abraham, paid tithes to Melchizedek, further marking the superiority of the order of Melchizedek.

The greatness of Melchizedek is further articulated in 7:3 in which he is said to have been "without father, without mother, without genealogy, having neither beginning of days nor end of life, but made like the Son of God, remains a priest continually." Here is a classic example of a typical Hebrew argument from silence. Our author would not have argued with the fact that Melchizedek was most likely one of a line of priest-kings with predecessors and successors. But this was beside the point he was trying to make, namely, that the silence of Scripture about his parentage, genealogy, birth, and death is to be read as a statement that Melchizedek is a type of Christ. In the Scripture, because of this silence, Melchizedek remains a priest continually. How much more, then, does Jesus abide as a priest forever, exalted at the right hand of God. This kind of argument was typical for the Hebrew, though it remains a bit foreign to Western logic.

Our writer goes on to argue that the new priesthood of Jesus in this new order was needed because of the imperfections of the old priesthood under Aaron (7:11-14). The very fact that God gave to Jesus a priestly order of His own, apart from the line of Aaron, simply points to the inadequacy of the old order. And since the priesthood changed, the law also changed. This is akin to Paul's view in Romans and Galatians that the law had the limited function of preparing us for the gospel. In the fullness of time, it was changed, though not abolished.

Beginning with 7:15, our writer decribes the superiority of the new priesthood, reiterating its tie to the order of Melchizedek (vv. 15-19), the new oath of a better covenant (vv. 20-22), the permanence guaranteed by the resurrection of Jesus (vv. 23-25), and the unmatched superiority of the moral perfection of Jesus (vv. 26-28).

Having established the uniqueness and superiority of the priesthood of Jesus, based largely upon the development of the order of Melchizedek, the writer now proceeds to develop the ministry of Jesus as

High Priest through the themes of the covenant, the sanctuary, and the sacrifices (8:1–10:18). As the Aaronic priesthood must give way to the new order of Melchizedek, so the old covenant must be superseded by the new, the earthly sanctuary must be replaced by the heavenly, and the many sacrifices will be completed with one sacrifice, "once and for all." The bottom line of the entire passage is that Christ our High Priest, having made the complete sacrifice on the model of the Day of Atonement, is now continuing His priestly ministry from the heavenly sanctuary at the right hand of God. All that we have learned of the tabernacle and sacrifices and priesthood in Leviticus are portrayed as the "copy and shadow of the heavenly things" (Heb. 8:5). Here again is a Hebrew way of thinking. The tabernacle was the dwelling place for God in the midst of God's people on earth. Therefore, it would be logical to assume that the earthly dwelling would be a model of the heavenly dwelling place. This is much more than mere typology. Everything in Leviticus was crucial to that time, but was also "a shadow of the good things to come" (Heb. 10:1). Jesus is seen as ministering not in any earthly sanctuary but in the heavenly dwelling place, and thus with a superior ministry to anything on earth (8:6).

In Heb. 8:8–13, the long history of Israel's ups and downs with the covenant is recalled, pointing to the new reality of the new covenant. This passage echoes Jer. 31:31–34. What was new about the new covenant? Not so much the substance as the reality of its power to change the hearts of people. Jeremiah had suggested that the life-changing reality of a transforming personal experience with God was not a normal product of the old covenant. This intimate, personal knowledge and experience of God by each member of the community is the essence of the new covenant. Here we can hearken back to the need for annual repitition of the Day of Atonement. Life under the old covenant seemed to be stuck on dead center.

Heb. 9:1–5 is a review of what we have learned in Exodus and Leviticus about the sanctuary under the old covenant, and 9:6–10 is a reminder that the worship in that sanctuary was always incomplete until there could be full access to the Holy of Holies. Now (9:11–14) Christ has brought to its fullness that access to God by shedding His own blood, having "entered the Most Holy Place once for all, having obtained eternal redemption." The ritual of the Day of Atonement is clearly linked to Christ's death on the cross. In His death, the redemption lasts not until next year but eternally.

The writer of Hebrews has no quarrel with the adequacy of the sacrifices in Leviticus to cleanse the tabernacle and its equipment from the uncleanness abhorrent to God. The ritual cleansing that we learned in Leviticus was real and effective for the day-to-day life of the people of God, but it only copied the heavenly reality. What the old worship could not do was cleanse the hearts and lives of the people themselves. The imagery of the Day of Atonement permeates the continuing affirmations of Heb. 9:23–10:18, with the central picture being that of Jesus as the great High Priest entering the Holy of Holies, both as priest and as sacrifice, once and for all.

The ultimate picture of the meaning of Christ's death in the context of the Day of Atonement is found in each of the three synoptic Gospels with the observation that at the moment of the death of Jesus "the veil of the temple was torn in two from top to bottom" (Mark 15:38; Matt. 27:51; Luke 23:45). What a powerful statement! Across the centuries, the Holy of Holies, the earthly dwelling place of God, had been screened off from the people and the priests, for no one could see God and live. Only the high priest could enter once each year, and then only under a cloud of smoke. But now, with Christ's death, the barrier has been removed, torn from the top to the bottom, obviously the work of God from above. Now, indeed, God is with us, Immanuel. We have been given access to the very presence of God through the atoning work of Jesus Christ on the cross.

> Therefore, . . . since we have confidence to enter the Most Holy Place by the blood of Jesus, by a new and living way opened for us through the curtain, that is, his body, and since we have a great priest over the house of God, let us draw near to God with a sincere heart in full assurance of faith, having our hearts sprinkled to cleanse us from a guilty conscience and having our bodies washed with pure water. Let us hold unswervingly to the hope we profess, for he who promised is faithful. And let us consider how we may spur one another on toward love and good deeds. Let us not give up meeting together, as some are in the habit of doing, but let us encourage one another—and all the more as you see the Day approaching.
>
> *Heb. 10:19–25, NIV*

Note well that the writer of Hebrews judiciously avoids the traps in applying Leviticus to the present. Excessive typology is avoided, but clear and contemporary application is the end product. Here, indeed, is a model for us to follow.

I can't conclude this addendum without returning once more to the scapegoat on the Day of Atonement. I've already mentioned that the New Testament writers made no reference to that part of the ritual of the Day. Not until the Epistle of Barnabas, around the beginning of the third century, do we have any linkage of the symbol of the scapegoat with Christ. I stubbornly hold to the right to draw that parallel, for I find it to be a rich symbol of the work of Christ. As the goat went out into the wilderness, bearing the people's sins, so Christ died "outside the city" bearing the sins of the whole world. This vivid picture of the meaning of Christ's death, it seems to me, enriches our understanding of the reality of Christ's taking away our sins.

The words of Charles Wesley are ringing in my heart as I reflect anew on the meaning of Christ's death in the light of the Day of Atonement:

> And can it be that I should gain
>   An interest in the Savior's blood?
> Died He for me, who caused His pain?
>   For me, who Him to death pursued?
> Amazing love! how can it be
>   That Thou, my God, shouldst die for me?
>
> He left His Father's throne above,
>   So free, so infinite His grace!
> Emptied Himself of all but love,
>   And bled for Adam's helpless race!
> 'Tis mercy all, immense and free,
>   For, O my God, it found out me.
>
> No condemnation now I dread:
>   Jesus, and all in Him, is mine!
> Alive in Him, my living Head,
>   And clothed in righteousness divine,
> Bold I approach th'eternal throne,
>   And claim the crown, through Christ my own.
>
> Amazing love!
>   how can it be
> That Thou, my God,
>   shouldst die for me!

CHAPTER FIVE

THE HOLINESS CODE

LEVITICUS 17:1–26:46

We come now to the longest single section in the Book of Leviticus, commonly called the Holiness Code. Though it may have once been an independent unit, the form in which we have it is clearly a composite of once separate units. In the early chapters of Leviticus, we were given the institution of the priesthood and the details of the sacrificial system. Then came the Great Day of Atonement, the annual day of cleansing and forgiveness. We have already learned that the central theme of Leviticus is holiness in worship and in life. Its focus is upon the full meaning of God's grace and redemption. God invites men and women to walk in humble obedience with him. Some interpreters have suggested that chapters 1 through 16 are really a summary of the first part of the Golden Rule, "Thou shalt love the Lord thy God" and that the remaining chapters (17–26) apply the meaning of "thou shalt love thy neighbor as thyself."

As we move into the Holiness Code, it will help to review the meaning of holiness. The basis of holiness is rooted in the nature of God. God is "other." God is infinite in love, goodness, justice, mercy, and power. We are to be holy because God is holy (Lev. 10:10, 11:44–47). But holiness is also grounded in the sense that God is present and active in all of life. When we forget or ignore God's presence, we are most likely to miss the mark of God's standards for the abundant life. Down through the centuries, countless men and women have discovered that "practicing the presence of God" is a vital element in spirituality. Through regular times of prayer and worship, reading and reflecting upon Scripture, and consciously cultivating a growing awareness of God's presence, the desire for holiness grows. Developing regular patterns of worship with the community of faith, along with disciplines of the use of our time and money, also nurtures spiritual growth in holiness.

Nowhere is this expressed more dramatically than by David in the ancient psalm:

> O Lord, You have searched me and known me.
> You know my sitting down and my rising up
> You understand my thought afar off.
> You comprehend my path and my lying down,
> And are acquainted with all my ways.
> For there is not a word on my tongue,
> But behold, O Lord, You know it altogether.
> You have hedged me behind and before,
> And laid Your hand upon me.
> Such knowledge is too wonderful for me;
> It is high, I cannot attain it.
>
> Where can I go from Your Spirit?
> Or where can I flee from Your presence?
> If I ascend into heaven, You are there;
> If I make my bed in hell, behold, You are there.
> If I take the wings of the morning,
> And dwell in the uttermost parts of the sea,
> Even there Your hand shall lead me,
> And Your right hand shall hold me.
> If I say, "Surely the darkness shall fall on me,"
> Even the night shall be light about me;
> Indeed, the darkness shall not hide from You,
> But the night shines as the day;
> The darkness and the light are both alike to You. . . .
>
> Search me, O God, and know my heart;
> Try me, and know my anxieties;
> And see if there is any wicked way in me,
> And lead me in the way everlasting.

Psalm 139

Note well how the sense of God's presence, everywhere, in everything, and in every situation, leads David to cry out for holiness in his own life at the conclusion of the psalm.

The ancient Hebrew did not consider holiness to be an impossible and unattainable ideal, but a reality made possible through obedience to God in the power of the Holy Spirit. The quest for holiness was not regarded as an effort to become something they were not, but rather to become who they really were. For them, obedience to God in worship and in life was not an effort to achieve God's grace and acceptance. Rather, it was an effort to live out in gratitude what God had given them. For the Hebrew, obedience to the Holiness Code was essential, not in order to become holy, but to demonstrate the holiness that God had already placed within them. This is the key to our understanding of the Holiness Code.

The question that we must keep asking all through Leviticus is, What about us today? Are we to keep each of these laws? Were they given for all times and places? In response to these questions, I have to say first of all that in studying Leviticus, there is no question in my mind that the laws were given by God to the Hebrews. And there is no subsequent indication that the laws were declared invalid.

But the plain fact is that, with few exceptions, neither Jews nor Christians today follow these laws in every detail as originally given. It seems to me that the clues are to be found in the Sermon on the Mount. Jesus both affirms the laws of the Hebrew Scriptures and just as clearly calls for changes. At no point does Jesus in any way minimize the demands of the law for his followers. Instead, he always calls upon them to move beyond the letter of the law to a greater responsibility.

While many of the laws given to God's people long ago are not binding upon us in an entirely different world, the overriding principle of the holiness of God and of the people of God is unchanging. Ours is the continuing challenge of discovering the principles of holiness underlying the ancient laws in order to be God's holy people in the midst of our complex world of the late twentieth century.

THE SANCTITY OF BLOOD

17:1   And the LORD spoke to Moses, saying,
    2 "Speak to Aaron, to his sons, and to all the
children of Israel, and say
    to them, 'This *is* the thing which the LORD has com-
manded, saying:
    3 "Whatever man of the house of Israel, kills an
ox or lamb or goat in the camp, or who kills *it* outside
the camp,

4 "and does not bring it to the door of the tabernacle of meeting, to offer an offering to the LORD before the tabernacle of the LORD, bloodguilt shall be imputed to that man. He has shed blood; and that man shall be cut off from his people.

5 "to the end that the children of Israel may bring their sacrifices which they offer in the open field, that they may bring them to the LORD at the door of the tabernacle of meeting, to the priest, and offer them *as* peace offerings to the LORD.

6 "And the priest shall sprinkle the blood on the altar of the LORD *at* the door of the tabernacle of meeting, and burn the fat for a sweet aroma to the LORD.

7 "They shall no more offer their sacrifices to demons, after whom they have played the harlot. This shall be a statute forever for them throughout their generations."'

8 "And you shall say to them: 'Whatever man of the house of Israel, or of the strangers who sojourn among you, who offers a burnt offering or sacrifice,

9 'and does not bring it to the door of the tabernacle of meeting, to offer it to the LORD, that man shall be cut off from among his people.

10 'And whatever man of the house of Israel, or of the strangers who sojourn among you, who eats any blood, I will set My face against that person who eats blood, and will cut him off from among his people.

11 'For the life of the flesh *is* in the blood, and I have given it to you upon the altar to make atonement for your souls; for it *is* the blood *that* makes atonement for the soul.'

12 "Therefore I said to the children of Israel, 'No one among you shall eat blood, nor shall any stranger who sojourns among you eat blood.'

13 "And whatever man of the children of Israel, or of the strangers who sojourn among you, who hunts and catches any animal or bird that may be eaten, he shall pour out its blood and cover it with dust;

14 "for *it is* the life of the flesh. Its blood sustains its life. Therefore I said to the children of Israel, 'You

shall not eat the blood of any flesh, for the life of all
flesh is its blood. Whoever eats it shall be cut off.'
    15 "And every person who eats what died *natu-
rally* or what was torn *by beasts, whether he is* a native
of your own country or a stranger, he shall both wash
his clothes and bathe in water, and be unclean until
evening. Then he shall be clean.
    16 "But if he does not wash or bathe his body,
then he shall bear his guilt."

Lev. 17:1-16

The laws in this part of the Holiness Code are a continuation of the
ceremonial rules relating to clean and unclean foods in chapter 11.
The laws given here bring into play the two themes of holiness that
we have already observed: difference and separateness. Though the
chapter is addressed to Aaron and his sons, the priests, its ultimate
application is to the people, pertaining to the necessity of bringing
their sacrifices to the tabernacle and the prohibition against eating
meat with the blood still in it. The basic theme of the chapter is stated
in verses 10-14, a theme that is still central among Jewish people, that
of the consumption of blood in eating meat. The laws of kosher are
designed to protect them from eating meat from which the blood has
not been properly drained.
    We have already seen that the Hebrews' worship of God was an
integral part of their daily lives. They did not separate the sacred and
the secular as we do. For many Christians today, the world is neatly
divided into two categories, the spiritual and the material. This often
results in the view that the church should be concerned only with the
spiritual realm and should not become involved in matters of a social
or political nature. Not so for the Hebrews. For them, everything was
sacred. Every aspect of life, including the preparation and eating of
food, was connected with their relationship with God. Thus, there are
two important and timeless principles concerning the preparation
and the killing of animals and the consumption of meat.
    The first principle is articulated in verses 1-9 and emphasizes the
importance of the central place of worship. While much contemporary scholarship uses this to date Leviticus in the time of the second
temple after the exile, others make a strong case to the contrary. The
Hebrew scholar Yehezkel Kaufmann (*The Religion of Israel*, University

of Chicago Press, 1960, p. 182) insists that Leviticus 17 does not oppose one sanctuary to several, but rather affirms sanctuary to nonsanctuary, sacrifice to God as opposed to sacrifice to demons (v. 7). Kaufmann argues that the only sanctuary known to the writers of Leviticus was the tabernacle of meeting, represented here not as law but as historical fact. The legitimacy of several places of worship is given full recognition after the entry into Canaan, as in Judges 19–21 where four places of worship are recognized in Bethel, Mizpah, Shiloh, and an undefined place in the hill country of Ephraim. Here, in the wilderness, Israel is encamped, and the tabernacle of meeting is in the middle of the camp.

Whenever an unblemished animal ox, lamb, or goat was killed, inside or outside the camp, it was to be taken *"to the door of the tabernacle of meeting"* for a peace offering or a burnt offering. The animal was killed. Its blood was collected by the priest in a bowl and then sprinkled either on the ground or on the sides of the altar. After burning the fat, the priest would take his allotted portion of the meat, returning the rest of the meat to the worshiper to be taken home for consumption within the time limitations prescribed by the law.

Apparently, some of the people were killing their animals for meat outside of the camp and not at the tabernacle as required. And they were accused of offering *"their sacrifices to demons, after whom they have played the harlot"* (v. 7). Contemporary translations suggest that the reference here is to "goat idols," possibly to Azazel, whom we met in chapter 16.

The penalty for slaughtering an animal anywhere but at the door of the tabernacle of meeting was severe: *"that man shall be cut off from among his people"* (vv. 4, 9). Interpretations of this penalty include the death penalty by execution or lifelong expulsion from the nation. It is certainly the most feared of all possible punishments. Such severity of punishment points to the seriousness with which this matter was taken. There does not appear to be any possibility of restoration to the community, as was the case with those with serious skin diseases who were banished to live outside the camp.

Why was this regarded as a matter of holiness? For the simple reason that the people of God were to be different from their neighboring cultures. Killing animals outside the camp gave the same appearance as other cultures who killed their animals wherever they wished and often did so as an act of worship to their gods, sometimes in degrading ways. The Hebrews were to demonstrate their difference in all of life, including the killing of livestock, by linking everything to their center of worship. We, for whom the eating of meat is quite routine, do well to recognize that the eating of meat was probably a rare luxury for these folks.

Perhaps we should view the tabernacle-centered, and later temple-centered, worship as a model for us today. Living in a community of lovely golf courses, I've met my share of those who insist that they can worship God on the golf course, or while "communing with nature," just as well or better than they can in church. This is much more an expression of Western individualism than it is of biblical faith and contradicts the entire history of the people of God. Salvation in the Bible always involves incorporation into the family of God. Solidarity with the community of faith in the worship of God is always central.

As an illustration I can think of one of the outstanding couples in my congregation, both of whom had served in many ways in the life of the church and reflected all of the signs of vital, contagious life in Christ. They purchased their second home in a resort setting and indicated to me that they wouldn't be in church very often, as they needed their weekends for relaxation in that idyllic setting. But before too many weeks had gone by, they found themselves experiencing spiritual atrophy. They concluded that the elimination of corporate worship with the community of faith on the Lord's Day was at the root of the matter. They located a vital congregation near their weekend retreat and began worshiping there, now considering themselves to be an active part of two congregations. I believe that this kind of dual membership may well become a part of the lives of many such Christians in the future. (I'm well aware of the many problems raised by this kind of affluence. But as a pastor, I also have to deal with the realities around me, realizing that ultimately each of us must give his own accounting to God. I stubbornly resist linking salvation to such matters.)

The second principle in this chapter comes with the repetition of the prohibition against eating the blood of any animal (vv. 10–16). The reason for this is given in verse 11: "*For the life of the flesh is in the blood, and I have given it to you upon the altar to make atonement for your souls; for it is the blood that makes atonement for the soul.*" You will recall from our previous discussions of the meaning of sacrifices and offerings, along with the role of the blood in the sacrifices, that it was their clear understanding and belief that the blood belonged to God alone.

In this section, we have the most comprehensive statement to be found in Leviticus for not consuming the blood. The prohibition from eating blood (eating meat from which the blood had not been properly drained) is repeated five times in this section, and the gravity of the offense is articulated twice — He shall be cut of from his people (vv. 10, 14) — the most serious punishment other than death. This prohibition goes back to the time of Noah (Gen. 9:4), though Kaufmann holds that the command to Noah was relative to eating meat from animals that had not been killed, citing primitive practices of the cultures around Israel.

In Deut. 12:1–25, the people are being given instructions for living in the Promised Land, prior to crossing the Jordan under Joshua's leadership. They are told that in Canaan they will be free to kill their animals for eating in any of their towns. The prohibition from eating blood, however, remains in effect: "However, you may slaughter and eat meat within all your gates, whatever your heart desires, according to the blessing of the LORD your God which He has given you; the unclean and the clean may eat of it, of the gazelle and the deer alike. Only you shall not eat the blood; you shall pour it out on the earth like water. . . . When the LORD your God enlarges your border as He has promised you, and you say, 'Let me eat meat,' because you long to eat meat, you may eat as much meat as your heart desires. If the place where the LORD your God chooses to put His name is too far from you, then you may slaughter from your herd and from your flock which the LORD has given you, just as I have commanded you, and you may eat within your gates as much as your heart desires. Just as the gazelle and the deer are eaten, so you may eat them; the unclean and the clean alike may eat them. Only be sure that you do not eat the blood, for the blood is the life; you may not eat the life with the meat" (Deut. 12:15–16; 20–23). Notice what changes and what doesn't change. In Canaan, they will be scattered over a much larger territory, and the requirement that they kill all of their meat for eating in the central place of worship is no longer in force. Only the sacrifices must be made in the central place of worship. But the ban on eating meat from which the blood has not been properly drained remains in force, even though the blood is to be poured out on the ground.

We see the same principle during the time of Samuel and Saul (1 Sam. 14:31–35). The Israelites are in pursuit of the Philistines in the hill country of Ephraim and have them pretty much on the run. Saul has commanded them to go without food for the entire day, apparently wanting to press the battle without interruption. After the successful day's battles, the famished men "rushed on the spoil, and took sheep, oxen, and calves, and slaughtered them on the ground; and the people ate them with the blood. Then they told Saul, saying, 'Look, the people are sinning against the LORD by eating with the blood!' And he said, 'You have dealt treacherously; roll a large stone to me this day.' And Saul said, 'Disperse yourselves among the people, and say to them, "Bring me here every man's ox and every man's sheep, slaughter them here, and eat; and do not sin against the LORD by eating with the blood."' So every one of the people brought his ox with him that night, and slaughtered it there. Then Saul built an altar to the LORD. This was the first altar that he built to the LORD" (1 Sam. 14:32–35). While Saul's hasty erection of the altar clearly indicates that the older principle of the central place of worship is no longer observed, the principle of not eating the blood is still taken with utmost seriousness.

Two reasons are given here in Leviticus 17 for this prohibition. The first is " ' "For the life of the flesh is in the blood, and I have given it to you upon the altar to make atonement for your souls; for it is the blood that makes atonement for the soul." . . . for it is the life of all flesh. Its blood sustains its life. Therefore, I said to the children of Israel, "You shall not eat the blood of any flesh, for the life of all flesh is its blood. Whoever eats it shall be cut off" ' " (vv. 11, 14). The life of an animal is identified with its blood. While our understanding of life has become much more complex, the principle still holds. When a living being loses its blood, it dies. We now transfuse blood in order to save life. Blood is thus held in high regard, perhaps with the ancients to the point of mysterious awe because it was obviously essential to life. When we see the news photo or television shot of a body lying in a pool of blood, we are immediately aware that a death has probably occurred. It seems safe to assume that there is a principle of respect for life in operation here though it is not stated. Even the lives of animals are not to be taken casually. Life, and thus blood, has been given by God.

The other reason given for not eating blood relates also directly to God: "For the life of the flesh is in the blood, and I have given it to you upon the altar to make atonement for your souls; for it is the blood that makes atonement for the soul" (Lev. 17:11). You may wish to refer again to our discussion of the role of blood in the sacrifices in conjunction with the burnt offering (Leviticus 1). Recall that the word for atonement can mean two things, cleansing or paying a ransom price. Here the latter is the apparent meaning. The penalty for many sins was death, but the death of an animal could be substituted for the death required by the law. The animal thus became the ransom price for the redemption of the guilty person. Interestingly, in Exod. 21:30, a person could be redeemed by a monetary payment from the death penalty incurred by being the owner of an ox that had gored another person to death, even though it had been known beforehand that the ox was prone to such behavior. This seems to be the only exception to the necessity of blood sacrifice for atonement.

On this point of the requirement of the shedding of blood for the atonement of sins the writer of the Book of Hebrews developed the magnificent passage on the meaning of Christ's death as an atonement for sin, once and for all (Hebrews 8–10). The section is summarized in 9:24–28:

"For Christ has not entered the holy places made with hands, which are copies of the true, but into heaven itself, now to appear in the presence of God for us; not that He should offer Himself often, as the high priest enters the Most Holy Place every year with blood of another—He then would have had to suffer often since the foundation of the world; but now, once at the end of the ages, He has appeared to put away sin by the sacrifice of Himself. And as it is appointed unto men to die once, but after this the judgment, so Christ was offered once to bear the sins of many. To those who eagerly wait for Him He will appear a second time, apart from sin, for salvation."

CALLED TO BE DIFFERENT

Chapters 18–20 constitute the heart of the Holiness Code. In studying them, we are again faced with two dangers in interpretation and application. On the one hand, a literal application would be impossible in the communities where most of us live. When someone asks me, "Do you believe in the Bible, literally?" I must reply, "Not if you include Leviticus 18–20!" While many of the behaviors set forth in chapters 18 and 19 are still being practiced among us, the penalties set forth in chapter 20, such as the death penalty for both parties involved in marital infidelity, are not likely to be recommended by most contemporary pastors.

The danger, however, of merely relegating these chapters to the dust bins of ancient customs must also be avoided. We do well to study these chapters in the light of their place in history, to be sure, but we do justice to them as Scripture by listening for the word of God to us through them. And how better do this than by attempting to discover the principles underlying the specifics? I urge you to wrestle seriously with these chapters as Scripture in need of practical application to our lives today. To me, the best starting point is to deal with their opening and closing paragraphs.

THE BASIS OF HOLINESS

18:1 Then the LORD spoke to Moses, saying,

2 "Speak to the children of Israel, and say to them: 'I am the LORD your God.

3 'According to the doings of the land of Egypt, where you dwelt, you shall not do; and according to the doings of the land of Canaan, where I am bringing you, you shall not do; nor shall you walk in their ordinances.

4 'You shall observe My judgments and keep My ordinances, to walk in them: I *am* the LORD your God.

5 'You shall therefore keep My statutes and My judgments, which if a man does, he shall live by them: I *am* the LORD.

20:22 'You shall therefore keep all My statutes and all My judgments, and perform them, that the land where I am bringing you to dwell may not vomit you out.

23 'And you shall not walk in the statutes of the nation which I am casting out before you; for they commit all these things, and therefore I abhor them.

24 'But I have said to you, 'You shall inherit their land, and I will give it to you to possess, a land flowing with milk and honey." I *am* the LORD your God, who has separated you from the peoples.

25 'You shall therefore distinguish between clean
beasts and unclean, between unclean birds and clean,
and you shall not make yourselves abominable by
beast or by bird, or by any kind of living thing that
creeps on the ground, which I have separated from
you as unclean.

26 'And you shall be holy to Me, for I the LORD *am*
holy, and have separated you from the peoples, that
you should be Mine.

27 'A man or a woman who is a medium, or who
has familiar spirits, shall surely be put to death; they
shall stone them with stones. Their blood *shall be* upon
them.'"

Lev. 18:1–5; 20:22–27

They were called to be different! This, as we have seen, is the
central theme of Leviticus: "*You shall be holy to Me, for I the Lord am
holy, and have separated you from the peoples, that you should be Mine*" (20:26).

The history of cultures is the history of human disobedience. From
the beginning, men and women have been questioning God. "Has
God indeed said?" (Gen. 3:1) has been the universal question that has
prompted human disobedience, ever seeking alternatives to the revealed will of God.

Egyptian culture, from which they had been delivered, and
Canaanite culture, to which they were going, are both declared to be
deviant from the standards set by God. God's very reason for driving
the Canaanites out of their land is because of their customs and
culture, shaped by principles other than God's declared will. To adopt
Egyptian or Canaanite standards was to curry the displeasure of God,
even to the point of possible banishment from the land (20:22).

The issue of the nature of the community is critical to our understanding of the holiness required of God's people. The people of God
are to be a special kind of community, very different from other
communities. With the passage of time, the nature of that special
community will become increasingly clear. It will be called the Kingdom of God and be characterized by folks whose love for God will
express itself in love for each other, in genuinely caring for the whole
of God's creation, and even loving and caring for the alien and the
enemy, unheard of in other cultures.

God's call to them, the call to holiness, was a call to be a very special community. And is not God's call to us the same? It has become increasingly difficult for many in American culture to hear this call because of a tendency to equate patriotism with loyalty to God. Such thinking may lead to the conclusion that being loyal to the government is the same as being obedient to God. We have been fortunate that our government has recognized the right of conscientious objection to military service, but I can remember all too well the disdain in some Christian circles during World War II for young men who chose that option because of their faithful convictions. Blurring the distinction between loyalty to country and loyalty to the Kingdom of God becomes the death of true holiness. The values of the culture, however much in common they may have with Kingdom values, are ultimately grounded in self-interest and thus antithetical to the Kingdom of God. "No servant can serve two masters. . . . You cannot serve God and mammon" (Luke 16:13) was Jesus' way of making this clear.

The Holiness Code is best seen as partially descriptive of what this special community should look like. And it deals, first of all, with the way that men and women should relate to each other as males and females.

HOLINESS AND SEXUALITY

6 'None of you shall approach anyone who is near of kin to him, to uncover his nakedness: I *am* the LORD.

7 'The nakedness of your father or the nakedness of your mother you shall not uncover. She *is* your mother; you shall not uncover her nakedness.

8 'The nakedness of your father's wife you shall not uncover; it *is* your father's nakedness.

9 'The nakedness of your sister, the daughter of your father, or the daughter of your mother, *whether* born at home or elsewhere, their nakedness you shall not uncover.

10 'The nakedness of your son's daughter or your daughter's daughter, their nakedness your shall not uncover; for theirs *is* your own nakedness.

11 'The nakedness of your father's wife's daughter, begotten by your father— she *is* your sister— you shall not uncover her nakedness.

209

12 'You shall not uncover the nakedness of your father's sister; she *is* near of kin to your father.

13 'You shall not uncover the nakedness of your mother's sister, for she *is* near of kin to your mother.

14 'You shall not uncover the nakedness of your father's brother. You shall not approach his wife; she *is* your aunt.

15 'You shall not uncover the nakedness of your daughter-in-law – she *is* your son's wife – you shall not uncover her nakedness.

16 'You shall not uncover the nakedness of your brother's wife; it *is* your brother's nakedness.

17 'You shall not uncover the nakedness of a woman and her daughter, nor shall you take her son's daughter or her daughter's daughter, to uncover her nakedness. They *are* near of kin to her. It *is* wickedness.

18 'Nor shall you take a woman as a rival to her sister, to uncover her nakedness while the other is alive.

19 'Also you shall not approach a woman to uncover her nakedness as long as she is in her *customary* impurity.

20 'Moreover you shall not lie carnally with your neighbor's wife, to defile yourself with her.

21 'And you shall not let any of your descendants pass through *the fire* to Molech, nor shall you profane the name of your God: I *am* the LORD.

22 'You shall not lie with a male as with a woman. It *is* an abomination.

23 'Nor shall you mate with any beast, to defile yourself with it. Nor shall any woman stand before a beast to mate with it. It *is* perversion.

24 'Do not defile yourselves with any of these things; for by all these the nations are defiled, which I am casting out before you.

25 'For the land is defiled; therefore I visit the punishment of its iniquity upon it, and the land vomits out its inhabitants.

26 'You shall therefore keep My statutes and My judgments, and shall not commit *any* of these abominations, *either* any of your own nation or any stranger who sojourns among you

27 '(for all these abominations the men of the land have done, who *were* before you, and thus the land is defiled),

28 'lest the land vomit you out also when you defile it, as it vomited out the nations that *were* before you.

29 'For whoever commits any of these abominations, the persons who commit *them* shall be cut off from among their people.

30 'Therefore you shall keep My ordinance, so that *you* do not commit *any* of these abominable customs which were committed before you, and that you do not defile yourselves by them: I *am* the LORD your God.'"

Lev. 18:6–30

Whatever else may be said about this section, most obviously all types of sexual behavior by individuals, other than those between a woman and a man in the marriage relationship, are expressly forbidden. The sixteen variations of male/female sexual relationships pretty well cover all of the possibilities, and there are added the male/male and the human/animal variations as well.

Sexual relationships are forbidden with:
1. Any close relative (6)
2. One's mother (7)
3. One's stepmother (8)
4. Sister, or stepsister of stepmother (9)
5. Granddaughter (10)
6. Stepsister born of father (11)
7. Aunt (through father or mother) (12, 13)
8. Wife of uncle (14)
9. Daughter-in-law (15)
10. Brother's wife (16)
11. Both a woman and her daughter or granddaughters (17)
12. Wife's sister (18)
13. A woman during her menstrual period (19)
14. A neighbor's wife (20)
15. A man (22)
16. An animal (23)

To be sure, the passage indicates that the ancients were just as adept at sexual promiscuity and variations as we are. (All of the prohibitions were addressed to males, except the one relating to bestiality, which included women, v. 23.) The underlying principles, however, must be the same for us as for them. Sexual integrity begins at home, with complete respect and integrity required of each member for the others. In a day when we are becoming painfully aware of widespread sexual abuse in all too many American homes, the importance of the underlying principles of this ancient code is obvious.

How often, as a pastor, I have agonized with some of our dear people through the pain that comes with brokenness growing out of sexual relations outside of their marriage vows. It shouldn't shock or surprise us that these things are happening with what seems to be greater frequency. Not only have community standards become more permissive, as expressed in the casual way that sexual relations are portrayed in contemporary drama and literature (in which, by the way, few incur disease or become pregnant). New lifestyles in business and professional life in which men and women are together more in the context of business activity, including travel away from home, have also encouraged permissiveness. How crucial it is for each couple to work diligently at maintaining a high level of intimacy and integrity within the marriage commitment against the trends that make lifetime marriage more difficult.

The brief reference to the burning of children in the fire of Molech is probably a reference to a practice among the Canaanites in which newborn babies were sacrificed to the glory of some god! As we have seen throughout Leviticus, the children of Israel were called to many radical differences from the cultures around them.

As with all sexual relations outside of marriage, homosexuality and bestiality are likewise forbidden. Dealing with the complex questions surrounding homosexuality is, indeed, one of the tough issues of our time. Clearly, the culture around us is moving toward a much wider acceptance of homosexual behavior. Such acceptance is grounded in the belief that homosexuality is an orientation quite beyond the control of the individual, thus making it unjust to condemn anyone for something over which he or she had no choice.

Biblical passages are used on all sides of the debate, and the issue of whether or not homosexuals should be accepted by the church through ordination is a source of sharp division in many denominations. A comprehensive discussion, dealing with all of the references in the Bible to homosexuality, is to be found in the *Interpreter's Dictionary of the Bible*, in the article on homosexuality.

It seems to me that in the heat of the arguments, debaters forget that in the Bible sexuality is always portrayed as given by God in creation for the intimate union of a man and a woman in marriage, both for the bonding of intimacy and for the creation of new life from such a union. For those of us who hold such a view, believing it to be shaped by the views set forth in the Scriptures, we will increasingly find ourselves in a countercultural position. Clearly, the culture has moved through radical changes in its views of sexuality. How do we live when in sharp disagreement with such cultural norms? Above all, I think we must exercise great caution and show deep compassion toward those whom we consider to be deviant or immoral. We are called to be people who are different in loving our neighbor — and the neighborhood was defined by Jesus as including everyone. As God's people, we are called to be holy in our sexual behavior because of God's holiness, but we are never given license to be anything other than loving to others.

Frankly, I find myself often in great pain over the issue of the ordination of homosexuals as clergy or church officers. I haven't been convinced by any of the efforts I have heard to interpret the Scriptures as affirming homosexuality as ordained by God in creation. Nor do I find any means, using Scripture, to find encouragement for or support of homosexual behavior in any relationship (any more than I do for heterosexual intimacy apart from marriage). Nor am I yet convinced that homosexuality is genetically determined. Thus, for me to support the ordination of homosexuals who insist upon the practice of homosexual behavior is contrary to my basic understanding of Scripture and tradition. But, at the same time, I want to demonstrate genuine love for all homosexuals as persons created and loved by God. Though I have not been convinced that their orientation as homosexuals is created by God, I do believe that they are to be regarded fully as human beings, irrespective of that orientation. Practically, in the light of Scripture, I can't call upon the church to condone homosexual behavior any more than I can to endorse heterosexual behavior outside of marriage. Yet I find no basis for regarding homosexual deviations in behavior any differently from heterosexual deviance. In all of this, I have had to deal with my own cultural homophobia to bring it under God's call to love my neighbor as myself.

A critical question to me focuses upon the issue of the possible reorientation of homosexuals. I'll never forget a social evening in the home of a friend with Dr. Victor Frankl, world-renowned psychiatrist and one of the few students of Sigmund Freud then living. We discussed at length this issue of possible ordination. His most meaningful statement to me was, "If your church ordains homosexuals, you will remove all hope from the vast majority of homosexuals who have not declared their orientation and who desparately want to be healed." How to hold out the hope of change without being judgmental and censorious — that is the question with which I live.

In the midst of the many sexual deviations forbidden is the strange word about the sacrifice of children to Molech (v. 21). So to sacrifice is a profanation against God's name. Wenham cites recent discoveries in a former temple in Amman (in the land of the Ammonites, whose god was Molech) of evidence of child sacrifice dating back to the time of the Conquest. Molech worship was widespread in northern Africa in pre-Christian centuries, apparently with origins in Phoenicia. It has never been fully determined whether the children were thrown alive into the fire or killed first. The practice is referred to and condemned in 2 Kings 23:10 and Jer. 32:35.

Verses 24–28 strengthen the appeal of the prohibitions by adding that disobedience in these areas actually defiles the land. Here is a fascinating metaphor which personifies the land and portrays it as vomiting out the Hebrews.

The chapter concludes with verses 29–30, repeating the penalty for those who transgress these laws of being cut off from the nation.

THREE BASICS

19:1 And the LORD spoke to Moses, saying,

2 "Speak to all the congregation of the children of Israel, and say to them: 'You shall be holy, for I the LORD your God *am* holy.

3 'Every one of you shall revere his mother and his father, and keep My Sabbaths: I *am* the LORD your God.

4 'Do not turn to idols, nor make for yourselves
molded gods: I *am* the LORD your God.

Lev. 19:1–4

This delightful summary of the Law could well be a text for a
sermon on Mother's or Father's Day. Awareness of the holiness of
God produces a certain style of life. Three of the ten commandments
are amplified at this point, as illustrative of this reality. Reverence for
parents, observance of the Sabbath, and the rejection of idols are the
three commandments underscored.

In their experiences as nomads in the Sinai desert, and later in the
land of Canaan, the Hebrews had experienced firsthand people who
were rough and brutal, who practiced child burning as religious
sacrifice, who copulated randomly with each other as well as with
animals, who practiced gross cruelty during times of both war and
peace, who treated slaves and animals with vicious cruelty, and who
abused women and children utterly. The constant repetition of the
phrase "the Lord spoke to Moses" reminds us that we have a word
from God in these matters, not just a new human idea about the good
life. This radical contrast in lifestyle is God's disclosure of what human beings are meant to be.

The fifth commandment is cited first, indicating that the honoring
of parents is of vital importance to the life of the community. The
ordering of family life stood in marked contrast to the chaos in human
relationships characteristic of the pagan tribes. Must this not
become a high priority for our churches today? Our need to bring
order out of chaos in family relationships is obvious. This is increasingly difficult because of the many shifts within the culture
in which we live. Take as an example the growing number of
single-parent households in the United States. It is now estimated
that more than 50 percent of all children who grow up in our
country during the next twenty years will have lived all or most of
their developmental years with only one of their parents. This
need not mean that they will be unable to "honor their father and
mother," but it certainly requires some new ways of thinking
about families.

While we certainly must do everything we can by way of pre-
venting divorce, we are also going to have to heighten our efforts

to support and help all who fail in their marriages. As a pastor, I was always aware of the tension involved in this dichotomy. With the passage of time, I have found that some of the most difficult sermons to prepare were those on marriage and family life — not because the standards have changed but because the culture has changed. When we preach and teach with clarity and strength, affirming the biblical standard of marriage as a lifelong relationship of one man with one woman, we are obviously declaring what needs to be heard by those who are married and those yet to enter into marriage. But what do we have to say to those who have failed in a marriage and who now have the primary responsibility for one or more children? What word do we have for those presently in a second or subsequent marriage? What do we have to say for those contemplating a marriage after divorce? What hope do we bring to people in later years whose marriage and family journeys have been disastrous? These are the questions to which we must respond in faithfulness to the gospel. And let's not forget that the gospel of God's grace and mercy in Jesus Christ is always good news.

Keeping "My Sabbaths" is perhaps the most casually and frequently violated commandment in our day. Many people born between 1920 and 1940 recall rigid and slavish rules about the Sabbath or Sunday in which a simple pleasure like reading the Sunday comics was forbidden. To such, liberation from legalism has come like a breath of fresh air. Sleeping in, shopping, and watching sports is felt to be vastly superior to the old constrictions.

Perhaps the pendulum has swung too far. Slavish restrictions on Sabbath-keeping indeed missed the mark of the intention of the biblical Sabbath. But so does our "anything goes" approach. I have no interest in dictating to anyone else, especially outside of the Christian community, how they should conduct themselves on the Lord's Day. But we who are God's people are specifically enjoined to honor the Sabbath as a holy day — a day set apart to God.

We best begin by recognizing the Sabbath as a gift, not as a burden. The Sabbath was no human invention. In the pagan cultures, slaves were driven seven days a week with only an occasional holiday. All work and no play not only make Jack a dull boy, but all work and no rest or worship also make for social breakdown and chaos. Both the French and the Russian revolutions tried to eliminate the Sabbath in order to increase worker efficiency. Both had to abandon the effort. It's past time for us who name Christ's name to renew our commitment to the Sabbath principle: one day in seven, preferably the day of Christ's resurrection, the first day of the week, as a day devoted to rest, corporate worship with Christ's people, prayer, reflection, and spiritual renewal.

To be sure, the seventh day of the week was the Hebrew sabbath, recognizing the order in the creation narrative. It is most likely that the early Christians continued to observe the Sabbath of their Jewish tradition, as is stated in passages such as Acts 13:14 and 14:1. They also gathered each Sunday morning, apart from the synagogue, to celebrate the resurrection of Jesus, which had been on the first day of the week. To them, the first day of the week became the Lord's Day. And with the passage of time, and the growing separation between the Christian community and the synagaogue, Jewish worship on the Sabbath and Christian worship on the Lord's Day became the norm, with Sunday coming to be the Christian Sabbath.

One approach to recovering the Sabbath that seems culturally and biblically sound has been tried by a number of our families: regarding Sunday as a family day. This requires a strong commitment by the parent(s) to plan special times for the entire family, be it two people or seven. The day begins with the larger family, the church, with worship, learning, and fellowship. This is followed by family activities such as picnics, day trips, family recreation, or whatever. Sometimes other families are invited to join together. The emphasis is upon being together, rather than merely using the day to do our own different things. With careful and creative planning, these become special days, eagerly anticipated. And the earlier a family begins this pattern, the better the chance of success.

The third commandment singled out pertains to idolatry. The repertoire of idols is not concluded with the making of molten or ceramic images. Idolatry occurs whenever we put anything or anyone on the same level as or a higher level than God in our lives. Trusting for our well-being in anything or anyone other than God, or along with God — be it wealth, marriage, career, or nation — is idolatry!

I suspect that few people on the contemporary scene witness the tragedies of idolatry more regularly than American pastors in affluent communities. I heard the story not long ago. She sat in my study with her teenage daughter, both of them in visible anguish. How did it happen? Just two years ago they had moved into their dream home, the result of years of hard work and sacrifice. Within a year, the condo in the mountains was added, and the good life was a reality. To be sure, the properties took a lot of time and energy and pretty well commanded the family resources, but life was exhilarating. Then, without notice, husband/father moved out to begin anew with someone else. "It's very clear to me now," she said, "that I put my faith in the false gods of wealth and possessions. I really believed that we had found our happiness and security in them. And now, I feel betrayed in every way!" The false gods promise much more than they ever deliver. We need to see them for what they really are: idols.

SHARING AND CARING

5 'And if you offer a sacrifice of peace offering to the LORD, you shall offer it of your own free will.
6 'It shall be eaten the same day you offer *it*, and on the next day. And if any remains until the third day, it shall be burned in the fire.
7 'And if it is eaten at all on the third day, it *is* an abomination. It shall not be accepted.
8 'Therefore *everyone* who eats it shall bear his iniquity, because he has profaned the hallowed *offering* of the LORD; and that person shall be cut off from his people.
9 'When you reap the harvest of your land, you shall not wholly reap the corners of your field, nor shall you gather the gleanings of your harvest.
10 'And you shall not glean your vineyard, nor shall you gather *every* grape of your vineyard; you shall leave them for the poor and the stranger: I *am* the LORD your God.

Lev. 19:5–10

I prefer to read this section as a whole, linking verses 5–8 with 9–10, since the rules for the peace offering had already been given. Here the emphasis is upon the offering being voluntary, along with the necessity of eating it without undue delay. Then follows the code requiring the farmer to leave what later Jewish writers would call "the sixteenth" of the harvest for the poor. In the deepest sense, this, too, was a voluntary action.

Here is a delightful emphasis upon genuine, practical caring for and sharing with the poor and the hungry, both in worship and in work. As we have seen (Leviticus 3), the peace offering is to be eaten with one's friends, and requiring it to be eaten within a day encouraged the invitation of others to share, thus broadening the circle of blessing. The harvest rule incorporated the same principle of sharing.

A most memorable portrayal of the harvest rule in action is in the Book of Ruth, the tender and moving story of the poor widow so graciously cared for by Boaz. With the death of her husband Elimelech, a Hebrew woman by the name of Naomi was left in the land of Moab (east of the Dead Sea and away from her home town of Bethlehem) with her two sons, Mahlon and Kilion. They married women from Moab, Orpah and Ruth, and died about ten years later, leaving the three women widowed. Hearing that a famine was over in Judah, Naomi decided to return to Bethlehem. As she was returning with her daughters-in-law, she urged them to return to their homes in Moab, where they would both have a better chance of marrying again. After much painful discussion, Orpah did return, but Ruth insisted on staying with Naomi with her well-known words: "Wherever you go, I will go, and wherever you lodge I will lodge; your people shall be my people, and your God, my God" (Ruth 1:16). Arriving in Bethlehem at the beginning of the barley harvest, Naomi and Ruth were widely noticed and warmly welcomed. The story moves to the fields of Boaz, a leading citizen of Bethlehem, who was a relative of Naomi's former husband, Elimelech. Urging Naomi and Ruth to glean in his fields, we see the harvest law in action. These two widows were able to collect enough grain to sustain them through the provision of this law. The story, as you might expect, has even greater significance, for ultimately Boaz arranges with integrity and care to provide for Naomi and marry Ruth, according to the rather complicated customs of their time. And they had a son whose name was Obed, who had a son whose name was Jesse, who had a son whose name was David! And Ruth was one of the four mothers listed (along with Tamar, Rahab, and "Uriah's wife") in the forty-two-generation genealogy of Matthew (Matt. 1:1–16).

Feeding the hungry and caring for the poor is meant by God to be a normal activity of God's people. The plight of the homeless needy has become a growing part of the American scene in recent years. A Christian layman in our community purchased a home and hired a trained couple to supervise a shelter for families in need of temporary housing and rehabilitation to work. Part of the program enables members of nearby churches to provide the evening meal for the residents, sometimes up to five families. Instead of sending the meal over, the providers are required to join the group for the meal and the evening worship that follows.

The joy that comes from such an experience has provided a rich source of sharing among many of our people. So much so, in fact, that there is now a waiting list for those wanting to participate. We're beginning to discover part of what Jesus meant when he said, "It is more blessed to give than to receive" (Acts 20:35).

LOVING ONE'S NEIGHBOR

11 'You shall not steal, nor deal falsely, nor lie to one another.

12 'And you shall not swear by My name falsely, nor shall you profane the name of your God: I *am* the LORD.

13 'You shall not defraud your neighbor, nor rob *him*. The wages of him who is hired shall not remain with you all night until morning.

14 'You shall not curse the deaf, nor put a stumblingblock before the blind, but shall fear your God: I *am* the LORD.

15 'You shall do no injustice in judgment. You shall not be partial to the poor, nor honor the person of the mighty. *But* in righteousness you shall judge your neighbor.

16 'You shall not go about *as* a talebearer among your people: nor shall you take a stand against the life of your neighbor: I *am* the LORD.

17 'You shall not hate your brother in your heart. You shall surely rebuke your neighbor, and not bear sin because of him.

18 'You shall not take vengeance, nor bear any
grudge against the children of your people, but you
shall love your neighbor as yourself: I *am* the LORD.

Lev. 19:11–18

Now we have a focus upon three more commandments, the third, eighth, and ninth. Honesty in our dealings with rich and poor is the basic standard designed by God. Stealing, false dealing, lying, and false oaths have a way of going together. One often leads to or grows out of the other. These injunctions are followed by warnings against oppressive and inhumane cruelty.

Oppression of a neighbor can take many forms. One form that is much in the news these days is sexual harassment in the marketplace. A woman from whom sexual favors are demanded, under threat of losing her job or being denied promotion, certainly deserves better treatment.

Delay in the payment of wages is also a form of oppression. In that day, it was the practice to pay the laborer at the end of each working day. Only then could the poor worker purchase the evening meal for his family. To delay payment was to inflict hardship. Caring for the poor in that way was a radical innovation in the world of that day.

Cruel treatment, whether in mockery of the deaf or in taunting the blind, was never to be any part of the life of the people of the community of faith. This principle has now born fruit in our growing concern for the physically, as well as the mentally, handicapped. Special parking places, ramps for access, acoustical aids, and expanded sanitary facilities are all ways in which we can express our love and care for those who must live with limitations. Every church should be in the process of making those provisions that say to all who are handicapped, "We love you, and we want you with us!" I was surprised when this became a matter of controversy in our congregation. It began when we added to our office facilities. In order to obtain a building permit, we had to make provisions for people with physical disabilities. This led to the conviction among many of us that we should review all of our facilities to make such provisions throughout. The opposition arose from many, primarily on the grounds that "we can't afford it!" I'm grateful to those folks who took the high road of principle and made every provision deemed necessary. I can't tell you that we now have hundreds of disabled folks rushing to our church, but I know in my heart that our people did what was right.

The summary conclusion regarding human relationships is stated in what surely is the best-known sentence in all of Leviticus: "You shall love your neighbor as yourself" (19:18). It is quoted by Jesus in the Sermon on the Mount (Matt. 5:43), in his conversation with the rich, young ruler (Matt. 19:19), and in the parable of the good Samaritan (Luke 10:27). Jesus also referred to it as the "second" commandment in his answer to the lawyer's question: "Which is the great commandment in the law?" (Matt. 22:36).

When Jesus quoted this verse in the Sermon on the Mount, he said, "You have heard that it was said, `You shall love your neighbor, and hate your enemy'" (Matt. 5:43). The obvious question one asks is when the "hate your enemy" got added. It was not, as far as we can tell, in the original version of Leviticus. All that we know for sure is that this was the way it was quoted at the time of Jesus, perhaps an interesting example of how great truths can become distorted with the passage of time. However the change took place, Jesus changed it, radically and dramatically, to incorporate both the love of neighbor *and* the love of enemy.

Many contemporary expositions emphasize the loving of oneself as the first step toward loving one's neighbor. However, this may result in a self-love that never gets to the loving of others. To be sure, a low self-image plagues and even cripples many folks today, and our highly competitive society often adds to their burden, but many of them can be helped through psychotherapy, pastoral counseling, and caring small groups. But a low self-image need not be a block to loving others and certainly is never an excuse for failure to do so.

As a matter of fact, I'm convinced that one of the best ways to deal with a negative self-image is to act intentionally in love toward someone else, no matter how one feels about oneself. This is surely what God is calling us to do in this verse. The literal meaning of the Hebrew does *not* mean that we are to love others *just* as we love ourselves, but, rather, that we are to love others as people *like* ourselves: people who are hurting, scared, insecure, guilty, longing to be noticed, loved, and cared for. Far from an invitation to preoccupation with how we feel about ourselves, this is a mandate to self-giving love. It really translates into what we have come to call the Golden Rule: "Whatever you want men to do to you, do also to them" (Matt. 7:12).

As a pastor, I have been invited into the painful struggles of count-less people, many of whom are crippled by difficulties with self-image. I've walked alongside Harold for a number of years. Seldom have I known anyone with such a low view of personal worth. Psychi-atric hospitalization, psychotherapy, and a small group of fellow be-lievers have all been helpful to him in his struggle for a wholesome sense of self-worth. But he told me that the greatest single source of joy in his entire journey is when he gives of himself to others through intentional acts of service or caring. "It may sound crazy," he said to a friend, "but sometimes when I'm feeling most worthless, I seek some way to help someone who's in need, and I'm helped in helping them."

I'm absolutely convinced that loving one's neighbor as another human being just like oneself is a necessity built into the grain of our being by God. And that means regarding our enemies in the same way, whether they live next door or on another continent. I'm further convinced that one good road toward an improving self-image is in serving and helping others.

Trivia and Practicum

19 'You shall keep My statutes. You shall not let your livestock breed with another kind. You shall not sow your field with mixed seed. Nor shall a garment of mixed linen and wool come upon you.

20 'Whoever lies carnally with a woman who *is* betrothed as a concubine to *another* man, and who has not at all been redeemed nor given her freedom, for this there shall be scourging; *but* they shall not be put to death, because she was not free.

21 'And he shall bring his trespass offering to the LORD, to the door of the tabernacle of meeting, a ram as a trespass offering.

22 'The priest shall make atonement for him with the ram of the trespass offering before the LORD for his sin which he has done. And the sin which he has done shall be forgiven him.

23 'When you come into the land, and have planted all kinds of trees for food, then you shall

count their fruit as uncircumcised. Three years it shall
be as uncircumcised to you. *It* shall not be eaten.

24 'But in the fourth year all its fruit shall be holy,
a praise to the LORD.

25 'And in the fifth year you may eat its fruit, that it
may yield to you its increase: I *am* the LORD your God.

26 'You shall not eat *anything* with the blood, nor
shall you practice divination or soothsaying.

27 'You shall not shave around the sides of your
head, nor shall you disfigure the edges of your beard.

28 'You shall not make any cuttings in your flesh
for the dead, nor tattoo any marks on you: I *am* the LORD.

29 'Do not prostitute your daughter, to cause her
to be a harlot, lest the land fall into harlotry, and the
land become full of wickedness.

30 'You shall keep My Sabbaths and reverence My
sanctuary: I *am* the LORD.

31 'Give no regard to mediums and familiar
spirits; do not seek after them, to be defiled by them: I
am the LORD your God.

32 'You shall rise before the gray headed and
honor the presence of an old man and fear your God:
I *am* the LORD.

33 'And if a stranger sojourns with you in your
land, you shall not mistreat him.

34 '*But* the stranger who dwells among you shall
be to you as one born among you, and you shall love
him as yourself; for you were strangers in the land of
Egypt: I *am* the LORD your God.

35 'You shall do no injustice in judgment, in
measurement of length, weight, or volume.

36 'You shall have just balances, just weights, a
just ephah, and a just hin: I am the LORD your God,
who brought you out of the land of Egypt.

37 'Therefore you shall observe all My statutes and
all My judgments, and perform them: I *am* the LORD.'"

Lev. 19:19–37

Commentaries on Leviticus give various names to this section,
ranging from "Miscellaneous Regulations" to "Principles of Neigh-
borliness" to "A Practical Handbook." To us, some of these codes

might seem more likely to be found in a game of Trivial Pursuit, while others are quite practical, even today.

The transition from loving one's neighbor (19:18) to not letting *"your livestock breed with another kind"* (19:19) might well bring a grin, even to the most serious among us. That injunction, followed by commands not to *"sow your field with mixed seed,"* nor to wear a *"a garment of mixed linen and wool,"* tend to baffle us. As trivial as these mandates may seem to us, they were of enough significance to them to be included in the Scriptures. Holiness, as we have seen, meant separateness and purity. These regulations were expressions of purity in every realm. We must not overlook the fact that God is portrayed as being concerned with all of the details of our lives, even those which to us may seem almost routine and trivial.

Adultery comes into the picture again (19:20–22), this time in a case involving a free man and a slave woman who have slept together though she had been promised to another man. On technical grounds, a sin offering was to be substituted for the death penalty, because the woman had not yet been given her freedom, and, presumably, there was an intention for marriage all along. Such technicalities are beyond our understanding, though we cannot miss the fact that sexual relationships outside of marriage are never condoned.

The law about eating the fruit of fruit trees (19:23–25) may exist because the fruit in the initial years of a tree does not reach its full potential. The fruit of the fourth year—the initial year of its mature production—is regarded as belonging solely to God. This is another of the constant reminders that everything we are and have belongs to God, so vital to our understanding of stewardship.

Linked to the prohibition of eating meat from which the blood has not been properly drained (v. 26), is the ban against divination and soothsaying. The cultures around them abounded in magic and incantations for every imaginable reason, including the control of nature and the prediction of the future. The Hebrews were expressly forbidden to practice any kind of magic. God's will was to be revealed to them through the words of the prophets or through the priests with the Urim and Thummim (Exod. 28:29–30; Lev. 8:8).

Verses 27–28 are generally taken to refer to cultic mourning practices in pagan culture. They were not denied the right to mourn in times of loss and grief, but any rituals that might involve the disfiguring of their God-given bodies were considered trespasses against

225

God. This view of the sanctity of the body was certainly instrumental in the striking metaphor of Paul likening the body of the believer to a temple of the Holy Spirit, a place in which God dwells (1 Cor. 6:19–20).

Verses 29–30 can be linked, since both emphasize reverence for the central place of worship. Temple prostitutes were in abundance among many ancient religions, but the people of Israel were to be totally different in this matter because of their high view of human sexuality and dignity. Referring again to Paul's metaphor of the body as a temple of the Holy Spirit, this temple must be kept free from all sexual impurity.

Verse 31 confronts the practice of calling up spirits from the dead to seek guidance for the future. Even Saul, who had banned such practices in Israel, when confronted with the silence of God as he faced the awesome might of the Philistines from his encampment at Gilboa, disguised himself and sought the counsel of the witch at Endor. To our perplexity, Samuel was raised by the witch, only to give Saul a scathing message for his disobedience, not in consulting the medium, but in having failed to carry out God's total wrath against the Amalekites (1 Sam. 28:1–25). Is there any substance to the claims of mediums and witches? Whether there is or not, the people of God are to have nothing to do with them.

The command to respect the elderly as an act of reverence to God in verse 32 needs to be heard in every age. One suspects that Asian culture has done better with this than have we. How wise the proverb: "Listen to your father who begot you, and do not despise your mother when she is old. Buy the truth, and do not sell it, also wisdom and instruction and understanding. The father of the righteous will greatly rejoice, and he who begets a wise child will delight in him. Let your father and mother be glad, and let her who bore you rejoice" (Prov. 23:22–25).

Verses 33–34 apply the truth of "loving your neighbor as yourself" to the alien living among them. They are never to forget that at one time they were aliens in Egypt and treated very poorly. When I was a drill instructor in the Marine Corps, some of the toughness dished out was, indeed, designed to instill the kind of obedience essential both for survival and success in combat. But I've never been convinced that some of it was not also produced by a sense of "this is what they did to me; now I'm going to do it to you!" How different from the spirit of this command which says, "remember how poorly you were treated; now treat others with love and kindness!"

Verses 35–36 call for honesty and integrity in the marketplace as a badge for the people of God. Amos had scathing words for those who were circumspect about keeping Holy Days and Sabbaths and yet were quick to boost prices dishonestly and to cheat with dishonest scales and measures as a means of profiting at the expense of the poor (Amos 8:4–6). The track record of American businesses in recent years, even in doing business with the government, to say nothing of the poor, hasn't been all that admirable. Not infrequently, the decisions that shape those practices are made by men and women who frequent our churches.

The chapter closes with verse 37, a summary appeal to obedience, often repeated in Leviticus.

While some of these laws have no possible validity for us because of vast changes across the centuries, the central principle remains timeless: love for God and neighbor must be the governing principle in all of our relationships and activities.

PENALTIES FOR DISOBEDIENCE

20:1 Then the LORD spoke to Moses, saying,
2 "Again, you shall say to the children of Israel: 'Whoever of the children of Israel, or of the strangers who sojourn in Israel, who gives *any* of his descendants to Molech, he shall surely be put to death. The people of the land shall stone him with stones.
3 'I will set My face against that man, and will cut him off from his people, because he has given *some* of his descendants to Molech, to defile My sanctuary and profane My holy name.
4 'And if the people of the land should in any way hide their eyes from the man, when he gives *some* of his descendants to Molech, and they do not kill him,
5 'then I will set My face against that man and against his family; and I will cut him off from his people, and all who prostitute themselves with him to commit harlotry with Molech.
6 'And the person who turns after mediums and familiar spirits, to prostitute himself with them, I will set My face against that person and cut him off from his people.

7 'Sanctify yourselves therefore, and be holy, for I *am* the LORD your God.

8 'And you shall keep My statutes, and perform them: I *am* the LORD who sanctifies you.

9 'For everyone who curses his father or his mother shall surely be put to death. He has cursed his father or his mother. His blood *shall be* upon him.

10 'The man who commits adultery with *another* man's wife, *he* who commits adultery with his neighbor's wife, the adulterer and the adulteress, shall surely be put to death.

11 'The man who lies with his father's wife has uncovered his father's nakedness; both of them shall surely be put to death. Their blood *shall be* upon them.

12 'If a man lies with his daughter-in-law, both of them shall surely be put to death. They have committed perversion. Their blood *shall be* upon them.

13 'If a man lies with a male as he lies with a woman, both of them have committed an abomination. They shall surely be put to death. Their blood *shall be* upon them.

14 'If a man marries a woman and her mother, it *is* wickedness. They shall be burned with fire, both he and they, that there may be no wickedness among you.

15 'If a man mates with a beast, he shall surely be put to death, and you shall kill the beast.

16 'If a woman approaches any beast and mates with it, you shall kill the woman and the beast. They shall surely be put to death. Their blood *is* upon them.

17 'If a man takes his sister, his father's daughter or his mother's daughter, and sees her nakedness and she sees his nakedness, it *is* a wicked thing. And they shall be cut off in the sight of their people. He has uncovered his sister's nakedness. He shall bear his guilt.

18 'If a man lies with a woman during her sickness and uncovers her nakedness, he has discovered her flow, and she has uncovered the flow of her blood. Both of them shall be cut off from their people.

19 'You shall not uncover the nakedness of your mother's sister nor of your father's sister, for that would uncover his near of kin. They shall bear their guilt.

20 'If a man lies with his uncle's wife, he has uncovered his uncle's nakedness. They shall bear their sin; they shall die childless.

21 'If a man takes his brother's wife, it *is* an unclean thing. He has uncovered his brother's nakedness. They shall be childless.

22 'You shall therefore keep all My statutes and all My judgments, and perform them, that the land where I am bringing you to dwell may not vomit you out.

23 'And you shall not walk in the statutes of the nation which I am casting out before you; for they commit all these things, and therefore I abhor them.

24 'But I have said to you, 'You shall inherit their land, and I will give it to you to possess, a land flowing with milk and honey." I *am* the LORD your God, who has separated you from the peoples.

25 'You shall therefore distinguish between clean beasts and unclean, between unclean birds and clean, and you shall not make yourselves abominable by beast or by bird, or by any kind of living thing that creeps on the ground, which I have separated from you as unclean.

26 'And you shall be holy to Me, for I the LORD *am* holy, and have separated you from the peoples, that you should be Mine.

27 'A man or a woman who is a medium, or who has familiar spirits, shall surely be put to death; they shall stone them with stones. Their blood *shall be* upon them.'"

Lev. 20:1-27

As is apparent, this chapter prescribes the punishments for the violation of some of the laws in the previous chapters of the Holiness Code. These punishments seem extremely harsh to us moderns, if not contradictory to the spirit of Jesus himself. To many today, capital punishment is inhumane and unacceptable. The execution of people for worshiping a foreign god, for cursing parents, for adultery and other sexual sins, for homosexual acts, and for witchcraft would seem to be unduly severe and without redeeming potential. I know of no one who advocates capital punishment for anything other than the most heinous of violent crimes which take or incapacitate human life. In this chapter, other sins have less severe penalties ranging from being cut off from the community (presumably a form of banishment) to being doomed to childlessness, both considered horrible punishments in their time.

The chapter begins with the establishment of death by stoning for anyone giving a child to Molech (vv. 2–5). Though the law was placed in the middle of chapter 18, it is given prominence here. The execution is to be done by the people of the community, emphasizing that such an act as child sacrifice to a foreign god is a threat to the entire community. It is further stated that such a practice is also a desecration of the tabernacle and a profanation of God's name. The enforcement of this matter is the responsibility of the entire community, and anyone failing to report this offense makes himself and his family liable to being cut off from their people. A puzzling aspect of the punishment is in the statement that the person guilty of child sacrifice to Molech will be cut off from his people *after* being stoned to death. This may indicate that the cutting off had greater implications than banishment from the nation, such as eternal separation from God's people.

Turning to mediums and spiritists (v. 6) is called the prostitution of one's self and will result in being cut off from one's people.

Verses 7–8 insert the repeated formula calling for obedience grounded in the recognition of God's sovereignty and goodness.

Verses 9–21 list the penalties for violations of most of the laws given in chapter 18. Some commentators point out that we have no way of knowing how often the death penalty was actually carried out against such offenders, suggesting that this might have been equivalent to our "maximum" and "minimum" sentences. The death penalty is prescribed for one who curses father or mother. Obviously, this had to do with more than uttering a few oaths against one's parents. This must have meant a perpetual rejection of parental authority and respect, a literal demeaning of one's parents, totally detrimental to family life and thus to the community. The central place given to the recognition of parental authority, along with the responsibility this places upon parents, is consistently affirmed throughout the Scriptures. Paul articulated this conviction clearly and eloquently when he wrote to the church in Ephesus: "Children, obey your parents in the

Lord, for this is right. 'Honor your father and mother,' which is the first commandment with promise: 'that it may be well with you and you may live long on the earth.' And you, fathers, do not provoke your children to wrath, but bring them up in the training and admonition of the Lord" (Eph. 6:1-4).

As with much of Leviticus, we simply have to face the fact that it's different for us than it was for the Hebrews. It makes all of the difference in the world when you live in a culture that does not support parental authority. It's as though the tone was set back in the 1950s when the slogan became vogue, "There are no bad kids, just bad parents." And thus began the development of what someone called teenage tyranny. For all too many parents, there must be the sense of having all of the responsibility but little of the authority. Somehow, we must break this pattern, and I can't think of any better place than in our churches — not by trying to replace teenage tyranny with parental tyranny, but by eliminating all tyranny. Our resource is the power of love. We must help one another in learning what love really looks like and feels like, as we learn it in the light of God's love. We must help parents and children alike learn in experience "the more excellent way" that Paul celebrates in 1 Corinthians 13. And let's be careful that we always do this in realistic ways that recognize that we live in a fallen and broken world in which the active power of sin and evil is as present as it was in the world of the Bible. Sometimes, beyond our understanding, the best of parental love is met with rejection. Across the years, I've seen some of the best kids coming from what appear to be the worst family situations, just as I've seen some of the worst kids coming from what appear to be the best homes. Within the family of the church we need to be careful lest we place a burden of guilt and failure upon each other for our children who choose the way of rebellion. Since we're not likely to advocate the death penalty for our young rebels, let's hold on to each other and love them, love them, love them — they just may return, like the younger son in Jesus' parable (Luke 15).

Verses 10-21 prescribe the penalties for twelve of the violations of sexual deviations named in chapter 18. Adultery with a neighbor's wife (v. 10) is punishable by the death of both persons involved, which makes us wonder why only the woman caught in the act of adultery was brought to Jesus (John 8:1-11). Sexual relations with a man's stepmother or daughter-in-law (vv. 11-12) likewise warrant the death penalty for both parties. Sexual intimacy between two males (v. 13) is punishable by the death of both men. The punishment prescribed for a man who marries both a mother and her daughter (v. 14) is death by burning for all three. The same punishment is indicated for the daughter of a priest who becomes a prostitute (Lev. 21:9). This means of punishment is seen elsewhere in the Bible. In Genesis 38:24, the death of Tamar by burning is called for by Judah when confronted with the pregnancy of his daughter-in-law. The sentence was suspended, however, when Judah's own complicity was revealed. In the intrigue surrounding Samson, the Philistines burned his wife and her father to death (Judg. 15:1–8). And we have a reference to cremation, when the bodies of Saul and his sons were taken down from the wall of Beth-Shean and burned.

Both men and women who relate sexually to animals (vv. 15–16) are to be put to death with the animals. The "cutting off" penalty is prescribed for both parties in a marriage of a man and his stepsister (v. 17), and for both persons having sex during the menstrual period (v. 18). In the latter case, we see again the sense of mystery related to blood, even the normal flow of blood during the menstrual period. Sexual relationships with a stepsister are further discouraged (v. 19), but with no physical punishment. If a man sleeps with his aunt (v. 20), the penalty is childlessness for both, as is the penalty for a man marrying his brother's wife (v. 21). The final punishment is given in verse 27: death by stoning for mediums or spiritists.

What do we do with this chapter? This is a tough question for all who affirm the Scriptures as the word of God to us. The fact is that we, by and large, have simply chosen to ignore this part of the Bible, or consigned it merely to historical interest. And I might say that I'm grateful. I would rebel against being the enforcer and executor of these sentences. I'm afraid that literal enactment of these penalties would reduce the population of our communities rather drastically, to say nothing of church membership.

The best way that I have found to read this chapter with any sanity and meaning is to read it in the light of verses 22–26. Here is a reprise of the theme of holiness as measured by separateness from the pagan culture. The issue was clear. They were to move into the land of the Canaanites and be different from them. Any violation of that difference was a matter of utmost gravity, with punishment to match. Adoption of pagan practices or the least absorption of such customs was to be strenuously avoided. The punishment, to them, was fitting to the crime. To hold that such punishments were therefore prescribed for all subsequent times and places is, to me, unwarranted and certainly not substantiated by Jesus. Above all, they were to make constant and continuing distinctions between the clean and the unclean, the holy and the profane. "you shall be holy to Me, for I the LORD am holy, and have separated you from the peoples, that you should be Mine" (v. 26).

In his handling of the embarrassing situation with the woman taken in the very act of adultery (John 8:1–11), with due respect for the textual problem, Jesus departed radically from the law. According to tradition, the woman (as well as the man who had been conveniently overlooked by these male enforcers) was to be stoned to death. Jesus tied the execution of the death sentence to the moral purity of the executioners. The woman was set free.

RULES FOR THE PRIESTS' BEHAVIOR

21:1 And the LORD said to Moses, "Speak to the priests, the sons of Aaron, and say to them: 'None shall defile himself for the dead among his people,

2 'except for his relatives who are nearest to him: his mother, his father, his son, his daughter, and his brother;

3 'also his virgin sister who is near to him, who has had no husband, for her he may defile himself.

4 '*Otherwise* he shall not defile himself, *being* a chief man among his people, to profane himself.

5 'They shall not make any bald *place* on their heads, nor shall they shave the edges of their beards nor make any cuttings in their flesh.

6 'They shall be holy to their God and not profane the name of their God, for they offer the offerings of the LORD made by fire, *and* the bread of their God; therefore they shall be holy.

7 'They shall not take a wife *who is* a harlot or a defiled woman, nor shall they take a woman divorced from her husband; for the priest is holy to his God.

8 'Therefore you shall sanctify him, for he offers the bread of your God. He shall be holy to you, for I the LORD, who sanctify you, *am* holy.

9 'The daughter of any priest, if she profanes herself by playing the harlot, she profanes her father. She shall be burned with fire.

10 'And *he who is* the high priest among his brethren, on whose head the anointing oil was poured and who is consecrated to wear the garments, shall not uncover his head nor tear his clothes;

11 'nor shall he go near any dead body, nor defile himself for his father or his mother;

12 'nor shall he go out of the sanctuary, nor profane the sanctuary of his God; for the consecration of the anointing oil of his God *is* upon him: I *am* the Lord.

13 'And he shall take a wife in her virginity.

14 'A widow or a divorced woman or a defiled woman *or* a harlot—these he shall not marry; but he shall take a virgin of his own people as his wife.

15 'Nor shall he profane his posterity among his people, for I the Lord sanctify him.'"

16 And the Lord spoke to Moses, saying,

17 "Speak to Aaron, saying: 'No man of your descendants in *succeeding* generations, who has *any* defect, may approach to offer the bread of his God.

18 'For any man who has a defect shall not approach: a man blind or lame, who has a marred *face* or any *limb* too long,

19 'a man who has a broken foot or broken hand,

20 'or is a hunchback or a dwarf, or *a man* who has a defect in his eye, or eczema or scab, or is a eunuch.

21 'No man of the descendants of Aaron the priest, who has a defect, shall come near to offer the offerings made by fire to the Lord. He has a defect; he shall not come near to offer the bread of his God.

22 'He may eat the bread of his God, *both* the most holy and the holy;

23 'only he shall not go near the veil or approach the altar, because he has a defect, lest he profane My sanctuaries; for I the Lord sanctify them.'"

24 And Moses told *it* to Aaron and his sons, and to all the children of Israel.

Lev. 21:1–24

Until now, the Holiness Code (17–26) has dealt with the holiness that is to characterize all of the people of God. In chapters 21–22, the focus turns to special requirements for the priests. One did not choose to be a priest. Priesthood was a special calling, ordained by God, in earliest times through a particular family. The office carried special responsibilities, for in the highest sense the priest represented both God to the people and the people to God.

The structure of this chapter is clearly delineated by one phrase that occurs three times, "I the Lord, sanctify them" (vv. 8, 15, and 23). Chapter 21 is also marked by the use of this phrase three times. It is used only one other time, in Lev. 20:8.

In verses 1–8, we are given rules for the priests pertaining to rites of burial and to marriage. These rules are given because " ' "for they offer the offerings of the LORD made by fire, and the bread of their God; therefore they shall be holy. Therefore you shall sanctify him, for he offers the bread of your God. He shall be holy to you, for I the LORD, who sanctify you, am holy" ' " (vv. 6, 8). The emphasis upon the sacrifices as food for God calls for special cleanness and holiness of those who handle the food. Touching any person's dead body made a person ceremonially unclean for seven days (Num. 19:11). Ceremonial bathing was required on the third and seventh days as a condition for reentering the tabernacle, and failure to do so resulted in being "cut off." Thus it was incumbent upon the priest to avoid possible contact with dead bodies, with the exception of his closest relatives, mother, father, son, daughter, brother, or unmarried sister dependent on him. This would mean that a married sister would be taken care of by her husband or his family. The sentence in verse 4 is difficult to translate, but seems best in this context to refer to the priests' exclusion from the burial rites of those related to him by marriage.

We have already seen (19:27–28) that though the shaving and body cutting indicated here (vv. 5–6) were a normal means of mourning in times of grief in that culture, it was not permitted in Israel. Here the same rule for the laity is applied to the priests.

The priest was required to be circumspect in the choice of his wife. He could not marry a woman who had been involved in prostitution nor one who had been divorced (v. 7). We must recall that with temple prostitution a widespread practice in the world around them, many women would have been involved at one time or another.

Thus, the prostitute in this context should not be thought of as the professional "hooker" of ours. Nor should a divorcée be regarded as morally suspect, for in that time a man could divorce his wife for almost any reason with a simple declaration that cast her out. However, to avoid any possible conjecture, the priest was to avoid both of them. This was not a judgment upon particular women but a statement of the special standards of the priesthood. By modern Western standards, this is a most unfair generality, but they didn't live in our time.

Before dealing with special rules for the high priest, the text inserts a word about priests' daughters who become prostitutes (v. 9). Again, remember that the most likely form of prostitution had to do with cultic rituals. However, such a girl was to be burned by fire, a stern and grim reminder to all of the seriousness of such sin. As I have suggested, in our time it is more likely that the priest would be castigated for the behavior of his daughter.

Even stricter standards are placed upon the high priest (vv. 10–15). He is not allowed to indulge even in the simplest form of mourning that involves only messing up the hair or tearing the clothing (v. 10). Such actions would most likely deface the special garments (Exod. 28–29, Lev. 8) and thus call into question his ordination and consecration to that high office. We might observe here that these people, as in other cultures around us, developed outward patterns for expressing their grief. We have discovered in recent years that it is healthy to express such emotions openly and freely.

The high priest is not allowed to risk any contamination by contacting dead bodies, even those of father or mother (v. 10). Thus, he is not even to participate in their burial rites. He must marry only a virgin of his own people (v. 13). This, apparently, stresses the importance of keeping the line of priestly descent absolutely pure. None of his descendants with any physical defect, though born as priests, shall participate in the actual sacrifices (vv. 16–23). They may eat the food and, presumably, perform other services in the tabernacle, but they are strongly and expressly forbidden to approach the curtain or the altar. Not all of the defects listed are capable of contemporary medical identification, but we have seen throughout Leviticus that only that which is without blemish, be it sacrificial animal or the person making the sacrifice, can come before God directly with the offerings. Again, we must be careful here not to regard people with infirmities or disabilities as second-class citizens on the basis of this distinction in the worship rites of the tabernacle. This was a technical matter based upon their understanding of holiness and not a judgment upon the worth or dignity of persons.

Rules for the Sacrifices

22:1 Then the Lord spoke to Moses, saying,

2 "Speak to Aaron and his sons, that they separate themselves from the holy things of the children of Israel, and that they do not profane My holy name *in those things* which they sanctify to Me: I *am* the Lord.

3 "Say to them: 'Whoever of all your descendants throughout your generations, who goes near the holy things which the children of Israel sanctify to the Lord, while he has uncleanness upon him, that person shall be cut off from My presence: I *am* the Lord.

4 'Whatever man of the descendants of Aaron, who *is* a leper or has a discharge, shall not eat the holy offerings until he is clean. And whoever touches anything made unclean *by* a corpse, or a man who has had an emission of semen,

5 'or whoever touches any creeping thing by which he would be made unclean, or any person by whom he would become unclean, whatever his uncleanness may be —

6 'the person who has touched any such thing shall be unclean until evening, and shall not eat the holy *offerings* unless he washes his body with water.

7 'And when the sun goes down he shall be clean; and afterward he may eat the holy *offerings*, because it *is* his food.

8 'Whatever dies *naturally* or is torn *by beasts* he shall not eat, to defile himself with it: I *am* the Lord.

9 'They shall therefore keep My ordinance, lest they bear sin for it and die thereby, if they profane it: I the Lord sanctify them.

10 'No outsider shall eat the holy *offering*; one who sojourns with the priest, or a hired servant, shall not eat the holy thing.

11 'But if the priest buys a person with his money, he may eat it; and one who is born in his house may eat his food.

12 'If the priest's daughter is married to an outsider, she may not eat of the holy offerings.

13 'But if the priest's daughter is a widow or divorced, and has no child, and has returned to her father's house as in her youth, she may eat her father's food; but no outsider shall eat it.

14 'And if a man eats the holy *offering* unintentionally, then he shall restore a holy *offering* to the priest, and add one-fifth to it.

15 'They shall not profane the holy *offerings* of the children of Israel, which they offer to the LORD,

16 'or allow them to bear the guilt of trespass when they eat their holy *offering*; for I the LORD sanctify them.'"

17 And the LORD spoke to Moses, saying,

18 "Speak to Aaron and his sons, and to all the children of Israel, and say to them: 'Whatever man of the house of Israel, or of the strangers in Israel, who offers his sacrifice for any of his vows or for any of his freewill offerings, which they offer to the LORD as a burnt offering —

19 '*you shall offer* of your own free will a male without blemish from the cattle, from the sheep, or from the goats.

20 '*But* whatever has a defect, you shall not offer, for it shall not be acceptable on your behalf.

21 'And whoever offers a sacrifice of peace offering to the LORD, to fulfill *his* vow, or a freewill offering from the cattle or the sheep, it must be perfect to be accepted; there shall be no defect in it.

22 'Those *that are* blind or broken or maimed, or have an ulcer or eczema or scabs, you shall not offer to the LORD, nor make an offering by fire of them on the altar to the LORD.

23 'Either a bull or a lamb that has any limb too long or too short you may offer *as* a freewill offering, but for a vow it shall not be accepted.

24 'You shall not offer to the LORD what is bruised or crushed, or torn or cut; nor shall you make *any offering of them* in your land.

25 'Nor from a foreigner's hand shall you offer any of these as the bread of your God, because their corruption *is* in them, *and* defects *are* in them. They shall not be accepted on your behalf.'"

26 And the LORD spoke to Moses, saying:

27 "When a bull or a sheep or a goat is born, it shall be seven days with its mother; and from the eighth day and thereafter it shall be accepted as an offering made by fire to the LORD.

28 *"Whether it is* a cow or ewe, do not kill both her and her young on the same day.

29 "And when you offer a sacrifice of thanksgiving to the LORD, offer *it* of your own free will.

30 "On the same day it shall be eaten; you shall leave none of it until morning: I *am* the LORD.

31 "Therefore you shall keep My commandments, and perform them: I *am* the LORD.

32 "You shall not profane My holy name, but I will be hallowed among the children of Israel. I *am* the LORD who sanctifies you,

33 "who brought you out of the land of Egypt, to be your God: I *am* the LORD."

Lev. 22: 1-33

Having given the special rules for the priests, concluding with the physical impediments that would disqualify a priest from actual participation in the sacrifices, the text now addresses questions pertaining to the eating of the food devoted to the priests and the qualities necessary in animals to be used for the offerings.

The chapter is divided in the same way as chapter 21, with the threefold use of the phrase "I the LORD sanctify them," in verses 9, 16, and 32.

No priest in a state of uncleanness is ever to be allowed to offer a sacrifice or to eat priestly food (vv. 2-3). To do so incurs the penalty of being "cut off." The uncleanness may arise from the sources set forth in chapters 11-15, such as serious skin disease, genital discharges, touching a dead body, touching swarming animals, or touching an unclean man (vv. 4-6). The previously required cleansing rites must be observed before the priest can be restored to active participation in the tabernacle services. An additional reminder of the prohibition of eating animals whose death was natural or who had been killed by other animals is appended (v. 8), prior to the recurring phrase, "I the LORD sanctify them" (v. 9).

Verses 10–16 deal with questions concerning who may eat the food that is dedicated to the priests, as described in Leviticus 6–7. You recall that the tithes and parts of the sacrifices were given to the priests as their sole income, since they were not to be allotted land in the distribution after the Conquest. The families of the priests were entitled to share in the food given to them, but definition is needed for who properly constitutes the priest's family. No outsider qualifies, even though employed by the priest (v. 10). A slave purchased by the priest, however, did qualify (v. 11). A priest's daughter who married no longer qualified (v. 12), as she now belonged to the household of her husband. However, if she returned home, widowed or divorced and without children, she was again treated as a member of the priest's family (v. 13). If anyone should eat of the priestly food unintentionally, a like amount must be returned, with a 20-percent penalty added, along with a trespass offering (vv. 14–16). The section concludes with the phrase, "For I the LORD sanctify them" (v. 16).

Physical defects make animals ineligible for sacrifice. This principle has been articulated consistently in chapters 1–4. Just as the priests must be without blemish, so must the animals to be sacrificed. Verses 17–25 list the kinds of imperfections disqualifying the use of particular animals. Blindness, broken bones, cuts, discharges, skin diseases, castration, and damaged animals bought from foreigners are listed. An interesting conjecture is offered by Wenham, based largely on the work of Douglas, that in the thinking of the Hebrews there was a parallel order of animals and humans. This scheme holds that unclean animals are to the animal world what Gentiles are to the world of people, clean animals are like the Hebrews, and unblemished animals are like the priesthood.

Verses 26–30 can be read within the general context of what we today call environmentalism. Animals must be at least eight days old before being sacrificed. A calf or lamb is not to be sacrificed on the same day as its mother (v. 28); an ox or a sheep must not be slaughtered on the same day as its young (v. 29). Other laws, such as in Exodus 23:19, the prohibition from cooking a kid in its mother's milk; Deut. 20:19–20, forbidding the unrestrained chopping of trees; and Deut. 22:6–7, banning the taking of a bird and its eggs, seem to echo a reverence for nature expressed through the reponsible use of its God-given resources. There is a repetition of the necessity of eating the meat of the animals in a timely manner as prescribed more throughly in Leviticus 7. The concluding phrase is repeated, "I am the LORD who sanctifies you (v. 32).

Two things stand out in my mind as I read this section. As one who has the privilege of teaching pastors-in-training in seminary, I am often privy to strong protests about the double standard imposed on the clergy. "Why should we be expected to live up to higher standards than the lay people?" And my answer, quite undemocratic, is deeply rooted in this ancient tradition.

As we have seen in the text, the priests of Israel were not allowed to mourn for the dead the same way as others. Contact with the dead could make one unfit for the assigned round of priestly service. Separate standards for priests also applied to personal relationships. The priest could only marry a particular type of woman, and the high priest could marry only a virgin. Any immorality in the family of a priest was to be punished with severity. All of the priest's domestic relationships were required to be above reproach. Even physical blemishes excluded one from the exercise of priestly ministry. His attention to every detail in the sacrifices was to be undivided.

A higher standard was required of priests because of the unique role of the priesthood. Without relaxing the standards expected of the members of the community, the priests were given a more demanding code. That tradition, in my judgment, must continue in the community of God's people. The ordination vows taken by ministers of the Word (ordained clergy) in every denomination and group that I know require higher standards than those placed upon members of the church. This does not make ministers morally superior to parishioners, but it does require of them a greater accountability to the church and to the Lord. And rightly so!

But if you're not ordained, don't pass this off as of no consequence. For the second reality growing out of the biblical tradition is that all of us are now called to be priests. Recall again Peter's statement: "You are a chosen generation, a royal priesthood" (1 Pet. 2:9). While we have every right to demand higher standards of exemplary living by our clergy leadership, we must never forget that each of us, ordained and nonordained alike, are called to be priests by Christ himself. Thus to each of us, the high standards of priestly ministry are relevant.

One of our men's Bible study groups had become involved in a series of discussions on the differences between the clergy and the laity. According to Al, it was there that he began to undergo a profound change. Al is an attorney who had come to faith in Christ recently. He had first come to our church because his children began attending our Sunday school and asked him to come with them. Considering himself a lifelong atheist (or at least a convinced agnostic), he came for the sake of the kids, certain that he was quite immune to anything that might be going on in the religious establishment. He was impressed, however, with the fact that these people were not only intelligent and normal, but that they were clearly enthused about being part of the church. His attendance became more regular, and he began to observe and listen with much more interest.

He made an appointment with me for a conversation and asked for some guidance in exploring the faith. We began meeting together around some agreed-upon reading of both the Bible and C. S. Lewis. His interest grew to the point of joining with a group of men, through which he came to a deep commitment to Christ. Before long he was baptized and joined the church.

He then experienced a major change in thinking and living through a discussion on clergy and laity. It was there that he realized his own call to the priesthood, as a minister of Jesus Christ in his legal practice. It's challenging to hear him describe how he now sees and relates to his clients as he views them through his "priestly" perspective. When appropriate, he shares his faith with clients and colleagues, and he devotes regular hours to a free legal clinic, providing legal services for needy people.

Why all this emphasis upon high and holy standards for all of God's priests? The closing sentence of each of the four concluding verses of chapter 22 states only: "I am the LORD." We are called to be holy because God is the Lord. No other reasons need be given. Welcome to the priesthood!

THE PATTERN FOR WORSHIP

Having covered the sacrifices and the priesthood, and the regulations for ceremonial and moral holiness, the people of God are now given a structure for regular worship beginning with the weekly

Sabbath and providing for special celebrations throughout the year along with periodic festivals over the years.

As we journey through these fascinating chapters (23–25), we need not only become more familiar with the patterns of the worship of Israel, but we do well to examine our own patterns of worship and celebration to enhance our own walk with God and our service in the world.

Through the centuries, various Christian traditions have developed similar patterns and cycles of worship, often called the liturgical or church year. Beginning with Advent and continuing through Christmas, Epiphany, Lent, Holy Week, Easter, and Pentecost, the liturgical year celebrates the full meaning of the Gospel.

In these chapters of the Holiness Code, the pattern for the worship of Israel is established. The number seven provides the basis for the entire scheme of things, for to the Hebrews seven was the perfect number, the number of completion and wholeness. We well know that in the creation stories of Genesis it was on the seventh day that God completed the creation, declared it to be very good, and rested. Thus, the seventh day of each week was the fundamental time for worship, rest, and renewal. The fourteenth day (two sevens) of the first month of the year was to be set aside for the Passover, the beginning of their "liturgical year." This was followed by the seven-day Feast of Unleavened Bread. Seven weeks (fifty days) after this feast came Pentecost, variously called Firstfruits or the Feast of Weeks. During the seventh month, considered the most sacred month, three special celebrations were held: on the first day, the Feast of Trumpets; on the tenth day, the Great Day of Atonement; and on the fifteenth day, the seven-day Feast of Tabernacles.

As periodic observances, every seventh year was to be observed as a Year of Sabbath, during which time the land was to remain fallow for rest and renewal. After seven seven-year periods, the design called for a Year of Jubilee, the crown of the entire cycle.

The Sabbath

23:1   And the Lord spoke to Moses, saying,
2   "Speak to the children of Israel, and say to them: 'The feasts of the Lord, which you shall proclaim *to be* holy convocations, these *are* My feasts.

3 'Six days shall work be done, but the seventh
day *is* a Sabbath of solemn rest, a holy convocation.
You shall do no work *on it*; it *is* the Sabbath of the
LORD in all your dwellings.

Lev. 23:1–3

Verses 1–2 serve as the introductory statement to this chapter
which concludes with the words, "So Moses declared to the children
of Israel the feasts of the LORD" (23:44). The reiteration of the Sabbath
law (v. 3) is a reminder that the cornerstone of the entire worship life
of Israel is the Sabbath.

All of the special days and seasons of worship are called "holy
convocations" or "sacred assemblies." Basic and central to each of
them was the observance every week of the Sabbath. On this day, no
work was to be done, and special focus was to be placed upon the
worship of God, personally and collectively. There is reason to believe
that the Sabbath principle was a source of special joy to these people
who had been driven to endless toil as slaves in Egypt. Imagine the
luxury of being given one full day for rest, worship, and renewal. Far
from a burden, the Sabbath was initially a very special gift of joy. The
only other day in which no work was to be done was the annual Day
of Atonement.

Sadly, with the passage of time, the Sabbath was made into a
troublesome thing, bound with numerous, perhaps more than 400,
rules and regulations defining what could and couldn't be done.
Ultimately the real purpose of the Sabbath was lost.

For Christians, it was natural for the first day of the week, the day
of Christ's resurrection, to become the Sabbath. Early, it came to be
called the Lord's Day, the day set aside each week for personal and
corporate worship, rest, and renewal.

In our own culture, Sundays became loaded with the baggage of
rules and regulations by well-meaning Christians, making it into a
day of heaviness and boredom, rather than discovering its intended
joy and renewal. And now the pendulum has swung about as far as
possible the other direction for perhaps the vast majority of Christians, for whom the day is devoid of deep spiritual intention and
focus. To absent ourselves regularly from the gathered worship of the
Christian community is to forfeit the potential for renewal that God
intends for us. And to become absorbed in activities of whatever kind,

to the exclusion of personal prayer, worship, and renewal, is to deprive oneself of this God-given privilege. The recovery of the potential of the Sabbath principle must become a high priority if there is to be genuine spirituality and renewal within and among us.

Perhaps those of us most in need of such a recovery are clergy men and women. It didn't occur to me until after many years in the pastorate that Sundays were not exactly Sabbath rests for me or for my family. My clergy colleagues will know exactly what I mean when I say that Sunday for us begins in earnest sometime on Saturday afternoon or evening and continues through Sunday night. I have yet to find a way to teach or preach with conviction and passion on Sunday that does not absorb most of my energy and concentration during that twenty-four-hour span. To be sure, it is a day of joyous celebration and worship with the people of God, but when you carry a large measure of responsibility for the planning and leadership of the services, it's not the same as for others. I wish I could tell you that I discovered and implemented the perfect solution. I can't because I didn't. A partial solution for me was to schedule regularly a day in the middle of the week to be alone and quiet, a day for prayer, reading, and reflection. It meant getting away from the church and the house, without distractions. That principle of one day in seven for withdrawal has become the practice through which I have discovered part of the rich meaning of the Sabbath as a holy convocation to the Lord.

I'm not satisfied that we ever got there fully with the family. For years, Saturday was the only day that the children were not in school, and the combination of weddings on many Saturday afternoons along with that mounting pressure of Sunday's sermon and additional responsibilities made a family Sabbath rest on Saturday an impossibility. That left what energy I could muster on Sunday afternoon as the only other time, and we never found that our best time for the family. Summer vacations without distractions and occasional long weekends with the family became some of our compensations, along with the constant discipline of trying to be really present when at home. We have been wonderfully blessed, and we're truly pleased with and grateful for each of our young adult daughters (with two delightful grandchildren), but I have to say that we celebrate them by God's grace, in spite of our inability during those years to develop a full day of Sabbath rest and renewal with our family. It is my hope that more frank and open dialogue between pastors and their families and congregations could encourage the development of much more creative approaches to genuine Sabbaths for clergy families.

THE PASSOVER AND THE FEAST OF FIRSTFRUITS

4 'These *are* the feasts of the LORD, holy convocations which you shall proclaim at their appointed times.

5 'On the fourteenth *day* of the first month at twilight *is* the LORD's Passover.

6 'And on the fifteenth day of the same month *is* the Feast of Unleavened Bread to the LORD; seven days you must eat unleavened bread.

7 'On the first day you shall have a holy convocation; you shall do no customary work on it.

8 'But you shall offer an offering made by fire to the LORD for seven days. The seventh day *shall be* a holy convocation; you shall do no customary work *on it.*'"

9 And the LORD spoke to Moses, saying,

10 "Speak to the children of Israel, and say to them: 'When you come into the land which I give to you, and reap its harvest, then you shall bring a sheaf of firstfruits of your harvest to the priest.

11 'He shall wave the sheaf before the LORD, to be accepted on your behalf; on the day after the Sabbath the priest shall wave it.

12 'And you shall offer on that day, when you wave the sheaf, a male lamb of the first year, without blemish, as a burnt offering to the LORD.

13 'Its grain offering *shall be* two-tenths *of an ephah* of fine flour mixed with oil, an offering made by fire to the LORD, for a sweet aroma; and its drink offering *shall be* of wine, one-fourth of a hin.

14 'You shall eat neither bread nor parched grain nor fresh grain until the same day that you have brought an offering to your God; *it shall be* a statute forever throughout your generations in all your dwellings.

Lev. 23: 4–14

The first feast of the annual worship cycle was the celebration of the Passover on the fourteenth day of the first month of their calendar year (at the time of our March/April). It was followed immediately by a seven-day celebration called the Feast of Unleavened Bread. In studying this section, it is essential to read Exodus 12:1–13:16 for the story of the first Passover and the initial giving of the law for keeping the Passover.

From Exodus 12 and 13 it is clear why the Passover begins the year of worship: "this month is to be for you the first month, the first month of your year" (Exod. 12:2). This is like our contemporary saying: "today is the first day of the rest of your life." For them, life began with God's creation, but in a personal sense it began with their deliverance from slavery at the time of the first Passover. Thus, the Passover celebration was to them as Independence Day is to Americans, only much more so. Passover was the time to remember God's sovereign love and goodness. It was the time to rehearse with their children the story of their beginning. "When your children ask you, `What do you mean by this service?' that you shall say, `It is the Passover sacrifice to the LORD, who passed over the houses of the children of Israel in Egypt when He struck the Egyptians and delivered our households'" (Exod. 12:26–27).

Verse 5 assumes that the meaning of the Passover is widely known. The Passover begins before sundown, but it is believed that its observance really began in mid-afternoon, around 3:00 P.M. This would allow more time to kill all of the lambs before dark. The fourteenth day of the first month (Nisan) would ordinarily come during the latter part of March or early part of April in our calendar. Traditionally, it was believed that the Jewish calendar was a lunar calendar with 29 or 30 days in each month, necessitating the addition of an extra month every three years to reconcile the lunar year with the solar year. More recently, it was discovered that the Qumran community (of Dead Sea scroll fame) used a "Jubilees" calendar with a year of exactly 52 weeks (364 days) and with each year beginning on Wednesday (possibly because the sun and moon were created on the fourth day to mark the seasons [Gen. 1:14]). If so, the Feast of Unleavened Bread, the Feast of Trumpets, and the Feast of Tabernacles all began on Wednesdays. The day following Passover (v. 6) marked the beginning of the seven-day Feast of Unleavened Bread. During this entire week, only unleavened bread could be eaten, and all yeast was to be removed from their dwellings, as a remembrance of their hasty departure from Egypt when there had not been time for the normal leavening of bread (Exod. 12:14–20). No normal work was to be done on the first and last days of the feast, and a worship celebration was held on each (vv. 7–8).

Looking ahead beyond the conquest of Canaan, they will bring a sheaf of the first harvest as a wave offering on the day after the Sabbath (vv. 9–11). It is still debated in the Jewish community whether "the day after the Sabbath" means the Sunday after the beginning of the Feast of Unleavened Bread or the day after the first day of the feast when no work was done. The wave offering was to be followed by a burnt offering (v. 12) and the grain and drink offerings (vv. 13–14).

For the Christian, the celebration of the Lord's Supper, Holy Communion, has its roots in the Hebrew Passover. It was at the Passover celebration that Jesus announced his impending death. Imagine the drama and the mystery when, at the Passover meal, "Jesus took bread . . . and said, `Take, eat; this is My body.' Then He took the cup, and when He had given thanks He gave it to them, and they all drank from it. And He said to them, `This is My blood of the new covenant, which is shed for many'" (Mark 14:22–24). Paul captured the full meaning of that memorable Passover: "Christ, our Passover, was sacrificed for us" (1 Cor. 5:7). The meaning of Christ's death can only be understood in the light of the meaning of the Passover. For us, that Passover feast in an upper room in Jerusalem long ago began the new Passover celebration. It is that which Christians celebrate on Maundy Thursday of Holy Week, and it is also celebrated many times daily around the world by believers who "eat the bread and drink the cup" in Jesus' name until he comes again (1 Cor. 11:26). Jesus Christ is our Passover Lamb. And let us not forget to tell our children the meaning of this holy sacrament.

The Firstfruits observance celebrated with the wave offering was used by Paul as a metaphor of Christ's resurrection. Christ's resurrection is portrayed as the assurance of our resurrection yet to come (1 Cor. 15:20–23).

Our understanding and experience of the full meaning of Christ's death and resurrection can only be heightened and enhanced by growing in our knowledge of these beautiful celebrations in Israel's annual worship cycle.

THE FEAST OF WEEKS

15 'And you shall count for yourselves from the day after the Sabbath, from the day that you brought the sheaf of the wave offering: seven Sabbaths shall be completed.

16 'Count fifty days to the day after the seventh Sabbath; then you shall offer a new grain offering to the LORD.

17 'You shall bring from your habitations two wave *loaves* of two-tenths *of an ephah*. They shall be of fine flour; they shall be baked with leaven. *They are* the firstfruits to the LORD.

18 'And you shall offer with the bread seven lambs of the first year, without blemish, one young bull, and two rams. They shall be *as* a burnt offering to the LORD, with their grain offering and their drink offerings, an offering made by fire for a sweet aroma to the LORD.

19 'Then you shall sacrifice one kid of the goats as a sin offering, and two male lambs of the first year as a sacrifice of peace offering.

20 'The priest shall wave them with the bread of the firstfruits *as* a wave offering before the LORD, with the two lambs. They shall be holy to the LORD for the priest.

21 'And you shall proclaim on the same day *that* it is a holy convocation to you. You shall do no customary work *on it. It shall be* a statute forever in all your dwellings throughout your generations.

22 'When you reap the harvest of your land, you shall not wholly reap the corners of your field when you reap, nor shall you gather any gleaning from your harvest. You shall leave them for the poor and for the stranger: I *am* the LORD your God.'"

Lev. 23:15–22

Following the Passover and the Feast of Unleavened Bread, they were to count off seven full weeks after the Firstfruits offering and set aside the fiftieth day for a day featuring special offerings and celebrations, marking the end of the wheat harvest, and called the Feast of Weeks. The New Testament name for this harvest festival was Pentecost, from the Greek word for fiftieth.

As Firstfruits, in connection with Passover, marked the beginning of the barley harvest, the Feast of Weeks marked the conclusion of the wheat harvest (vv. 15–16). Two loaves of freshly baked bread, baked with yeast, were to be presented as a Firstfruits wave offering (v. 17). This was to be accompanied by a burnt offering of seven year-old male lambs, one young bull, and two rams, with accompanying grain and drink offerings (v. 18). Then is to follow a sin offering of a male goat and a peace offering of two year-old lambs, offered as a wave offering with the bread of the firstfruits (vv. 19–20). No regular work is to be done on that day, and a worship celebration is its culmination (v. 21). The lavishness of the sacrifices is fitting for a harvest celebration, a national time of thanksgiving. The section concludes with an amended version of the law of gleaning, for the benefit of the poor (Lev. 19:9–10).

It was on the day of Pentecost that the Holy Spirit was poured out upon the believers in Jerusalem in a special way (Acts 2:1–4). For Christians since then, Pentecost has become a celebration of a different kind of harvest, a celebration of the gracious gift of God's Spirit to the people of the first Christian community, empowering and equipping them for ministry and service throughout the world. It might be called the birthday of the church.

Many Christian traditions refer to Pentecost as Whitsunday. That's because many churches found Pentecost an appropriate time to receive new members into the fellowship. It became traditional for those to be baptized and received into the church to dress in white, symbolizing their cleansing by Christ. Thus, the day came to be called White Sunday, later shortened to Whitsunday.

The Feast of Trumpets

23 Then the LORD spoke to Moses, saying,
24 "Speak to the children of Israel, saying: 'In the seventh month, on the first *day* of the month, you shall have a sabbath-*rest*, a memorial of blowing of trumpets, a holy convocation.

25 'You shall do no customary work *on it*; and you
shall offer an offering made by fire to the LORD.'"

Lev. 23:23–25

No reason is specified for this Feast. The summer was past, and it
was now the seventh month of the worship cycle. Almost four months
had passed since Pentecost. The grapes and olives have been harvested, the hot summer is moderating, and the rains are soon to come.
Now, on the first day of the seventh month, a special day of rest with a
sacred assembly was to be celebrated, announced by the blowing of
trumpets and concluding with a burnt offering. The seventh month
was regarded as the most sacred month, and the Feast of Trumpets
will be followed by three other special celebrations within the month.
The seventh month in the worship cycle was also the first month in
the civil calendar (Tishri), thus the Feast of Trumpets also marked the
New Year—and came to be called Rosh Hashanah. To this day Rosh
Hashanah is the Jewish New Year celebration and occurs during
September/October of our calendar. You will want to review the
joyous description of the celebration of the exiles upon their return to
Jerusalem on the Feast of Trumpets, which they extended for seven
days (Nehemiah 8)! So thrilled were they to be back in their own land
after more than seventy years, and so eager were they to again hear
the Book of the Law that they had Ezra read it to them from daybreak
until noon. As he read, they shouted their "Amens" and wept with
overwhelming joy. And when did this happen? On the first day of the
seventh month!

THE GREAT DAY OF ATONEMENT

26 And the LORD spoke to Moses, saying:
27 "Also the tenth *day* of this seventh month *shall
be* the Day of Atonement. It shall be a holy convocation for you; you shall afflict your souls, and offer an
offering made by fire to the LORD.
28 "And you shall do no work on that same day,
for it *is* the Day of Atonement, to make atonement for
you before the LORD your God.

29 "For any person who is not afflicted *of soul* on that same day, he shall be cut off from his people.

30 "And any person who does any work on that same day, that person I will destroy from among his people.

31 "You shall do no manner of work; *it shall be* a statute forever throughout your generations in all your dwellings.

32 'It *shall be* to you a sabbath of *solemn* rest, and you shall afflict your souls; on the ninth *day* of the month at evening, from evening to evening, you shall celebrate your sabbath."

Lev. 23:26–32

The next of the four seventh-month festivals was the Day of Atonement. We have already studied it in detail in our chapter on Leviticus 16. This came to be the day of days of the entire year of worship. Though, as we have seen, little was said of the scapegoat in the New Testament, I still cling to the idea that the goat ritual must have been an annual event greatly anticipated and celebrated, and certainly enriching to our understanding of Christ as our sin-bearer.

Here there is a strong emphasis on acts of personal denial (vv. 27, 29, 32), presumably through fasting or other confessional actions. Failure to do so requires being "cut off." The day is to be observed strictly as a Sabbath of rest, focusing upon a sacred assembly with burnt offerings. I've often wondered if Jesus might have had this passage in mind when he called people to discipleship with the words, "If anyone desires to come after Me, let him deny himself" (Luke 9:23).

THE FEAST OF TABERNACLES

33 Then the LORD spoke to Moses, saying,

34 "Speak to the children of Israel, saying: 'The fifteenth day of this seventh month *shall be* the Feast of Tabernacles *for* seven days to the LORD.

35 'On the first day *there shall be* a holy convocation. You shall do no customary work *on it*.

36 '*For* seven days you shall offer an offering made by fire to the LORD. On the eighth day you shall have a holy convocation, and you shall offer an offering made by fire to the LORD. It *is* a sacred assembly, *and* you shall do no customary work *on it*.

37 'These *are* the feasts of the LORD which you shall proclaim *to be* holy convocations, to offer an offering made by fire to the LORD, a burnt offering and a grain offering, a sacrifice and drink offerings, everything on its day—

38 'besides the Sabbaths of the LORD, besides your gifts, besides all your vows, and besides all your freewill offerings which you give to the LORD.

39 'Also on the fifteenth day of the seventh month, when you have gathered in the fruit of the land, you shall keep the feast of the LORD *for* seven days; on the first day *there shall be* a sabbath-*rest*, and on the eighth day a sabbath-*rest*.

40 'And you shall take for yourselves on the first day the fruit of beautiful trees, branches of palm trees, the boughs of leafy trees, and willows of the brook; and you shall rejoice before the LORD your God for seven days.

41 "You shall keep it as a feast to the LORD for seven days in the year. *It shall be* a statute forever in your generations. You shall celebrate it in the seventh month.

42 'You shall dwell in booths for seven days. All who are native Israelites shall dwell in booths,

43 'that your generations may know that I made the children of Israel dwell in booths when I brought them out of the land of Egypt: I *am* the LORD your God.'"

44 So Moses declared to the children of Israel the feasts of the LORD.

Lev. 23:33–44

This, the third festival of the seventh month, was a unique seven-day celebration in which they lived in little lean-tos made of branches (booths), symbolic of their lives as nomads during the forty years of their journeys in the wilderness. The name of the Feast of Tabernacles is a bit misleading, since it refers not to the tabernacle as such but to the temporary huts ("booths," "tabernacles") in which they lived for the week.

Beginning on the fifteenth day of this festival month, the first day was to be a Sabbath, with no work to be done, and a sacred assembly to be held (vv. 33–35). Sacrifices are to be made by fire during the next seven days, culminating in another sacred assembly with a burnt offering on the eighth day, also to be observed as a Sabbath without work (v. 36). Verses 37–38 are a parenthetical reminder and summary statement of the laws pertaining to feasts and sacrifices. Verse 39 continues the instructions for the Feast of Tabernacles, indicating it to be a harvest festival, this being the time of the grape harvest. While this certainly reflects their life in Canaan after the Conquest, we must not forget that they were in the Sinai wilderness for forty years and certainly would have developed some cycles for planting and harvesting, as, for example, in Exod. 23:14–19. They were to observe a full Sabbath on the first and the eighth days, and with the choice fruit they were to bring palm fronds and branches from other trees to build "booths" in which they were to live for the week of the feast (vv. 40–42). Living in the booths was to serve as a reminder to their descendants that their progenitors had lived in temporary shelters after they had been delivered from their slavery in Egypt (v. 43).

I encourage you to let your imagination run a bit with this unusual celebration. Living as I do near Pasadena, California, we are accustomed to the camp-out that occurs every year along Colorado Boulevard, the route of the Rose Parade. Thousands of people begin gathering along the parade route two or three days prior, not just to get a front row seat on the curb, but for what they regard as the sheer fun of joining the crowd. Sometimes, the fun is marred by misconduct, but for the most part people just come to enjoy. While the occasion has no relationship to that for which the people of Israel gathered at this feast, I do believe that it can help us catch the flavor of this most celebrative festival.

Living for a week in this camp-out situation was a dramatic reminder of the primitive conditions in which an entire generation of their forebears had lived under Moses on the Sinai peninsula. And what an important reminder it was to them after they had become settled in comfortable homes—and perhaps some in estates—in the land of Canaan.

Some of us in suburbia are discovering that it's a good idea to move away from our comfortable, lavish homes to live in a village, or even barrio, setting to experience what it is like to be homeless or poor. To be sure, we return to our comforts, but at least with a heightened sensitivity to people who live all year long in shacks and hovels. And some, like Millard Fuller and the many volunteers working with Habitat for Humanity, devote more than a little of their time and resources to helping alleviate some of that homelessness in the building of adequate shelter with and for people in need.

HOLY LIGHT AND HOLY BREAD

24:1   Then the LORD spoke to Moses, saying:

2 "Command the children of Israel that they bring to you pure oil of pressed olives for the light, to make the lamps burn continually.

3 "Outside the veil of the Testimony, in the tabernacle of meeting, Aaron shall be in charge of it from evening until morning before the LORD continually; *it shall be* a statute forever in your generations.

4 "He shall be in charge of the lamps on the pure *gold* lampstand before the LORD continually.

5 "And you shall take fine flour and bake twelve cakes with it. Two-tenths *of an ephah* shall be in each cake.

6 "You shall set them in two rows, six in a row, on the pure table before the LORD.

7 "And you shall put pure frankincense on *each* row, that it may be on the bread for a memorial, an offering made by fire to the LORD.

8 "Every Sabbath he shall set it in order before the LORD continually, *being taken* from the children of Israel by an everlasting covenant.

9 "And it shall be for Aaron and his sons, and they shall eat it in a holy place; for it *is* most holy to him from the offerings of the LORD made by fire, by a perpetual statute."

Lev. 24:1–9

These specifics regarding oil for the lamps of the golden candlestick and the bread to be placed upon the table in the tabernacle seem to be out of place, belonging more to the regulations in the opening chapters of Leviticus. They do fill in some details not previously given. And we are reminded that the symbolism of light and bread certainly are a rich part of our experience and understanding of Jesus.

Verses 2–4 are a repetition of the instructions given in Exod. 27:20–21 for both the placing of the golden lampstand outside the curtain of the Holy of Holies and the necessity of keeping the lamps burning at all times. The details of the construction of the lampstand are found in Exod. 25:31–40 and 37:17–24. It was a magnificent treasure with its six branches and seven lamps, made of seventy-five pounds of pure gold! The responsibility for their continual burning is given to Aaron and his sons. This particular of the tabernacle is mentioned in Hebrews 9:2 without comment.

Verses 5–9 describe the making of the Bread of the Presence (v. 5), the placing of the bread on the gold-covered table (v. 6–7), the meaning of the bread (v. 8), and the eating of the bread (v. 9). While the table is described in detail in Exod. 25:23–29 and 37:10–16, this is the first time that instructions are given for the making of the Bread of the Presence. These were large loaves of bread, each being made of four quarts of flour! There were to be twelve of them, presumably symbolic of the twelve patriarchs and tribes of Israel. The table was approximately three feet long and eighteen inches wide. It was also to hold gold plates and dishes, pitchers and bowls for the drink offerings, and the bread. Obviously, the table was quite filled—even overloaded! Presumably, the huge loaves of breads were stacked in two piles. The Bread of the Presence was just that, set out before the Lord each Sabbath as a reminder of the lasting covenant, or presence, of God. This is why it was called the Bread of the Presence (Exod. 25:30, 35:13, 39:36), and the table was called the Table of the Presence (Num. 4:7). The bread was to be eaten by Aaron and his sons as a part of their regular share of the sacrifices. It would appear that these twelve huge loaves would be a good supply of bread each week.

There was an interesting encounter recorded in the New Testament in Mark 2:23–28 (with parallels in Matt. 12:1–8 and Luke 6:1–5). The disciples were observed by the Pharisees picking some heads of grain to eat as they walked through a field on the Sabbath. The Pharisees, angered by this clear violation of Sabbath law, made their complaint to Jesus. Jesus defended the actions of his disciples by citing an occasion when David and some of his companions actually ate the Bread of the Presence (1 Sam. 21:1–6) with the permission of the priest. The only requirement maintained by Ahimelech the priest was that the men be ceremonially clean with regard to abstinence from sexual relations. This, David assured him, was the case since soldiers on missions were not allowed to engage in sex. Jesus argues that since David violated the Levitical law by eating the Bread of the Presence, so Jesus took the liberty of violating the Levitical law by allowing his disciples to "harvest" grain on the Sabbath. In his statement to the Pharisees, Jesus not only puts himself on a par with David, but clearly declares himself above the law of Moses (Mark 2:27). We can hardly be surprised at the violent opposition of the Pharisees to Jesus.

TRAGIC BLASPHEMY

10 Now the son of an Israelite woman, whose father *was* an Egyptian, went out among the children of Israel; and this Israelite *woman's* son and a man of Israel fought each other in the camp.
11 And the Israelite woman's son blasphemed the name *of the* LORD and cursed; and so they brought him to Moses. (His mother's name *was* Shelomith the daughter of Dibri, of the tribe of Dan.)
12 Then they put him in custody, that the mind of the LORD might be shown to them.
13 And the LORD spoke to Moses, saying,
14 "Take outside the camp him who has cursed; then let all who heard *him* lay their hands on his head, and let all the congregation stone him.
15 "Then you shall speak to the children of Israel, saying: 'Whoever curses his God shall bear his sin.
16 'And whoever blasphemes the name of the LORD shall surely be put to death, *and* all the congregation shall certainly stone him, the stranger as well as him who is born in the land. When he blasphemes the name *of the* LORD, he shall be put to death.
17 'Whoever kills any man shall surely be put to death.

18 'Whoever kills an animal shall make it good,
animal for animal.

19 'If a man causes disfigurement of his neighbor,
as he has done, so shall it be done to him—

20 'fracture for fracture, eye for eye, tooth for
tooth; as he has caused disfigurement of a man, so
shall it be done to him.

21 'And whoever kills an animal shall restore it;
but whoever kills a man shall be put to death.

22 'You shall have the same law for the stranger
and for one from your own country; for I *am* the LORD
your God.'"

23 Then Moses spoke to the children of Israel; and
they took outside the camp him who had cursed, and
stoned him with stones. So the children of Israel did
as the LORD commanded Moses.

Lev. 24:10–23

Here is another of the few and unusual narrative sections in
Leviticus, a tragic story of a man who set himself against God and
perhaps tried to influence the community to join in his rebellion. We
must keep this in perspective by noting that the act of the man was
more than a casual swear word. The picture is that of blaspheming the
name of God with a curse, and curses were regarded as having special
power. Here, then, was a serious violation of the commandment
which holds God's name to be holy and sacred, to be used only in
worship and praise. This behavior must be understood as active rebellion designed to remove God from power. The penalty was severe,
but so was the violation.

This sudden return to the form of narrative reminds us of the basic
structure of Leviticus: (1) the statement of laws for life and worship
built upon the narrative of the Book of Exodus, (2) return to the
narrative form in chapters 8–10, (3) continuing statements of the law,
and (4) return to the narrative form here. This story of the blasphemer,
following the giving of the law regarding the lampstand and the
Bread of the Presence, could well illustrate the gravity of desecrating
that which is holy, especially the name of God. Growing out of a fight
in the camp, the son of an Israelite woman and an Egyptian father, for
some reason not stated, cursed the name of God (vv. 10–11). He was
placed in custody by Moses while divine guidance was sought as to

the appropriate disposition of the matter (v. 12). It was concluded that the blasphemer must be stoned to death outside the camp in the presence of and with the participation of the entire community (vv. 13-17). Out of that decision came the teaching of verses 17-22, prior to the record of the stoning of the man (v. 23).

Let us make two essential observations. First, we must remember, as we said earlier, that the violation must have been not just a casual use of a swear word but a serious profanation of the holiness of God through some rebellious action. Second, we must wrestle with the meaning of one of the more controversial statements of Scripture, the *lex talionis*, the classic eye-for-an-eye, tooth-for-a-tooth principle (24:20). Some scholars insist that this principle was intended to limit, not extend punishment. Here, the argument is that the *lex talionis* actually put restrictions on punishment. All too frequently, capital punishment was meted out to some poor person whose crime had been relatively minor. The positive way of looking at the principle emphasizes the just aspect of retribution, namely, that the punishment must not exceed the crime, a radical and most humane departure from many of the horrendous penal systems of the world around them.

To be sure, those who wish to use this passage in support of capital punishment in current political debate, have every right to claim that the Bible is on their side. However, we can't conclude the argument on the basis of this passage alone, because of Jesus. His commentary on this passage was a radical departure from the traditional view: "You have heard that it was said, `An eye for an eye, and a tooth for a tooth.' But I tell you not to resist an evil person. But whoever slaps you on the right cheek, turn the other to him also. If anyone wants to sue you and take away your tunic, let him have your cloak also" (Matt. 5:38-39). Certainly, Jesus is not suggesting that every offender should be allowed to be freed from the responsibility of all punishment and retribution, but neither does He encourage His followers to apply legal principles without mercy and genuine care for the ultimate well-being of the offender.

Certainly, Calvin's basic principle that Scripture must be interpreted in the light of other Scripture must come into play in such an issue as this. The interpretation of Lev. 24:20 is certainly a challenge confronting those opposed to capital punishment. At the same time, I find it more difficult to place Jesus on the side of the argument

supporting capital punishment. We owe it to each other, in this continuing debate among brothers and sisters in Christ, to recognize the
strength of the arguments on both sides, to avoid seeking simple one-
sided answers, and to respect our right to disagree and even work for
opposing causes.

THE SABBATH AND JUBILEE YEARS

The cycle of worship and celebrations included not only the seventh day and the seventh month but the seventh year as a special year.
This was not to become operative until they were settled in Canaan.
Here was to be a special year in which the land was to be renewed (as
in crop rotation) and in which the people would mark an entire year
for celebration and spiritual renewal. This was to be followed, after a
series of seven seven-year periods, by a fiftieth year of Jubilee in
which all land was to be restored to its original owners and all slaves
were to be set free and returned to their own clans. But we have no
record that the Jubilee Year was ever observed or put into practice.

THE SABBATH YEAR

25:1   And the LORD spoke to Moses on Mount Sinai,
saying,
2   "Speak to the children of Israel, and say to
them: 'When you come into the land which I give
you, then the land shall keep a sabbath to the LORD.
3   'Six years you shall sow your field, and six years
you shall prune your vineyard, and gather in its fruit;
4   'but in the seventh year there shall be a sabbath
of solemn rest for the land, a sabbath to the LORD. You
shall neither sow your field nor prune your vineyard.
5   'What grows of its own accord of your harvest
you shall not reap, nor gather the grapes of your
untended vine, *for* it is a year of rest for the land.
6   'And the sabbath *produce* of the land shall be
food for you: for you and your servant, for your
maidservant and your hired servant, for the stranger
who sojourns with you.

7 'for your livestock and the animals that *are* in
your land — all its produce shall be for food.

Lev. 25:1-7

Verse 1 places the giving of this law for the Sabbath Year at Mount
Sinai, a reminder of the initial statement of it in Exod. 23:10–11. There
the emphasis was upon the provision for the poor to get food from the
land during the Sabbath Year, and even for the wild animals to eat
from it what was left. The year was to be regarded as a gift from God
(v. 2) and also as a gift to God, "*a sabbath to the LORD*" (v. 4). There was
to be no sowing or reaping, even of what might grow of itself during
that year (vv. 4–5). Whatever might grow on the land during the year
was to be eaten as acceptable food by owners, servants, hired work-
ers, aliens, livestock, and wild animals. It would seem that this would
have been not only a year of Sabbath rest for the land, as stated in
verse 4, but also as a joyous year of rest for the people as well. This
concept of the Sabbath Year has obviously been the basis for the
Sabbatical Year given to professors in theological seminaries, and in
increasing measure to pastors of congregations.

A significant question raised by the Sabbath Year is resolved in
verses 18–22 of this chapter. The question is rightly raised whether
there will be enough to eat during the seventh year. God's promise is
that there will be an abundance in the sixth year that will be enough
for three years — the sixth, seventh, *and* eighth — while the new crops
are maturing!

THE YEAR OF JUBILEE

8 'And you shall count seven sabbaths of years
for yourself, seven times seven years; and the time of
the seven sabbaths of years shall be to you forty-nine
years.
9 'Then you shall cause the trumpet of the Jubilee
to sound on the tenth *day* of the seventh month; on
the Day of Atonement you shall make the trumpet to
sound throughout all your land.
10 'And you shall consecrate the fiftieth year, and
proclaim liberty throughout *all* the land to all its

inhabitants. It shall be a Jubilee for you; and each of you shall return to his possession, and each of you shall return to his family.

11 'That fiftieth year shall be a Jubilee to you; in it you shall neither sow nor reap what grows of its own accord, nor gather *the grapes* of your untended vine.

12 'For it *is* the Jubilee; it shall be holy to you; you shall eat its produce from the field.

13 'In this Year of Jubilee, each of you shall return to his possession.

14 'And if you sell anything to your neighbor or buy from your neighbor's hand, you shall not oppress one another.

15 'According to the number of years after the Jubilee you shall buy from your neighbor, and according to the number of years of crops he shall sell to you.

16 'According to the multitude of years you shall increase its price, and according to the fewer number of years you shall diminish its price; for he sells to you *according* to the number *of the years* of the crops.

17 'Therefore you shall not oppress one another, but you shall fear your God; for I *am* the LORD your God.

18 'So you shall observe My statutes and keep My judgments, and perform them; and you will dwell in the land in safety.

19 'Then the land will yield its fruit, and you will eat your fill, and dwell there in safety.

20 'And if you say, "What shall we eat in the seventh year, since we shall not sow nor gather in our produce?"

21 'Then I will command My blessing on you in the sixth year, and it will bring forth produce enough for three years.

22 'And you shall sow in the eighth year, and eat old produce until the ninth year; until its produce comes in, you shall eat *of* the old *harvest*.

23 'The land shall not be sold permanently, for the land *is* Mine; for you *are* strangers and sojourners with Me.

24 'And in all the land of your possession you shall grant redemption of the land.

25 'If one of your brethren becomes poor, and has sold *some* of his possession, and if his kinsman-redeemer comes to redeem it, then he may redeem what his brother sold.

26 'Or if the man has no one to redeem it, but he himself becomes able to redeem it,

27 'then let him count the years since its sale, and restore the balance to the man to whom he sold it, that he may return to his possession.

28 'But if he is not able to have *it* restored to himself, then what was sold shall remain in the hand of him who bought it until the Year of Jubilee; and in the Jubilee it shall be released, and he shall return to his possession.

29 'And if a man sells a house in a walled city, then he may redeem it within a whole year after it is sold; *within* a full year he may redeem it.

30 'But if it is not redeemed within the space of a full year, then the house in the walled city shall belong permanently to him who bought it, through-out his generations. It shall not be released in the Jubilee.

31 'However the houses of villages which have no wall around them shall be counted as the fields of the country. They may be redeemed, and they shall be released in the Jubilee.

32 'Nevertheless the cities of the Levites, *and* the houses in the cities of their possession, the Levites may redeem at any time.

33 'And if a man purchases a house from the Levites, then the house that was sold in the city of his possession shall be released in *the Year of* Jubilee; for the houses in the cities of the Levites *are* their posses-sion among the children of Israel.

34 'But the field of the common-land of their cities may not be sold, for it *is* their perpetual possession.

35 'And if one of your brethren becomes poor, and falls into poverty among you, then you shall help him, like a stranger or a sojourner, that he may live with you.

36 'Take no usury or interest from him; but fear your God, that your brother may live with you.

37 'You shall not lend him your money for usury, nor lend him your food at a profit.

38 'I *am* the LORD your God, who brought you out of the land of Egypt, to give you the land of Canaan *and* to be your God.

39 'And if *one of* your brethren *who dwells* by you becomes poor, and sells himself to you, you shall not compel him to serve as a slave.

40 '*But* as a hired servant *and* a sojourner he shall be with you, *and* shall serve you until the Year of Jubilee.

41 'And *then* he shall depart from you, *both* he and his children with him, and shall return to his own family; he shall return to the possession of his fathers.

42 'For they *are* My servants, whom I brought out of the land of Egypt; they shall not be sold as slaves.

43 'You shall not rule over him with rigor, but you shall fear your God.

44 'And as for your male and female slaves whom you may have — from the nations that are around you, from them you may buy male and female slaves.

45 'Moreover you may buy the children of the strangers who sojourn among you, and their families who are with you, which they beget in your land; and they shall become your property.

46 'And you may take them as an inheritance for your children after you, to inherit *them as* a possession; they shall be your permanent slaves. But regarding your brethren, the children of Israel, you shall not rule over one another with rigor.

47 'Now if a sojourner or stranger close to you becomes rich, and *one of* your brethren *who dwells* by him becomes poor, and sells himself to the stranger *or* sojourner close to you, or to a member of the stranger's family,

48 'after he is sold he may be redeemed again. One of his brothers may redeem him;

49 'or his uncle or his uncle's son may redeem him; or *anyone* who is near of kin to him in his family may redeem him; or if he is able he may redeem himself.

50 'Thus he shall reckon with him who bought him: The price of his release shall be according to the

number of years, from the year that he was sold to
him until the Year of Jubilee; *it shall be* according to
the time of a hired servant for him.

51 'If *there are* still may years *remaining*, according
to them he shall repay the price of his redemption
from the money with which he was bought.

52 'And if there remain but a few years until the
Year of Jubilee, then he shall reckon with him, *and*
according to his years he shall repay him the price of
his redemption.

53 'He shall be with him as a yearly hired servant,
and he shall not rule with rigor over him in your
sight.

54 'And if he is not redeemed in these *years*, then
he shall be released in the Year of Jubilee, *both* he and
his children with him.

55 'For the children of Israel *are* servants to Me;
they *are* My servants whom I brought out of the land
of Egypt: I *am* the LORD your God.

Lev. 25:8–55

What could have been more threatening and exciting than such a
year? Nothing could have made a more dramatic statement about
their belief that the land and their possessions belonged to God than
such a Year of Jubilee. This is probably the most radical social and
economic idea in all of the Bible.

Verses 8–13 define and describe the Year of Jubilee. It is clearly an
extension of the principle of the Sabbath into a larger time frame: the
seventh day, the seventh year, and now the year after seven cycles of
seven years. The Hebrew word translated "jubilee" probably comes
from the word for the ram's horn (later called the shofar) which was
the "trumpet" used to herald the beginning of the year. It is of special
significance that the year is to begin on the Day of Atonement, that
special day of new beginnings. Many of us are aware that the words
of verse 10: "Proclaim liberty throughout all the land to all its inhabitants," are inscribed on our Liberty Bell, now housed in Philadelphia.
It was to be a time of family reunions, with each person returning to
the family property of the tribe. And there was to be no sowing or
harvesting during the year. This has raised speculation as to the
feasability of having two years in a row (the Sabbath Year, the forty-

ninth, followed by the fiftieth) without sowing or reaping. Even with the bumper crop promised for the sixth year, it would certainly take some planning ahead to make this viable. Some have suggested a translation of verse 8 in which the Jubilee "year" becomes a cycle of 49 days added to the calendar at the end of the 49 years, which would also have the effect of collating the lunar and solar calendars. While such a theory makes the Jubilee Year more practical, it seems to be unwarranted by the text itself, nor does the adjustment of the calendar by one day per year over 49 years restore the lunar to the solar calendar, which differs by one year in four.

Verses 14–17 establish a most interesting basis for the exchange and selling of land. The price is to be based upon the number of crops left prior to the next Jubilee Year. Thus, land sold during the first year after the Jubilee would be sold for twice the price as land sold during the twenty-fifth year. And land sold during the last year or two prior to Jubilee would be sold for a mere fraction of its original price. Thus, speculative dealing in land was virtually ruled out by the principle of the Year of Jubilee.

Verses 18–22 provide both a general and a specific promise tied to the observance of the Jubilee Year. The general promise is that they will live safely and abundantly in the land that God is giving them if they are faithful to God's laws (vv. 18–19). The specific promise (to which we referred in conjunction with the Sabbath Year) is that God will provide enough in the sixth year to carry them through the seventh and eighth years (vv. 20–22).

Verse 23 gives the rationale for the Jubilee Year. It is to be a reminder that the land belongs to God, not to them. It is also to be a reminder that they are aliens and tenants—guests, as it were—on God's land. To those of us who live in a culture in which the private ownership of land is regarded as an inviolable human right, this concept in Leviticus is radically different. And yet, the basis of Christian stewardship is grounded in this principle that everything belongs to God.

The rights of the redemption of property are established in verses 24–34. If one must sell some property, it is the responsibility of the nearest relative to redeem it (v. 25), presumably to keep the property within the family and tribe. If, however, there is no one to redeem it, but the person is later able to purchase it back, an equitable formula is given by which the property may be redeemed based upon the number of crops (years) that have elapsed, measured by the remaining years to the next Jubilee (vv. 26–27). But if the person who was forced to sell the property is unable to redeem it, the property will not be returned until the Jubilee Year. Houses within walled cities are exceptions to this rule (vv. 29–31), remaining permanently sold. You will recall that the Levites were not to be given land as their own, other than forty-eight specific cities and adjoining pasture land, thus special exceptions were made for them (vv. 32–34), allowing them to redeem their houses at any time and forbidding them to sell any pasture land.

Rules for the redemption of persons who had to sell themselves, and for the purchasing of slaves, are given in the remainder of the chapter (vv. 35–55). In the case of a Hebrew who becomes poor to the point of being incapable of self-support (vv. 35–38), the community is to provide the assistance (as required of them with aliens and strangers) necessary to enable that one to continue living among them. In other words, a Hebrew should never have to sell himself or herself into slavery, for it was from slavery that they had been delivered. Not only were they to assist such persons, but they were to provide interest-free loans and food at actual cost (vv. 36–37). This was mandated on the basis of the oft-repeated statement: "*I am the* LORD *your God, who brought you out of the land Egypt, to give you the land of Canaan and to be your God*" (v. 38).

Verses 39–46 establish principles pertaining to the owning of slaves. Under no circumstances was a Hebrew to become a slave. Even if a Hebrew sold himself or herself to another Hebrew, that person was to be treated not as a slave but as a hired worker, and even then only until the Year of Jubilee, at which time such were to be returned to their own families and tribes (vv. 39–43). Though a Hebrew could, under no circumstances, own another Hebrew as a slave, ownership of slaves was not forbidden. Verses 44–46 allow the ownership of slaves as long as they are from other nations around them, or from among the aliens who had come to live among them (vv. 44–46). Such slaves could be male or female, could be indentured for life, and could be willed to their children as inherited property. This passage, by the way, was the basis of many proslavery sermons preached in the United States in the nineteenth century during the great emancipation debates.

Verses 47–55 deal with the situation in which a Hebrew must sell himself or herself to an alien or stranger who has become rich enough to own slaves. Any Hebrew sold into such slavery must retain the right of redemption, and such redemption should be exercised by a blood relative as soon as possible. Such redemption was to involve a fair financial settlement based upon the number of years remaining to the next Jubilee Year. Even if the Hebrew is not redeemed by someone in the family or tribe, he or she must be released in the Year of Jubilee. Verse 55 gives the emphatic reason for this; namely, every Hebrew is a servant of the Lord, brought out of slavery in Egypt by God, and thus to be slave to no other. Now we can understand with greater appreciation why Paul referred to himself frequently as a slave of Jesus Christ.

In summary, the Jubilee Year would prevent the massive accumulation of wealth by a small portion of the population. If a member of the community lost family land and freedom by falling into debt, restoration was granted in the Jubilee Year. Wealth, in other words, was to be redistributed without injustice or partiality. Many have suggested that the Year of Jubilee would have steered a course between the greedy excesses of unrestrained capitalism and the oppressive control of state communism. As the bottom line, the Jubilee Year was a test of faith in the promises of God. Peace and blessing were promised to those who would keep the Jubilee Year. Foregoing a year's harvest would require faith that God would provide enough in previous and succeeding years to sustain them.

There is little evidence that this radical concept was ever tried on a wide scale. It seems to have been shelved alongside other great ideals never realized because never attempted. Though there is no mention of the Year of Jubilee specifically in the New Testament, we certainly have an intimation of it when Jesus quotes from Isaiah 61 in the synagogue at Nazareth at the beginning of his public ministry (Luke 4:14–21). The closing phrases of the Isaiah passage, "to preach deliverance to the captives and recovery of sight to the blind, to set at liberty those who are oppressed, to preach the acceptable year of the LORD," certainly reflects the principles of the Year of Jubilee. And the early Christian community appears to have been influenced by the basic principles of the Jubilee when, early in their life together, many of them chose to share all of their possessions and goods in order to give to anyone in need. They sold their houses and lands and brought the money to the apostles for distribution (Acts 2:44–45 and 4:32–37). Because of the hypocrisy of Ananias and Sapphira (Acts 5:1–11), the ideal was aborted. But they really tried to develop a community in which all possessions were shared in common so that no one would be in need.

Should the ideal be ignored either because it was never tried or because it didn't work? I hope not! I long to be a part of a fellowship of believers who just might want to take some risks for the adventure of living out this kind of ideal. Maybe it will never work on this side of Christ's return, but it might be worth trying.

As we have walked through these festivals and celebrations of the Hebrew year and beyond, it is my prayer that our vision be renewed regarding the importance of regular worship and festivals as essential to continuing renewal. In recent years in our congregation, we have encouraged our people not only to be present on special Sundays and celebrations in our church year but also to give serious consideration to inviting special friends and neighbors to attend with them. Our culture has exploited our major festivals, Christmas and Easter, and even added a few of their own, such as Mother's Day and Father's Day (and more recently Grandparents' Day). Why shouldn't we piggyback on them for a change and use these occasions to plan special services that might have unusual appeal to our unchurched friends and neighbors?

Skip and Claudia, newly married, had moved next door to one of our church families. Neither had been around a church since their high-school days, and their faith had been pretty much unattended through the years of college and graduate school. When Dave invited Skip, over the backyard fence, to come with them to the Christmas Eve candlelight service, it brought back a warm memory from Skip's adolescence. At a recent new member's class, Skip and Claudia shared how at that service something stirred within them. They could hardly wait for next Sunday to "come home" to church. We hear these stories again and again, and we're convinced that these "holy days" are very important and often very significant to many. We had one family share recently that they first began to "come back" to church because the kids wanted to bring Mom to church on Mother's Day.

BLESSINGS AND CURSES

26:1 'You shall not make idols for yourselves;
neither a carved image nor a *sacred* pillar shall
you rear up for yourselves;

nor shall you set up an engraved stone in your
　　land, to bow down to it;
for I *am* the Lord your God.

2　　You shall keep My Sabbaths and reverence My
　　　sanctuary:
I *am* the LORD.

3　　'If you walk in My statutes and keep My com-
　　　mandments, and perform them,

4　　then I will give you rain in its season, the land
　　　shall yield its produce, and the trees of the
　　　field shall yield their fruit.

5　　Your threshing shall last till the time of vintage,
　　　and the vintage shall last till the time of sowing;
you shall eat your bread to the full, and dwell in
　　　your land safely.

6　　I will give peace in the land, and you shall lie
　　　down, and none will make *you* afraid;
I will rid the land of evil beasts,
and the sword will not go through your land.

7　　You will chase your enemies, and they shall fall
　　　by the sword before you.

8　　Five of you shall chase a hundred, and a hun-
　　　dred of you shall put ten thousand to flight;
your enemies shall fall by the sword before you.

9　　For I will look on you favorably and make you
　　　fruitful, multiply you and confirm My
　　　covenant with you.

10　　You shall eat the old harvest, and clear out the
　　　old because of the new.

11　　I will set My tabernacle among you, and My
　　　soul shall not abhor you.

12　　I will walk among you and be your God, and
　　　you shall be My people.

13　　I *am* the LORD your God, who brought you out of
　　　the land of Egypt, that *you* should not be their
　　　slaves;
I have broken the bands of your yoke and made
　　　you walk upright.

14　　'But if you do not obey Me, and do not observe
　　　all these commandments,

15　　and if you despise My statutes, or if your soul
　　　abhors My judgments, so that you do not

perform all My commandments, but break
My covenant,

16 I also will do this to you:
I will even appoint terror over you, wasting
disease and fever which shall consume the
eyes and cause sorrow of heart.
And you shall sow your seed in vain, for your
enemies shall eat it.

17 I will set My face against you, and you shall be
defeated by your enemies.
Those who hate you shall reign over you, and
you shall flee when no one pursues you.

18 'And after all this, if you do not obey Me, then I
will punish you seven times more for your sins.

19 I will break the pride of your power;
I will make your heavens like iron and your
earth like bronze.

20 And your strength shall be spent in vain;
for your land shall not yield its produce, nor
shall the trees of the land yield their fruit.

21 'Then, if you walk contrary to Me, and are not
willing to obey Me, I will bring on you seven
times more plagues, according to   your sins.

22 I will also send wild beasts among you, which
shall rob you of your children, destroy your
livestock, and make you few in number;
and your highways shall be desolate.

23 'And if by these things you are not reformed by
Me, but walk contrary to Me,

24 then I also will walk contrary to you, and I will
punish you yet seven times for your sins.

25 And I will bring a sword against you that will
execute the vengeance of *My* covenant;
when you are gathered together within your cities
I will send pestilence among you; and you
shall be delivered into the hand of the enemy.

26 When I have cut off your supply of bread, ten
women shall bake your bread in one oven,
and they shall bring back *to you* your bread by
weight, and you shall eat and not be satisfied.

27 'And after all this, if you do not obey Me, but
walk contrary to Me,

28   then I also will walk contrary to you in fury;
      and I, even I, will chastise you seven times for
          your sins.

29   You shall eat the flesh of your sons, and you
          shall eat the flesh of your daughters.

30   I will destroy your high places, cut down your
          incense altars, and cast your carcasses on the
          lifeless forms of your idols; and My soul shall
          abhor you.

31   I will lay your cities waste and bring your
          sanctuaries to desolation, and I will not smell
          the fragrance of your sweet aromas.

32   I will bring the land to desolation, and your
          enemies who dwell in it shall be astonished at it.

33   I will scatter you among the nations and draw
          out a sword after you;
      your land shall be desolate and your cities waste.

34   Then the land shall enjoy its sabbaths as long as it
          lies desolate and you *are* in your enemies' land;
      then the land shall rest and enjoy its sabbaths.

35   As long as *it* lies desolate it shall rest —
      for the time it did not rest on your sabbaths
          when you dwelt in it.

36   'And as for those of you who are left, I will send
          faintness into their hearts in the lands of their
          enemies;
      the sound of a shaken leaf shall cause them to
          flee;
      they shall flee as though fleeing from a sword,
          and they shall fall when no one pursues.

37   They shall stumble over one another, as it were
          before a sword, when no one pursues;
      and you shall have no *power* to stand before
          your enemies.

38   You shall perish among the nations, and the
          land of your enemies shall eat you up.

39   And those of you who are left shall waste away
          in their iniquity in your enemies' lands;
      also in their fathers' iniquities, which are with
          them, they shall waste away.

40   'But if they confess their iniquity and the iniq-
          uity of their fathers, with their unfaithfulness

272

in which they were unfaithful to Me, and that
they also have walked contrary to me,

41 and *that* I also have walked contrary to them and
have brought them into the land of their
enemies;
if their uncircumcised hearts are humbled, and
they accept their guilt—

42 then I will remember My covenant with Jacob,
and My covenant with Isaac and My covenant with Abraham I will remember; I will
remember the land.

43 The land also shall be left empty by them, and will
enjoy its sabbaths while it lies desolate
without them;
they will accept their guilt, because they de-
spised My judgments and because their soul
abhorred My statues.

44 Yet for all that, when they are in the land of their
enemies, I will not cast them away, nor shall I
abhor them, to utterly destroy them and
break My covenant with them;
for I *am* the Lord their God.

45 But for their sake I will remember the covenant of
their ancestors, whom I brought out of the land
of Egypt in the sight of the nations, that I
might be their God:
I *am* the Lord.'"

46 These *are* the statutes and judgments and laws
which the LORD made between Himself and
the children of Israel on Mount Sinai by the
hand of Moses.

Lev. 26:1–46

The concluding chapter of the Holiness Code is typical of ancier
Near East legal treaties which almost always concluded with pa
sages containing blessings upon those who observed them and curs
upon those who did not. We find similar passages in Exod. 23:25–3
Deut. 28:1–68, and Josh. 24:20.

There was little question in Hebrew thinking that to be obedient
God was to procure God's blessing and to be disobedient to God w
to invite God's judgment. They were undoubtedly delighted to

ceive the promise of God's blessing for obedience (vv. 3–13). But they must have shuddered as they received the warnings of God's judgment upon their disobedience (vv. 14–39).

Some prefer to link verses 1–2 with chapter 25, but it can just as well be regarded as an appropriate introduction to this concluding section of the Holiness Code. There is a reminder of the gravity of idolatry in any form and a repetition of the commands to observe the Sabbaths and to maintain the purity of the tabernacle.

Verses 3–13 articulate a series of blessings promised to them for continuing faithfulness and obedience to God. Rain in its season and an abundance of crops is promised first (vv. 3–5). The crops will be so plenteous that they will work throughout the year in a never-ending cycle of planting and reaping, providing all the food they could want as they dwell securely in their land. Peace and military security are promised in verses 6–8, the theme having been introduced in the last phrase of verse 5. Even the lions and bears will be removed from the land, and they will be able to defend themselves from their enemies: five will chase one hundred, and one hundred will chase ten thousand. Isaiah reversed this image, indicating that the faithless people of God would be routed by their enemies, one thousand of them fleeing from one, and all of them fleeing from five (Isa. 30:17). The promise of fruitfulness, both in offspring and in overabundant harvests is given in verses 9–10. Their problem will be surpluses. Verses 11–12 promise the very presence of God among them. Verse 11 could be translated, "I will tabernacle among you." As we have seen throughout Leviticus, the tabernacle was regarded as the dwelling place of God among them, and from the tabernacle, God regularly strolled in their midst. What a beautiful sense of God's presence! The promises conclude with the continuing reminder of God's faithfulness to them in delivering them from Egypt (v. 13), with the delightful concluding thought that they might walk with their heads held high. A powerful base for a healthy self-image is the knowledge that God is our lover and deliverer.

The list of curses for disobedience (vv. 14–45) is more than three times as long as the blessings for obedience. In a fallen and broken world, our proclivity toward disobedience seems to exceed our bent to obedience. Persistence in disobedience and violation of the covenant will be met with emotional and physical disease and the loss of their crops to their enemies who will conquer them (vv. 16–17). In contrast to the promised blessing, they will flee even when no one is pursuing them.

Continuing disobedience (vv.18–21) will bring multiplied punishment *"seven times more."* Seven is the number of completion, as in creation, but here it is reversed to signify complete punishment, as later by John in Revelation with the various series of seven judgments upon the world. The curse of drought is also threatened with the metaphor of an iron sky and bronze soil, making their agricultural endeavors fruitless.

This entire series of curses is based upon God's redemptive love, as is seen in the cycle of verses 18, 21, 27, 36, and 40. The increasing severity of punishment is designed not for retribution and punishment but for correction and redemption. The cycle continues here in verses 21–22. Continuing disobedience will be met with yet another sevenfold increase in afflictions along with attacks upon their children and cattle by wild animals. And yet another multiplication of affliction by seven is threatened for continuing disobedience (vv. 23–26). This is to be accompanied by war, plague, and famine. The disasters will continue to escalate in enormity if disobedience continues (vv. 27–35). In addition to another sevenfold punishment for sins, the devastating effects of war, plague, and famine will multiply, including cannibalism, mass slaughter with corpses stacked upon their idols, destruction of their cities and places of worship, total devastation of the land, and their dispersion to the nations around them. If they desecrate the Sabbath, the land will be left alone to rest and enjoy its Sabbaths after they have been removed (vv. 34–35). And to those few who may yet remain in the land, final destruction is forecast (vv. 36–39). The dramatic promise of verses 7–8 is totally reversed, for now they will flee in panic at the sound of a windblown leaf, and they will run away even when no one is pursuing them. If any are still left, they will merely waste away. What an overwhelmingly sad and somber picture of the end results of the rejection of God's redeeming love!

However! The infinite patience and love of God is still promised to all who will return to God with confession (vv. 40–45). God will never abrogate the covenant with Jacob, Isaac, and Abraham (v. 42). God will remember the covenant, even though they have been carried off to the land of their enemies. Sin must be atoned for, but God will never forget or turn upon God's people. The writer of 2 Chron. 7:14 may have had this passage in mind when, at the dedication of the temple, the word of God to Solomon was recorded: "When I shut up heaven and there is no rain, or command the locusts to devour the land, or send pestilence among My people, if My people who are called by my name will humble themselves, and pray and seek My face, and turn from their wicked ways, then I will hear from heaven, and will forgive their sin and heal their land" (2 Chron. 7:13-14).

The concluding summary for the entire Holiness Code is given in verse 46.

This chapter calls for careful study and interpretation. It must neither be used to incite us to obedience merely for the sake of gaining rewards and blessings nor to make us fearful of disobedience merely to escape God's judgment. We can be certain that God's grace is sufficient to cover all of our sins. Yet we must never presume upon his mercy and grace as though obedience to him is unimportant or as though disobedience is without consequences.

We must always be aware of the tension between the carelessness that can result from taking lightly the demands of God for obedience and the slavish fear that can result from living in fear of God's judgment upon our neglect or failure. We do well to reaffirm our hope in the words of Paul to the believers in Rome, "There is therefore now no condemnation to those who are in Christ Jesus, who do not walk according to the flesh, but according to the Spirit. For the law of the Spirit of life in Christ Jesus has made me free from the law of sin and death" (Rom. 8:1-2).

I never read this chapter or the Holiness Code without recalling the Spanish sonnet ascribed to Francis Xavier (1506–52):

> My God, I love Thee; not because I hope for
>   heaven thereby.
> Nor yet because those who love Thee not are
>   lost eternally.
>
> Thou, O my Jesus, Thou didst me upon the
>   cross embrace;
> For me didst bear the nails, and spear
>   and manifold disgrace.
>
> And griefs and torments numberless, and
>   sweat of agony;
> Yea, death itself; and all for me who was
>   Thine enemy.
>
> Then why, O blessed Jesus Christ, should I
>   not love Thee well?

Not for the sake of winning heaven,
   nor of escaping hell;

Not from the hope of gaining aught,
   not seeking a reward;
But as Thyself hast loved me,
   O ever-loving Lord.

So would I love Thee, dearest Lord,
   and in Thy praise will sing;
Solely because Thou art my God,
   and my most loving King.

CHAPTER SIX

VOWS AND TITHES

LEVITICUS 27

Most commentators agree that it is not at all clear why chapter 27, which deals with vows and tithes, appears in its present position. Chapter 26, with its blessings and curses, would have been the logical conclusion to the book. It is suggested by some that chapter 27 comes here because this is the way it was revealed at Sinai. Others hold that it was a later addition to the Holiness Code. But neither of these views really explains why, in the final editing, these laws on vows and tithes were placed here rather than somewhere else in the book.

One possible view is that chapter 26 constitutes God's vows to the people, promising what God will do for the people in response to their obedience or disobedience. Then, chapter 27 follows with the theme of how men and women make vows and promises to God. It seems best to recognize the difficulty, and that's why I have not included this chapter in the Holiness Code.

VOWS AND TITHES

27:1 Now the LORD spoke to Moses, saying,

2 "Speak to the children of Israel, and say to them: 'When a man consecrates by a vow certain persons to the LORD, according to your valuation,

3 'if your valuation is of a male from twenty years old up to sixty years old, then your valuation shall be fifty shekels of silver, according to the shekel of the sanctuary.

4 'If it *is* a female, then your valuation shall be thirty shekels;

5 'and if from five years old up to twenty years old, then your valuation for a male shall be twenty shekels, and for a female ten shekels;

6 'and if from a month old up to five years old, then your valuation for a male shall be five shekels of silver, and for a female your valuation shall be three shekels of silver;

7 'and if from sixty years old and above, if *it is* a male, then your valuation shall be fifteen shekels, and for a female ten shekels.

8 'But if he is too poor to pay your valuation, then he shall present himself before the priest, and the priest shall set a value for him; according to the ability of him who vowed, the priest shall value him.

9 'And if *it is* a beast such as men may bring as an offering to the LORD, all such that *any man* gives to the LORD shall be holy.

10 'He shall not substitute it or exchange it, good for bad or bad for good; and if he at all exchanges beast for beast, then both it and the one exchanged for it shall be holy.

11 'If *it is* an unclean beast which they do not offer as a sacrifice to the LORD, then he shall present the beast before the priest;

12 'and the priest shall set a value for it, whether it is good or bad; as you, the priest, value it, so it shall be.

13 'But if he *wants* at all *to* redeem it, then he must add one-fifth to your valuation.

14 'And when a man sanctifies his house *to be* holy to the LORD, then the priest shall set a value for it, whether it is good or bad; as the priest values it, so it shall stand.

15 'If he who sanctified it *wants to* redeem his house, then he shall add one-fifth of the money of your valuation to it, and it shall be his.

16 'And if a man sanctifies to the Lord *some part* of a field of his possession, then your valuation shall be according to the seed for it. A homer of barley seed *shall be valued* at fifty shekels of silver.

17 'If he sanctifies his field from the Year of Jubilee, according to your valuation it shall stand.

18 'But if he sanctifies his field after the Jubilee, then the priest shall reckon to him the money due according to the years that remain till the Year of Jubilee, and it shall be deducted from your valuation.

19 'And if he who sanctifies the field ever wishes to redeem it, then he must add one-fifth of the money of your valuation to it, and it shall belong to him.

20 'But if he does not want to redeem the field, or if he has sold the field to another man, it shall not be redeemed anymore;

21 'but the field, when it is released in the Jubilee, shall be holy to the LORD, as a devoted field; it shall be the possession of the priest.

22 'And if a man sanctifies to the LORD a field which he has bought, which is not the field of his possession,

23 'then the priest shall reckon to him the worth of your valuation, up to the Year of Jubilee, and he shall give your valuation on that day *as* a holy *offering* to the LORD.

24 'In the Year of Jubilee the field shall return to him from whom it was bought, to the one who *owned* the land as a possession.

25 'And all your valuations shall be according to the shekel of the sanctuary: twenty gerahs to the shekel.

26 'But the firstling of the beasts, which should be the LORD's firstling, no man shall sanctify; whether *it is* an ox or sheep, it *is* the LORD's.

27 'And if *it is* an unclean beast, then he shall redeem *it* according to your valuation, and shall add one-fifth to it; or if it is not redeemed, then it shall be sold according to your valuation.

28 'Nevertheless no devoted *offering* that a man may devote to the LORD of all that he has, *both* man and beast, or the field of his possession, shall be sold or redeemed; every devoted *offering is* most holy to the LORD.

29 'No person under the ban, who may become doomed to destruction among men, shall be re-deemed, *but* shall surely be put to death.

30 'And all the tithe of the land, *whether* of the seed of the land *or* of the fruit of the tree, *is* the LORD's. It *is* holy to the LORD.

31 'If a man wants at all to redeem *any* of his tithes, he shall add one-fifth to it.

32 'And concerning the tithe of the herd or the flock, of whatever passes under the rod, the tenth one shall be holy to the LORD.

33 'He shall not inquire whether it is good or bad, nor shall he exchange it; and if he exchanges it at all, then both it and the one exchanged for it shall be holy; it shall not be redeemed.'"

34 These *are* the commandments which the LORD commanded Moses for the children of Israel on Mount Sinai.

Lev. 27:1–34

It was often said in the Marine Corps, "There are no atheists in foxholes." Many vows were made to God in the heat of combat. Such practice has a long history, probably as long as human history itself. But all too often such vows are made in the desperation of the moment, and when the crisis has passed, the vows are soon ignored and forgotten. For the people of God, such an attitude toward vows was unacceptable. Thus, in Ecclesiastes stands the warning: "When you make a vow to God, do not delay to pay it; for He has no pleasure in fools. Pay what you have vowed. It is better not to vow than to vow and not pay" (Eccles. 5:4–5).

Verses 2–8 deal with vows in which persons were set apart to God. Apparently this was the vow in which one dedicated oneself to the service of God, literally as a slave to God. In their view, to be a slave to God would have meant working as slaves in the temple, but only the priests and Levites could be so involved. Therefore, they could keep such a vow by paying to the sanctuary for its upkeep and operation a price roughly equivalent to what they would have been worth on the slave market. In that market, different values were placed upon persons according to gender and age, and those values are reflected in verses 4–7.

Considering that the average wage for a worker was about one shekel per month, a range from fifty shekels to three shekels represented a significant commitment at both ends of the scale. The inclusion of children apparently indicates that one could pledge one's entire family to God.

Verses 9–13 deal with the vowing of animals to God. Since animal sacrifice was a regular part of their worship, the vowing of animals was not uncommon. With the vow, a particular animal could be named as the offering for that vow. A strong warning is given in verse 10 against offering an animal of lesser value when the time came to pay the vow. Unclean animals could be offered for a vow, subject to the valuation by the priest.

If the person later decided to purchase the animal back from the Temple, a 20 percent penalty was to apply.

Verses 14–15 deal with the dedication of houses to God. From persons and animals, we now move to the pledging of houses and land. This was a practice in which, as far as we can tell, a house was given to the sanctuary for the priests to do with as they wished. The 20 percent penalty was again applicable if one wished to purchase the house back.

Verses 16–25 deal with the dedication of land to God. Dedication of land was more complicated because of the rule that land reverted to the original family of ownership during the Year of Jubilee. The one who made the vow was expected to redeem the land prior to the Year of Jubilee by paying the 20 percent fee. The original valuation was determined by the priest based upon a formula taking account of the size of the field and the number of years until the next Jubilee. Failure to redeem the land released the land to the priest at the Year of Jubilee. Though the regulations appear to us to be complex, they were clearly designed to control what could have become sharp practice.

Verses 26–29 summarize various regulations. Since firstborn animals already belonged to God, one could not use them in the making of a vow, other than in the case of unclean animals.

The practices of banning and devoting were regarded as being much more sacrosanct than dedicating as a vow. Such practices were held to be irreversible.

Verses 30–33 deal with the tithes. Tithing, giving the first tenth, goes clear back to the patriarchs. When Abraham was met by the mysterious Melchizedek, after being blessed by him, "he gave him a tithe of all" (Gen. 14:20). At Bethel, Jacob made a vow: "If God will be with me . . . of all that You give me I will surely give a tenth to You" (Gen. 28:20–22). Thus, from the earliest times, tithes were regarded as a kind of vow. And the rules governing other vows apply to tithing as well.

Leviticus 27 and the New Testament

The tradition of making vows and tithing is obviously assumed in the New Testament as a part of the life of the people of God. Luke relates that Paul had his hair cut off before sailing for Syria because of a vow he had taken (Acts 18:18). In Jerusalem, to demonstrate that he was not advocating the abandonment of Mosaic customs, Paul joined four others who had taken a vow and shared in the purification rites, which involved shaving their heads (Acts 21:17-26). Jesus affirmed the Pharisees for giving tithes, but rebuked them for neglecting justice, mercy, and faithfulness (Matt. 23:23). Vows and tithes were normal parts of their lives.

While the specific ways and means of vowing are no longer of conceivable duplication, is there not still a fundamental principle for us growing out of these ancient traditions? Do we not tend to take our vows too lightly? Is there one of us who has not made some promises to God in a time of crisis which we failed to keep?

Perhaps our greatest loss is in the area of vows that are broken between persons. One of my heroes in the world of athletics was Branch Rickey, major league baseball executive and innovator. Indeed, the world was much simpler in the 1940s and 1950s when Rickey was in his prime, but he was always known to keep his word. No one ever accused him of reneging on a commitment, whether or not it was in writing. I recall one of his sharpest competitors saying of him, "His handshake is as good as a contract." Is simple honesty and integrity really outdated? Is it no longer possible to take one another at our word? Like the Hebrews of old, we are called upon to be different from those around us. In the straight and simple keeping of our promises, we can demonstrate a significant dimension of the Kingdom of God.

And whatever happened to tithing? Any tampering or withholding of any part of the first tenth of one's increase was considered to be a criminal act against God (see Mal. 3:8). While the New Testament does not specifically reiterate the tradition of tithing, it certainly never suspends it. The most comprehensive discussion of the principle of proportionate giving is found in 2 Corinthians 8 and 9, and it certainly is based upon the fundamental concept that everything that we have belongs to God. The tithe is best understood as the way in which we witness to that belief.

Too often, I'm afraid, the tithe is presented as though only the first 10 percent belonged to God. Not so. Giving the first 10 percent is our way of expressing our conviction that everything belongs to God. Anything less must still be seen as robbing God.

Over the years, I have yet to meet anyone who takes tithing seriously who does not witness to the sheer joy and satisfaction that grows out of the practice. In fact, I know of many folks who find joy in going beyond the tithe. Peter and Chris Geddes have been a tremendous inspiration and challenge to everyone in our congregation. More than fifty years ago, they began their marriage with a mutual vow to give the first tenth of everything they gained to Christ's work. Starting with a small printing business that grew considerably across the years, they increased the percentage of their giving from 10 percent to 20 percent, and then to 30 percent. Then they decided to make it 50-50. I know them well, and I can tell you that they could have supported a much more expansive lifestyle and could have lived in a much more lavish home, but they couldn't have received more joy and happiness than they have in supporting Christian missions and ministries around the world.

Here is another area, the management and stewardship of our money, in which we have the potential to be different from those around us and to demonstrate something very basic about the Kingdom of God.

*   *   *

With these laws on vows and tithing, we have come to the end of Leviticus. I hope that you have come with me to a new appreciation of what has been a much neglected and relatively unknown part of the Bible. What God gave to Moses and the Hebrew people long ago was meant for us as well. As Paul put it, "For whatever things were written before were written for our learning, that we through the patience and comfort of the Scriptures might have hope" (Rom. 15:4).

Holiness, the full consecration of all that we are and have to God, is that for which God has made us. Through Jesus Christ, our great High Priest, the final and complete sacrifice for sin has been made. We are redeemed by the shedding of His blood. Through His love, by the power of the Holy Spirit working in us and through us, we can be holy, for God is holy.

BIBLIOGRAPHY

COMMENTARIES

Bonar, A. A. *A Commentary on Leviticus.* London: Banner of Truth, London, reprint of 1861 edition, 1966.

Calvin, John. *Commentaries on the Four Last Books of Moses.* Grand Rapids: Eerdmans, reprint of 1852 translation.

Clements, R. E. *Leviticus.* Broadman Bible Commentary. Nashville/London: Broadman; Marshall, Morgan, and Scott, 1970.

Erdman, C. R. *The Book of Leviticus.* New York: Revell, 1951.

Harrison, R. K. *Leviticus.* Tyndale Old Testament Commentaries. Downers Grove, Ill.: InterVarsity Press, 1974.

Kellogg, S. H. *The Book of Leviticus.* The Expositor's Bible. New York: Armstrong and Son, 1903.

Knight, G. A. F. *Leviticus.* The Daily Study Bible. Philadelphia: Westminster, 1981.

Mays, James L. *Leviticus, Numbers.* The Layman's Bible Commentary. Atlanta: John Knox, 1964.

Micklem, N. *The Book of Leviticus.* The Interpreter's Bible. New York: Abingdon, 1953.

Milgrom. J. "The Book of Leviticus," *The Interpreter's One-Volume Commentary on the Bible.* Nashville: Abingdon, 1971.

Noth, Martin. *Leviticus.* The Old Testament Library. Philadelphia: Westminster, 1965.

Parker, Joseph. *Leviticus-Numbers XXVI.* The People's Bible. New York: Funk and Wagnalls, n.d.

Porter, J. R. *Leviticus.* Cambridge Bible Commentary. Cambridge: Cambridge University Press, 1976.

Snaith, N. H. *Leviticus and Numbers.* New Century Bible. London: Nelson, 1967.

Wenham, G. J. *The Book Of Leviticus.* The New International Commentary on the Old Testament. Grand Rapids: Eerdmans, 1979.

GENERAL AND BACKGROUND

Anderson, Bernhard. *Understanding The Old Testament.* Englewood Cliffs, N.J.: Prentice-Hall, 1966.

Bright, John. *The Authority of the Old Testament.* London: SCM, 1967.

Douglas, M. *Purity and Danger.* London: Routledge, 1966.

Harrison, R. K. *Introduction to the Old Testament.* Grand Rapids: Eerdmans, 1969.

Kauffman, Yehezkel. *The Religion of Israel.* Chicago: University of Chicago, 1960.

Milgrom, J. *Studies in Levitical Terminology*. Berkeley: University of California Press, 1970.

Morris, Leon. *The Atonement*. Downers Grove, Ill.: InterVarsity Press, 1983.

Noth, Martin. *The Laws in the Pentateuch and Other Studies*. Edinburgh: Oliver and Boyd, 1966.

Speiser, E. A. *Oriental and Biblical Studies*. Philadelphia: University of Pennsylvania, 1967.

Stott, John R. W. *The Cross of Christ*. Downers Grove, Ill.: InterVarsity Press, 1986.

Turner, V. W. *The Ritual Process*. London: Routledge, 1969.

ARTICLES

The Interpreter's Dictionary of the Bible. Supplementary Volume. Nashville: Abingdon, 1988:

"Aaron, Aaronides," Rivkin, E.

"Atonement in the Old Testament," Milgrom, J.

"Blood," Mc Carthy, D. J.

"Day of Atonement," Milgrom, J.

"Heave Offering," Milgrom, J.

"Homosexuality," Pope, M. H.

"Leviticus," Milgrom, J.

"Priests," Levine, B. A.

"Sabbatical Year," Wacholder, B. Z.

"Sacrifices and Offerings, OT," Milgrom, J.

"Sex, Sexual Behavior," Taber, C. R.

"Wave Offering," Milgrom, J.

The New Westminster Dictionary of the Bible. Philadelphia: Westminster, 1970:

"Aaron"

"Altar"

"Atonement, Day of"

"Azazel"

"Heave Offering"

"High Priest"

"Levites"

"Leviticus"

"Offerings"

"Priest"

"Jubilee"

"Sabbath"

"Tabernacle"

"Tabernacles, Feast of"

"Weeks, Feast of"